HANDBOOK TO
THE ROMAN WALL

D1614621

A

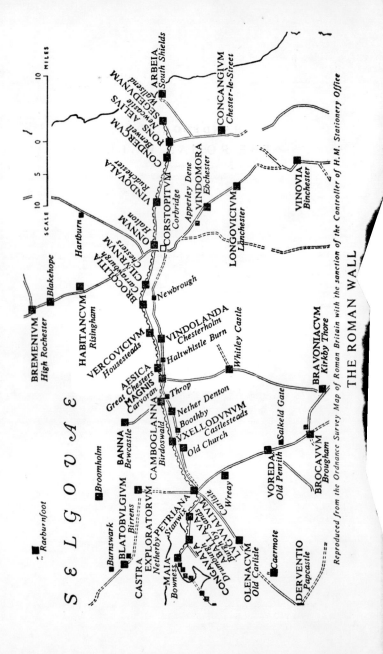

THE ROMAN WALL

Reproduced from the Ordnance Survey Map of Roman Britain with the sanction of the Controller of H.M. Stationery Office

HANDBOOK TO

THE ROMAN WALL

WITH THE

CUMBRIAN COAST AND OUTPOST FORTS

J. COLLINGWOOD BRUCE
LL.D., D.C.L., F.S.A.

Thirteenth Edition
EDITED AND ENLARGED
BY
CHARLES DANIELS
M.A., F.S.A.

HAROLD HILL & SON
NEWCASTLE UPON TYNE
1978

First Published 1863
Second Edition 1884
Third Edition 1885
Fourth Edition 1895
Fifth Edition 1907
Sixth Edition 1909
Seventh Edition 1914
Eighth Edition 1921: *Reprinted* 1925 *and* 1927
Ninth Edition 1933: *Reprinted* 1937
Tenth Edition 1947: *Reprinted* 1951
Eleventh Edition 1957
Twelfth Edition 1965
Thirteenth Edition 1978
Revised and Extended by C. M. Daniels

© Harold Hill & Son 1978

ISBN 090046 332 5

PRINTED IN SCOTLAND BY HOLMES MCDOUGALL LTD.
AT 24 CLYDEHOLM ROAD, GLASGOW, G14

CONTENTS

CHAPTER IV

LOCAL DESCRIPTION OF THE CUMBRIAN COAST

CHAPTER V

PREFACE

TO THE

THIRTEENTH EDITION

"JOHN COLLINGWOOD BRUCE was born in 1805 and, after graduating at Glasgow, became a schoolmaster in Newcastle upon Tyne. During the whole of a long and active life, until his death in 1892, he was an untiring student of Roman antiquities, and especially of the great Wall with which his memory will always be associated. Even more valuable than his work as a field archaeologist, however, were his services to the study of Roman inscriptions. He had the qualities of an epigraphist to an eminent degree: patience, pertinacity, a quick eye and a retentive memory were so combined in him with sound scholarship, that for many years he was the leading authority on Roman inscriptions in this country; and the British volume of the Berlin *Corpus Inscriptionum Latinarum* consists mainly of material which he supplied.

His *Handbook of the Roman Wall* was first written in 1863, when the materials for the definitive edition of his great book on *The Roman Wall* were practically complete. It has all the virtues of a small book written by a man who has his subject at his fingers' ends. Nothing is said but what is essential; the descriptions are vivid and terse: the style is rapid and eloquent; and the reader is carried along with a stride like that of the Wall itself—

> 'Hadrian's Wall, that strides from hill to hill
> Along the wave-crest of the great Whin Sill.'

Subsequent editions, interpolating and qualifying, did much to mar these fine qualities, and a reader who only knows the later editions is surprised, when he makes the acquaintance of the earlier, to find how good they are."

*   *   *

The foregoing paragraphs opened the preface to Professor Collingwood's Ninth Edition, and they were still retained, as an authoritative estimate of Dr. Bruce's work by one pre-eminently qualified to make it, Professor Sir Ian Richmond, in his successive editions of the Handbook. The present editor's task, on the basis laid by these great men, is to bring the work up to date by the inclusion of new discoveries, together with references to them in the bibliography. Since the last edition much that is new has been found, but much new thought and many new opinions have also emerged, with the result that some parts of the book have had to be extensively revised, and not a few alterations made. Some passages and descriptions omitted in recent editions have been reinstated, to give a fuller and, it is hoped, more enjoyable account of the Wall; but more, the Stanegate, the Cumbrian coast and the outpost forts have all been added, for they too are a part of the Wall system. Moreover, they are parts which Bruce did not hesitate to include in the early editions of this work. Sadly, succeeding editors have cropped them; but for a full appreciation of the whole of the great frontier work their inclusion is essential, and it is hoped that the pilgrim will find his visit to them enjoyable and rewarding.

Whenever possible the previous text has been left unaltered, as a tribute to the scholarship and the memory of that great Wall scholar Sir Ian Richmond. In places, however, a return has been made to the fuller descriptions of his Eleventh Edition in preference to the somewhat abbreviated Twelfth.

Most of the old illustrations have been retained, although a handful have been slightly altered, or brought up to date, while in other places new versions have been supplied. Elsewhere, illustrations have been revived from earlier editions, either to augment the existing ones, or to provide material for the added sites, for which new drawings have also been prepared as felt necessary. In addition to the sources acknowledged in previous editions I must thank Mr. J. P. Gillam and the late Mr. J. Tait for the illustrations on pages 49 and 86, Professor G. D. B. Jones for pages 210 and 259, and Dr. T. W. Potter for pages 261 and 284. My wife has drawn almost all the other new material, for which I am most deeply grateful. Finally, I wish to thank Mr. R. L. Bellhouse, Mr. M. Binns, Dr. D. J. Breeze, Miss D. Charlesworth, Mr. J. Dore, Mr. J. P. Gillam, Dr. M. G. Jarrett and Professor A. R. Birley, Professor G. D. B. Jones, Dr. T. W. Potter, Mr. G. Smith, and Mr. R. P. Wright for information unpublished at the moment of writing or for discussing points of interpretation. I must also thank Mr. Gillam for his continued assistance and encouragement and for placing his considerable experience and knowledge of the Northern Frontier of Britain at my disposal while preparing this edition.

*   *   *

The closing paragraph of R. G. Collingwood's preface is again used, out of love and respect for those two great masters of Wall studies who have employed it in successive editions of the Handbook; and with the belief that it echoes, better than anything substituted, the fitness of things concerning a Wall pilgrimage.

"A book like this has the singular privilege of not lying still all its days indoors, but travelling with its owner and sharing his fortunes of wind and weather. The privilege is doubly precious when the journey itself is a notable one, and those who have made it are agreed that there is something more than notable about the pilgrimage of the Wall. It is the editor's dearest wish that this book may long continue to accompany those who make that pilgrimage, honourably scarred and stained in their service; that it may remind them how many have travelled the Wall before them and have earned the right to say, with Camden, *Verily I have seene the tract of it over the high pitches and steepe descents of hilles, wonderfully rising and falling;* and that it may strengthen in them the will that these relics and this pilgrimage should be preserved for our posterity as part of their national heritage."

C. M. D.

Newcastle upon Tyne,
Eid. Nov. 1976,
Feriæ Iovi.

Alterations to this Edition have been made at page proof stage to incorporate, where relevant, material from F. G. Simpson's 1907-13 excavations, published in 1977 as *Watermills and Military Works on Hadrian's Wall.*
July, 1977
C. M. D.

Although considerable portions of the Wall system are accessible to the general public, some of the sites described remain in private ownership, and are inaccessible. Inclusion below, therefore, is no indication of public right of way.

x

HANDBOOK TO

THE ROMAN WALL

CHAPTER I

INTRODUCTORY

HE who contemplates a pilgrimage *per lineam Valli*, if he has a thorough love of antiquity, and duly appreciates the importance of the great structure which he is to see, will not enter upon the enterprise lightly. Before starting upon his journey he will probably wish to consult the authors who have written upon the Wall itself, and to refresh his acquaintance with the Roman chapter of our English history. In the belief that he will wish to carry with him some notes upon these points the following sections of this chapter are set before him.

I. EARLIER ACCOUNTS

The first important modern work is the survey by William Camden, the great Elizabethan antiquary, made in 1599 and first printed in the fifth edition (1600) of his *Britannia*. Camden journeyed the whole line of the Wall except for the central part, where he did not go because of the unsettled condition of the country; and he advanced a complete and logical explanation of the Wall and its attendant works which, though now superseded, held the field for 250 years.

The *Britannia*, written in Latin, was translated in 1610 by Philemon Holland, in consultation with Camden, and Holland's son, Henry, produced a new edition in 1637. The Holland translations long remained the standard works on the archaeology of Britain; and there were many revisions, notably those by Bishop Gibson (1695, 1722, 1753, 1772) and Richard Gough (1789, 1806). Gibson's later editions contain the results of a fresh examination of the Wall made in 1708-9 and for the first time an account of the entire line from end to end. The material contained in

1

Gibson's survey is good observation but poor historical theory. Gough, on the other hand, is based upon Horsley, the second great student of the Wall.

John Horsley (1685-1732) was a Presbyterian minister and schoolmaster at Morpeth. He was a man of deep learning, great industry and very unusual powers of observation, inference and judgment. His *Britannia Romana*, published in 1732 after his death, is still a prime treatise on the Roman antiquities of Britain. His account of the Wall has hardly been surpassed for careful and penetrating observation. His materials were used, quite without acknowledgment, by Alexander Gordon, Sir Walter Scott's 'Sandy Gordon', whose *Itinerarium Septentrionale* was published in 1726; and a plagiarised version of his actual description of the Wall was published by Warburton in 1753 under the title of *Vallum Romanum*.

William Stukeley's *Iter Boreale* was published in 1776, also posthumously, and it includes the memoranda of a journey made in 1725 in the company of Roger Gale, over western and northern England. It contained a new theory of the relation between the Wall and the Vallum, and a number of drawings most useful in showing the state of the remains in his time; but his fieldwork is very poor when compared with that of Horsley. Another short first-hand account of the Wall is that of John Brand, in an Appendix to the first volume of his *History of Newcastle* (1789).

In the year 1801 William Hutton of Birmingham, at the age of 78, walked the Wall from end to end and gave his enthusiastic observations to the world in *The History of the Roman Wall*. Six years later, in August 1807, the Rev. John Lingard walked from Wallsend to Gilsland, making manuscript notes entitled *Mural Tourification*, largely transcribed in 1929 by R. C. Bosanquet. The fourth volume of *Magna Britannia* (1816), by Daniel and Samuel Lysons, has an article on the Roman Wall and a good account of the Roman inscriptions of Cumberland.

Meanwhile, the Rev. John Hodgson, then incumbent of Jarrow and Heworth, had published, in *The Picture of Newcastle-upon-Tyne* (1812), a comprehensive and useful account of the Wall. In 1839 he devoted a very large part of the last volume of his *History of Northumberland* to the Walls of Hadrian and Antoninus. Everyone since Camden had thought that the Vallum was Hadrian's frontier-work and the Wall that of Severus; Hodgson, on the evidence of inscriptions, saw that this was untenable.

The difficulty was then to explain the relation between the Wall and the Vallum; and this was done by regarding them as contemporary and explaining the Vallum as a rearward defence, a theory partly anticipated by Stukeley.

Twelve years later came Bruce's *Roman Wall*, first edition, 1851; second, 1853; third, 1867. The third edition, a fine quarto, is a detailed description of the remains, excellent in the east and centre, less good in the west; with accounts of Roman sites in the neighbourhood of the Wall, inscriptions and other objects, and an important chapter on the question of who built the Wall. The great value of Bruce's work is that it summarised the results of excavation by John Clayton of Chesters, and publicised Hodgson's theory of the Wall's Hadrianic date. Bruce also produced the important *Lapidarium Septentrionale* in 1870-1875, which, contemporary with the *Corpus Inscriptionum Latinarum*, vol. vii, edited by Hübner in 1873, gave full descriptions of the inscriptions. Since then, fresh inscriptions up to 1954 have been published by R. G. Collingwood and R. P. Wright in *The Roman Inscriptions of Britain* (1965, hereafter abbreviated as RIB), and annually from 1921 to 1969 in the *Journal of Roman Studies*, thereafter in *Britannia*.

Bruce's later work was facilitated by the production in 1858 of the first accurate survey of the Wall, *A Survey of the Roman Wall*, made by Henry MacLauchlan in the years 1852-1854 for the third Duke of Northumberland and accompanied by an explanatory *Memoir*. In 1964 (second edition 1972) the Ordnance Survey published a magnificent special archaeological *Map of Hadrian's Wall*, at a scale of 2 inches to 1 mile, which anyone visiting the Wall will find invaluable, and is especially recommended for use with this *Handbook*. For greater detail the 2½ inches (1:25,000) O.S. sheets are also good: the new 1:50,000 series, however, is very poor for archaeological remains.

Finally, twentieth-century research and excavation on the Wall is published in *Archaeologia Aeliana* by the Society of Antiquaries of Newcastle upon Tyne, or in the Cumberland and Westmorland Archaeological and Antiquarian Society's *Transactions*. Summaries of the main conclusions have appeared in the *Journal of Roman Studies*, in articles called *Hadrian's Wall, a history of the problem* (1920); *Hadrian's Wall, 1921-1930* (1931); *The Turf Wall of Hadrian, 1895-1935* (1935); and *Hadrian's Wall, 1939-1949* (1950). The *Northumberland County History* has published descriptions of the Wall from Wallsend to Rudchester Burn (vol. xiii), thence to Matfen Piers (vol. xii) and to a little west of Halton (vol. x) and of the outpost forts to the north (vol. xv). Professor Eric Birley's *Research on Hadrian's Wall* (1961) contains a mass of detailed, specialist information.

In recent years popular Wall and site guides have proliferated. Most are brief and cheaply produced, especially in their illustrations. Two booklets, however, stand apart, these are: *The Building of Hadrian's Wall* (1970) and *The Army of Hadrian's Wall* (1972) by Drs. Brian Dobson and David Breeze. Together with Mr. John Gillam's *The Frontier after Hadrian, a history of the problem* (*Arch. Aeliana*⁵ ii, 1974, p. 1-16) they give an excellent outline of recent opinions and up to date thought on the Wall, its building and its subsequent history. Just published is *Hadrian's Wall* (Allen Lane 1976) by Drs. Breeze and Dobson. This is a full-length treatment of the subject which replaces their earlier work, and is to be recommended to the interested reader as a sound and scholarly treatment of the whole subject.

II. HISTORICAL SUMMARY

Britain was known to both Greeks and Romans from the middle of the fourth century B.C.; but was first reached by Roman military power when Julius Caesar invaded it in 55 and 54 B.C. Events in Gaul prevented Caesar consolidating his initial success, so that conquest was preserved for Claudius in A.D. 43. Even then it was a generation later before Roman troops first penetrated the northern regions. Julius Agricola, governor of Britain from 78 to 84/5, overran all the north of England and Scotland to the Moray Firth. The districts he conquered were linked by roads and studded with forts, thus cutting the land into small units and creating cordons to isolate native communities. One of these roads was that now known as the Stanegate, linking Corbridge with Carlisle.

Agricola's northernmost schemes of consolidation were never completely realised, and events following his recall are in many particulars obscure. His successors held Scotland south of the Highland line for a time and then, almost certainly because of the reduction of the provincial garrison following crushing defeats on the Danube in the middle 80s, became the instruments of a creeping withdrawal. This was probably carried out in stages, which soon brought the effective frontier back to Newstead and Oakwood in southern Scotland, and led to a reorganization of the Stanegate line. About the year 105 the situation worsened with the destruction of many, if not all, of the remaining forts north of the Tyne-Solway line, including Corbridge, probably at the hands of hostile tribesmen. The Emperor Trajan's reaction was to rebuild and strengthen the line of posts on the Stanegate, adding new forts, of both standard and sub-standard size, in the west-central area where the country is most difficult and the road negotiates several river and stream valleys; and perhaps also elsewhere. It is even possible that between Corbridge and Carlisle he created a developed frontier line (*limes*) complete with a regular system of interval forts and signal-stations.

Whatever the situation on Trajan's death, it was the new Emperor Hadrian, visiting Britain in 122, who decided to build a Wall from Tyne to Solway in order to create a continuous and permanent frontier barrier. This is the Wall of which the present volume gives some account; it marks the apogee of the system of cordon control, not only in Britain, but in the whole Empire. Whether it was a case of 'overkill', a successful solution, or an admission of failure to solve the British problem by its obvious solution—total conquest—need not delay us at this point, for it is a description of the barrier and not its evaluation which is our aim.

Hadrian did not remain in the province to see the completion of his work, and it was Aulus Platorius Nepos, legate of Britain from 122 until probably 126, who carried it forward and began the modification of the system which produced the arrangement we see today. The final touches to the scheme were not added until some years after 130. The first period of occupation of the Wall is known as Period 1A.

Antoninus Pius succeeded Hadrian in A.D. 138. In the next year preparations began, under Lollius Urbicus, for a new advance into Scotland, which was consolidated by a new Wall between Forth and Clyde. Hadrian's Wall was virtually abandoned, with the gates of the milecastles removed to allow free access across the Wall line, and the Vallum regularly breached. But peace seems to have been restless and precarious. There was apparently trouble by A.D. 155, when the first period of occupation on the Antonine Wall came to an end, and after an almost immediate reoccupation of at least some of the forts, the Antonine Wall was quickly and finally abandoned. Hereafter, it was Hadrian's Wall which was held, with outpost forts in both east and west. The reoccupation of the Wall opens Period 1B.

In 180, or so, under Commodus, the son of Marcus Aurelius, "the tribes within the island, having passed over the Wall which divided them from the Roman garrisons, committed much devastation, after killing a certain general and his soldiers. Commodus became alarmed, and sent Ulpius Marcellus against them" (The *Historia Augusta*). Until recently it was believed that the Wall in question was the northern one. A recent study of the samian pottery from Scotland by Mr. B. R. Hartley, however, has shown that most of Scotland had been abandoned as early as the mid-160s, which means that it must have been Hadrian's Wall which was crossed. Damage is archaeologically attested at the forts of Rudchester, Haltonchesters, Corbridge and Birdoswald towards the end of the second century or early in the third, and the damage at the first three of these sites, at least, was probably sustained at this time. The Wall was restored (beginning of Period II) but Risingham, at least, of the outpost forts was apparently not rebuilt, while Birrens, Newstead and Cappuck were abandoned.

Commodus was assassinated at the end of A.D. 192, and there soon followed a struggle for the Empire, in which Septimius Severus was ultimately triumphant. One of the rival claimants was Clodius Albinus, governor of Britain, who was defeated only after two violent battles near Lyons in 197. From 1929 until recently it was accepted without doubt that the withdrawal of at least part of the provincial garrison, to fight in Gaul, led to an overwhelming destruction of the northern frontier, and every piece of damage which can be dated to the late second or early third century has been interpreted as an orgy of pillage and destruction carried out by the northern tribes on the abandoned Wall in 197. However, the only literary reference to these events says no more than that Virius Lupus, the first governor sent by Severus to Britain, was obliged to buy off the tribes from beyond the Wall in exchange for prisoners they had taken. No mention of destruction is made, and it is unsafe to assume that it automatically followed any withdrawal of troops. Virius Lupus is attested rebuilding at Ilkley, Brough under Stainmore, Bowes and possibly Corbridge, but in no Wall fort. His work seems to have been to rebuild and consolidate in the Pennine area. A short time later, Alfenus Senecio strengthened the frontier defences by reconstructing the outpost forts of Risingham and High Rochester, and rebuilding at Benwell, Chesters and Birdoswald, as well as at Corbridge and forts further south. But the situation appears to have further declined. In fact, it is just conceivable that the great destruction of the Wall, above placed in 180, could have occurred as late as A.D. 205-8 (with a correspondingly later start to Period II), for Cassius Dio speaks of wars in Britain, while Herodian states that the governor wrote to say that the barbarians had risen and were over-running the country, carrying off booty and causing great destruction. This brought Severus to Britain in 208, with his sons Caracalla and Geta. In 209 he advanced against the Caledonians. The campaigns lasted two seasons, and had more success than ancient historians admit. A third campaign was preceded by the death of the old Emperor at York in February, 211. His two sons, Caracalla and Geta (Caracalla became Augustus in 198, Geta in 209), then arranged a peace with the northern tribes and returned to Rome. Accounts of these Caledonian wars are written to give an impression of failure, but it seems that one main objective at least was achieved: Severus taught the northern tribes so sharp a lesson that the frontier had peace for 100 years. The rebuilding or modernisation of forts along the line of the Wall continued for some time after his death; we have various records of work done in the reigns of Elagabalus (218-222), Severus Alexander (222-235), and even Gordian III (238-244); a spate of building activity which is paralleled in other provinces. One group of inscriptions, however, was set up by the army "out of their joint duty and devotion" (*pro pietate ac devotione communi*) under the governor Iulius Marcus in 213, to protest loyalty to Caracalla after the murder of Geta: an act which suggests widespread disapproval of this fratricide (see pp. 159 and 293).

Beyond the Wall the outpost forts were re-established (see p. 37). The principal routes to the north were held by very strong garrisons, and a wide sweep of territory was subjected to patrol by long-range scouts (*exploratores*). Relations with the tribes of southern Scotland became increasingly friendly, and their lands may be regarded as a Roman protectorate, for 8 places, *loca*, given in the *Ravenna List* merely as "in Britain" (*sunt autem in ipsa Britannia diversa loca*), appear to belong to this period. These stretch from southern Dumfriesshire to the Forth and Tay, and have been seen as sites of "lawful assembly recognised by Roman treaty or frontier regulation", where patrolling troops, or their officers, would meet with the local leaders on stipulated occasions. The defences of many native sites were slighted about this time, if not earlier, while the huts of others spread across their neglected fortifications; all of which was seen by Richmond as evidence that the "*Pax Romana,* under whose aegis the area (now) lay, plainly meant not merely protection from enemies but prohibition of incentives to civil war or revolt".

The third century saw crises in much of the Empire, but in Britain it was predominantly a time of peace and prosperity, so much so in the north that the Wall garrison was conspicuously reduced, and by the mid-290s South Shields, Wallsend, Rudchester, Haltonchesters and Birdoswald, at least, were in a state of partial ruin with many of their buildings, and in some cases even their defences in collapse. To this list Bowness and Greatchesters can probably be added. But Britain did not escape the disorders of the times completely; in the 270s raids from across the Chainel and the North Sea were increasing and in A.D. 287 the tranquility was further disturbed when Carausius, who had command of the fleet to repress piracy in the English Channel, revolted. He assumed the sovereignty of Britain, which he retained until 293, when his power was in turn usurped by Allectus, his finance minister.

In 296, Constantius Chlorus reconquered Britain and restored the province to the Empire. He decided to put the Wall again into fighting shape (beginning of Period III), and was responsible for substantial rebuilding, similar to that carried out nearly a century before. One of the pieces of evidence for this is an inscription from Birdoswald (*RIB* 1912) which records that "the commanding-officer's house, which was covered with earth and had fallen into ruin, and the headquarters building and the bath-house" were restored under the charge of the centurion in command. Ten years later Constantius was in Britain, residing at York, after a campaign in the farthest north, when he died in 306.

The reorganisation of the frontier defences gave Britain a continued period of peace and prosperity; but the situation was changing: a Pictish campaign was undertaken about 310, Constans had to cross the Channel in midwinter 343 to deal with serious trouble, in 360 Julian was forced to send Lupicinus against the Picts and Scots who had broken the terms imposed upon them, and 5 years later further frontier attacks are recorded. All culminated in the great disaster of 367, when a combination of barbarian invaders from overseas and the far north set upon Britain from all sides at once. Now, probably for the second time only in its history, the Wall fell to a direct attack upon it; but this time the attack was coupled with treachery, and is known as the Barbarian Conspiracy. The *areani*, who seem to have been the fourth-century successors of the *exploratores*, combined with the Picts, Scots, Saxons, Franks and Atacotti to overwhelm not only the Wall but the whole province. Fortifications were destroyed and troops annihilated: of the two army commanders the Count of the Saxon Shore fell in battle and the Duke of the British Provinces was rendered immobile, while large parts of Britain were overrun and devastated.

The situation was retrieved by Count Theodosius, who in 367 came post-haste to Britain, cleared out the invaders, and restored the fortifications. But relations with the Lowland tribes were irrevocably altered, and although the Wall was restored, the outpost forts beyond it, reduced in number before 367, were never held again.

The restoration of 369 opens Period IV, the last and shortest in the history of the Wall. Magnus Maximus is credited with northern campaigns, but in 383 he led the army of Britain in revolt against Gratian, and, passing over with his forces to the Continent, drained the island of its protectors. He either evacuated the Wall, or as Rudyard Kipling imagined in *Puck of Pook's Hill*, left it defended by only the barest of skeleton forces. Thereafter, archaeological evidence and historical record alike, are almost non-existant. Life, to be sure, continued, as witnessed by the trickle of late fourth-century pottery and coins, but our vision of the last days and final collapse of the Wall is as yet seen through the very darkest of glasses.

III. ANCIENT SOURCES

The Notitia

The *Notitia Dignitatum et Administrationum, tam civilium quam militarium, in partibus Orientis et Occidentis* records the distribution of Imperial officials, civil and military, throughout the Roman world. The document is of the early fifth century in date, but it draws upon earlier sources and gives at least a partial list of the forces in garrison on the Wall. The following, with some corrections in spelling, is that portion under the *dux Sritanniarum,* or commander-in-chief of the British Provinces; the section is headed *Item per lineam valli* — "Also, along the line of the Wall".

Tribune of the Fourth Cohort of Lingones at SEGEDUNUM (*Wallsend*).
Tribune of the First Cohort of Cornovians at PONS AELIUS (*Newcastle*).
Prefect of the First *Ala* of Asturians at CONDERCUM (*Benwell*).
Tribune of the First Cohort of Frisiavones at VINDOVALA (*Rudchester*).
Prefect of the *Ala Sabiniana* at ONNUM (*Haltonchesters*).
Prefect of the Second *Ala* of Asturians at CILURNUM (*Chesters*).
Tribune of the First Cohort of Batavians at BROCOLITIA (*Carrawburgh*).
Tribune of the First Cohort of Tungrians at VERCOVICIUM (*Housesteads*).
Tribune of the Fourth Cohort of Gauls at VINDOLANDA (*Chesterholm*).
Tribune of the Second Cohort of Asturians at AESICA (*Greatchesters*).
Tribune of the Second Cohort of Dalmatians at MAGNA (*Carvoran*).
Tribune of Hadrian's Own First Cohort of Dacians at . . .
. . . at CAMBOGLANNA (probably *Castlesteads*).
Prefect of the *Ala Petriana* at PETRIANA (*Stanwix*).
Prefect of a Unit of Aurelius's Own Moors at ABALLABA (*Burgh-by-Sands*).
Tribune of the Second Cohort of Lingones at CONGAVATA (*Drumburgh*).
Tribune of the First Cohort of Spaniards at UXELLODUNUM (probably *Netherby*).
Tribune of the Second Cohort of Thracians at GABROSENTIUM (*Moresby*).
Tribune of the First Cohort of Hadrian's Own Marines at TUNNOCELUM (Uncertain).
Tribune of the First Cohort of Morinians at GLANNIBANTA (*Ravenglass*).
Tribune of the Third Cohort of Nervians at ALIONIS (*Uncertain*).
Cavalry Formation of Sarmatians at BREMETENNACUM (*Ribchester*).
Prefect of the First *Ala Herculea* at OLENACUM (*Old Carlisle?*).
Tribune of the Sixth Cohort of Nervians at VIROSIDUM (*Bainbridge*).

Also part of the overall Wall system, although not included in the foregoing list, was:

Prefect of the Unit of Tigris Lightermen at ARBEIA (*South Shields*).

The great value of these entries, as Horsley first perceived, is that they supply the ancient names of 11 or 12 out of the 16 Wall forts, from Wallsend to Carvoran or Birdoswald. For the Wall the garrison described is usually taken to be that of the fourth century, which was, as inscriptions show, substantially that of the third century. The remaining names, not in strict geographical order, need not concern us here.

The Antonine Itinerary

This is a fourth-century edition of an early third-century road-book, describing the post-roads of the Empire, with names and intervening distances. The Wall is mentioned only because two roads cross its line: one to the east (later known as Dere Street), going from the outlying fort of High Rochester across the Wall at Portgate to Corbridge and the south; the other leaving the Wall at Carlisle and running south through Cumbria and beyond. The *Itinerary* therefore gives us the ancient names of Carlisle, Corbridge and a few other places near the Wall. It described the Wall alternatively as *limes* or *vallum*.

The Rudge Cup, Amiens Skillet and Ravenna List

The Rudge Cup, found at Rudge in Wiltshire, is a small enamelled cup once forming part of a set of ornamental souvenir bowls. Its decoration is a frieze comprising the Wall, with turrets and milecastles, crowned by the inscription A MAIS ABALLAVA VXEL(L)OD(VN)VM CAMBOGLAN(NI)S BANNA. These names are taken from an Itinerary of the Wall, from west to east. A comparable vessel, found in 1949 at Amiens, carries the words MAIS ABALLAVA VXEL(L)ODVNVM CAMBOGLA(NI)S BANNA ESICA.

The *Ravenna List* is a sixth-century copy of a road-map, derived from second-century sources in Britain. It gives the Wall forts from east to west, including those on the Rudge Cup and Amiens skillet, but in tabulated form.

IV. THE ARMY AND ITS OFFICERS

The Roman Imperial army was divided into two main classes of troops: the legions and the auxiliaries. The legions, each just over 5,000 strong, were composed exclusively of Roman citizens, highly-trained and heavily-armed infantry with a small cavalry detachment. Each legion was commanded by a *legatus legionis* of senatorial rank, holding his commission direct from the Emperor, the commander-in-chief of the army. Its second-in-command was the senior tribune, its third the *praefectus castrorum*. Next came 5 tribunes of the wealthy equestrian class, who, like the senior tribune, were receiving this experience of army life early in a career in the Imperial Service. But the backbone of the legion was the 60 centurions, each commanding a century (*centuria*) of 80 men; for upon them fell the real work of maintaining discipline and efficiency. Each centurion had under him an *optio* or understudy, and a *signifer* or standard-bearer. There was, in fact, an extremely elaborate system of subordinates forming an administrative, clerical and engineering staff. The length of service for the normal legionary was in theory 20 years, but in practice, always 25, with the possibility of re-enlistment.

The legion lived and acted as a unit, having its permanent quarters in a fortress, often situated some distance behind the actual frontier line. It fought, on the occasion of a campaign, either as a mobile striking force ready to invade enemy territory, or to counter-attack against an invader. In Britain, from Hadrian onwards, there were three legions: the Second *Augusta* at Caerleon-on-Usk, the Sixth *Victrix* at York, and the Twentieth *Valeria Victrix* at Chester.

The auxiliaries differed from the legionaries in many ways. Instead of being recruited from Roman citizens, they were raised among non-Roman tribes or frontier provincials. Instead of the heavy armour of the legionary, they generally carried lighter equipment, sometimes including their own old-established weapons: thus, the Hamians of Carvoran used the Syrian bow, and the Dacians of Birdoswald used their traditional curved sword. Instead of living in large units like the legion, they were grouped as cohorts of infantry or *alae* of cavalry, nominally either 1,000 strong (milliary) or 500 strong (quingenary). A further type of cohort was that which included a body of cavalry in addition to its infantry strength. This was distinguished by the adjective equitate, or part mounted. An infantry cohort was divided into 10 or 6 *centuriae* commanded by centurions, and an *ala* into 24 or 16 *turmae* commanded by decurions; an equitate cohort contained the normal force of infantry (that is either 10 or 6 *centuriae*), plus either 8 or 4 *turmae*. The large cohorts were normally commanded by a tribune, the smaller cohorts and all cavalry by a prefect. Here again there was an elaborate system of subordinates, although of course less complex than in the legions.

Each cohort or *ala* lived and fought as a unit, stationed on the frontier and taking the rough-and-tumble of frontier police work.

In campaigning, the auxiliaries were expected to take the first brunt of the fighting and, if possible, to achieve victory unaided by the legions. Their permanent forts resembled a legionary fortress in miniature: generally from 3 to 5 acres in extent and containing within their ramparts barrack buildings, quarters for the commanding officer, storehouses and administrative offices. All this was established in military manuals and scores of forts were built to more or less similar patterns.

Two other formations may be mentioned. A *vexillatio* was a detachment for some special purpose from the ranks of one or more legions or auxiliary regiments; perhaps as reinforcements, perhaps to discharge some special temporary duty. A *numerus* or "unit" was often levied from newly-conquered districts or from outside the Empire, was sometimes at least commanded by officers of its own people, and used wholly un-Romanised equipment. The *numeri* may be roughly described as native infantry units. Their cavalry counterparts were known as *cunei* or "formations".

V. HEIGHT ABOVE SEA-LEVEL OF PRINCIPAL POINTS ON THE WALL

These are taken from the Ordnance maps of Northumberland and Cumberland.

	Feet		*Feet*
Wallsend	95	Winshields	1,230
Newcastle Keep	94	Greatchesters	690
Newcastle Bridge	23	Walltown Crags	860
Benwell	415	Carvoran	700
Chapel House	371	Willowford Bridge	360
Rudchester	449	Birdoswald	515
Harlow Hill	495	Pike Hill	541
Down Hill	666	Hare Hill	427
Halton	610	King Water	140
Milecastle 23 (Stanley)	860	Walton	248
St. Oswald's	745	Castlesteads	177
Chesters	240	Newtown of Irthington	223
Limestone Corner	823	Stanwix	110
Carrawburgh	785	River Eden	35
Sewingshields Crags	1,068	Beaumont	75
Housesteads	850	Burgh-by-Sands	65
Hotbank Crags	1,074	Drumburgh	70
Cat Stairs	900	Bowness-on-Solway	54

CHAPTER II

A GENERAL ACCOUNT OF THE WORKS

THE Roman Wall or, as it used to be called, the Picts' Wall, is a great fortification intended not only to act as a fence against a northern enemy, but also as the basis of military operations in his territory; for not only was every fort and every milecastle along its course provided with gates opening towards the north, but there were outpost forts situated at first on two, and later on three, roads running north from the Wall.

This great fortification consists of 6 chief parts:

    i. A Stone Wall, with a large ditch on its north side.

    ii. Forts, Milecastles and Turrets, to accommodate the soldiery who manned the Wall.

    iii. An Earthwork, now known as the Vallum, south of the Wall and its associated structures.

    iv. The continuation in the form of Forts, Milefortlets and Towers down the Cumbrian coast.

    v. The Outpost Forts to the north.

    vi. Roads for communication and for transmission of military stores.

The Wall and Vallum proceeded from one side of the island to the other in a more or less direct line and in close association; generally 60 or 80 yards apart. Only beside Limestone Bank and near Birdoswald have they been shown to impinge on one another. On the high ground of the central region they are more widely separated: for there the Wall seeks the crest of the Whin Sill while the Vallum runs on the lower ground at its tail, thus avoiding the rock. Again, west of Carlisle, on the cliffs of the Eden and on the Solway shore, the Wall seizes the positions with the best northward outlook. The Vallum, which is neither a work of defence nor sited on ground chosen for defensive qualities, runs everywhere in long straight sectors. The Wall extends for 80 Roman miles from Wallsend on Tyne to Bowness-on-Solway, a distance of about 73½ English miles. Forts, milefortlets and towers continue the line down the Cumbrian coast

14

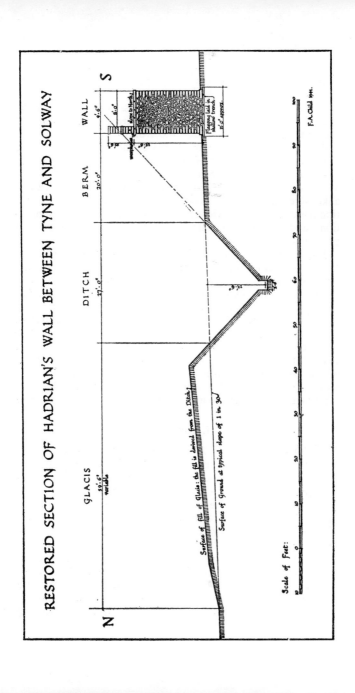

RESTORED SECTION OF HADRIAN'S WALL BETWEEN TYNE AND SOLWAY

N

S

GLACIS
59'.6"
variable

DITCH
27'.0"

BERM
20'.0"

WALL

Surface of fill of Glacis: the fill is derived from the Ditch

Surface of Ground at typical slope of 1 in 30

13'.6"

9'.6"

6'.0"

Scale of Feet:

F. A. Child del.

probably for a further 40 miles. The Vallum does not begin before Newcastle in the east, and terminates at Bowness in the west.

All earlier writers, from Bede onwards, considered that the Wall and Vallum were the work of different periods. Camden thought that the Vallum was the frontier work of Hadrian, and the Wall that of Severus. This view held the field until the nineteenth century, when Hodgson, Clayton and Bruce recognised, or found, inscriptions of Hadrian in the milecastles of the Wall, and evolved the theory that the Wall and the Vallum alike were Hadrian's and parts of a single scheme. Later excavation has confirmed this view, at the cost of adding new complications, and the Hadrianic date of both Wall and Vallum is now a proven fact.

The most striking feature in the planning of both Wall and Vallum is their straight course. The Wall takes the dominant position: shooting across country it seizes the commanding ground and the crests, changing direction on high points. For 19 miles out of Newcastle the Military or Carlisle road runs chiefly upon the foundations of the Wall, and gives the traveller, who passes from summit to summit on its course, a chance to observe the line stretching for miles before and behind him. Even in the central sector, where the Wall runs along the crags of the Whin Sill, a straight point-to-point course is mostly retained. Only where the crags are broken by gaps does the Wall take a re-entrant course, to ease the descent and increase defensive power.

I. THE WALL

A. *The Stone Wall as first planned and modified in building.*

As originally designed the Stone Wall was to be 10 Roman feet wide, built with coursed stonework, the faces of which were set in mortar, although the core, in places at least, was apparently set in puddled clay. The whole was based on a foundation of stone and puddled clay. Foundations to carry a Wall of this width were laid from Newcastle to the North Tyne, a distance of 23 Roman miles, and thereafter intermittently as far as the Irthing. The superstructure, begun from the east, had progressed some distance (but *perhaps* not even as far as Harlow Hill—milecastle 16), when it was decided to complete the work to a narrower gauge, and always to set the core in lime mortar. The actual building was carried out by legionary working parties, which proceeded at different paces in different areas, so that some of the individual gang lengths had been finished

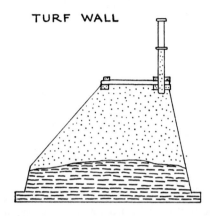

TURF WALL

BUILT IN COURSED TURVES, 18 × 12 × 6 INS. CUBE

0   5   10   15   20
FEET

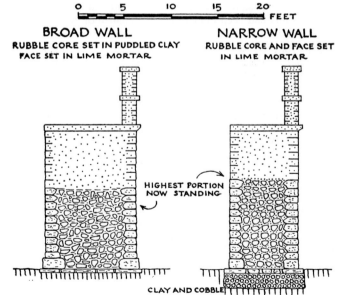

BROAD WALL
RUBBLE CORE SET IN PUDDLED CLAY
FACE SET IN LIME MORTAR

NARROW WALL
RUBBLE CORE AND FACE SET
IN LIME MORTAR

HIGHEST PORTION
NOW STANDING

CLAY AND COBBLE

to a 10 feet gauge in the area between Newcastle and the North Tyne. The spaces between these broad-gauge sections were then filled with narrow-gauge Wall, usually 8 Roman feet wide, but in some places as narrow as 6 Roman feet. These alterations in width occur from somewhere east of turret 24*b* all the way to the North Tyne. Elsewhere, they occur where turrets and mile-castles had been built, or begun, to the broad gauge, with wing walls projecting which were subsequently incorporated in Narrow curtain Wall. All of this Broad Wall construction was built before it was decided to move the forts on to the line of the Wall. At the same time as that decision was taken it was also decided to extend the Wall to Wallsend. Hence we have the following sequence —

(*a*) From Wallsend to Newcastle the Wall is *narrow*.

(*b*) From Newcastle to some point unknown, but before turret 24*b*, the Wall is *broad*, although some exceptions are recorded.

(*c*) From this point to the North Tyne there are variations in the width of the Wall from a *narrow* gauge of only 6 feet to the full 10 feet *broad* gauge. As further west, lengths of the broad foundation had been laid and milecastles and turrets had been built before the change of plan, ready to bond with the Broad Wall. These are of *broad* width.

(*d*) From the North Tyne to Willowford, the Wall is *narrow*, but in places it stands on foundations prepared for the Broad Wall. In this sector most of the milecastles and turrets and part of the east abutment of Willowford Bridge had been built before the change of plan occurred, and the wing-walls which project from them, ready to bond with the running work when it was built, are *broad*.

Two further variations in Wall construction occur in its lowest courses, indicating work by different legions.   These are —

Standard A: consisting of one course of large stones above the flag foundation, and then a single offset.

Standard B: consisting of three, or even four, courses of small stones above the foundation, then the offset.

B. *The Turf Wall, and its subsequent replacement in stone.*

West of the Irthing, there was a Turf Wall 20 feet thick at its base and built of cut turves laid in courses. The reason for this change in material is to be found in the local geology. West of

the Irthing limestone ceases at the Red Rock Fault, near milecastle 54. Lime for the grouting of the Wall could therefore no
longer be prepared at hand and the change in material was
made for convenience of organisation at the Irthing itself.
The milecastles of the Turf Wall were built in turf and timber:
the turrets were of stone. Replacement began quickly, and for a
stretch of some 5 miles west of the Irthing (that is, to about
turret 54*a*), the Turf Wall was soon replaced by the *narrow*
Stone Wall on exactly the same line, except between milecastles
49 (Harrow's Scar) and 51 (Wall Bowers), where the Stone
Wall took a course further north. Here, and here alone, Turf
Wall and Stone Wall can be studied in isolation and here their
relationship was determined in 1931-5. From west of milecastle 54
to Bowness, however, the replacement was deferred, and the
Stone Wall, as eventually supplied, was built to an *intermediate*
gauge of 9 Roman feet. This change took place before A.D. 180,
and was perhaps part of the preparation for the reoccupation
of Hadrian's Wall on the Antonine withdrawal from Scotland
(Period IB). Both replacements incorporated the stone turrets
of the Turf Wall, and supplied new stone milecastles.

C. *The height of the Stone and Turf Walls*

In no part of its course does the Wall now stand to full height.
Bede, whose home was the monastery of Jarrow, on the south
side of the Tyne almost opposite to Wallsend, is the earliest
author (A.D. 731) who gives dimensions. He described the
Wall, probably as he saw it in his own neighbourhood, as "eight
feet wide, and twelve high, in a straight line from east to west,
as is clear to beholders to this day" (*Hist. Eccl.* i, 12).

Subsequent writers give the height as greater. Christopher
Ridley, curate of Haltwhistle, wrote about 1572, "The bredth
iij yardis, the hyght remaneth in sum placis yet vij yardis".
An anonymous writer, deriving his information from Arch-
deacon Threlkeld in 1574, observed, "As towching Hadrians
Wall, begyning abowt a town called Bonus standing vppon the
river Sulway now called Eden . . . and there yet standing of the
heyth of 16 fote, for almost a quarter of a myle together, and so
along the river syde estwards." Camden, who visited the Wall
in 1599, says "Within two furlongs of Carvoran, on a pretty
high hill the Wall is still standing, fifteen feet in height, and nine
in breadth"; but it is possible that Camden had misread "xi"
as "xv". These statements leave an impression that Bede's

figure, if meant to apply to the original height of the Wall, is too low. Recent estimates, based on the discovery of flights of steps, have suggested 15 feet as the original height, to which most scholars would add a parapet and merlons, making an effective height of just over 20 feet in all. It must be added, however, that we do not know for certain that the Wall top was patrolled, and the evidence from other frontiers is mostly against such practice there. Nor do we know that the Wall was everywhere the same height.

The Turf Wall, whose turrets had no ladder platforms (see p. 219) and presumably therefore did not need them, is usually given as probably about 12 feet high to the rampart walk.

D. *The ditch*

Throughout its length, the Wall was protected on the north by a ditch, except where cliffs or the sea rendered this unnecessary. The flat space or berm between the two is normally 20 feet wide, but in association with the Turf Wall it is 6 feet wide, except in bad ground.

East of Heddon-on-the-Wall the rock-cut ditch, in weathered condition, is 34 feet wide and 9 feet deep; at Stanley, rock-cut, it is 26 feet wide and 11 feet deep; as it descends from Carvoran to Thirlwall it is 40 feet wide and 10 feet deep. At Haltonchesters east gate it was 29½ feet wide and not less than 8 feet deep; at Chesters 27 feet wide and 9 feet deep. At Birdoswald it has the width of 27 feet and a depth of 9 feet. To judge from the sections preserved in virtually the original condition (because soon filled) at Haltonchesters, Chesters and Birdoswald, it was a standard Roman military ditch, V-shaped in section, with a small square drainage-channel running along the bottom. Weathering, re-digging and difficult ground, have, however, produced wide variations.

The upcast from the ditch is normally thrown to the north to form a broad mound or glacis, which considerably heightens the outer slope or counterscarp of the ditch and tails away gently northwards so as to afford no cover to an enemy. But in some places, such as Wall Fell and Appletree, this work remains unfinished and upcast lies in tumbled heaps as dumped in baskets from the digging of the ditch. Nor is the ditch itself always completed. At Cockmount Hill it is dug only to half depth, while further west, at Allolee, it is not dug at all, though its absence is not warranted by the character of the terrain. But the

quadrangular fortlets normally varying from 50 to 60 feet in width
and from 57 to 75 feet in length, internally, although some of the

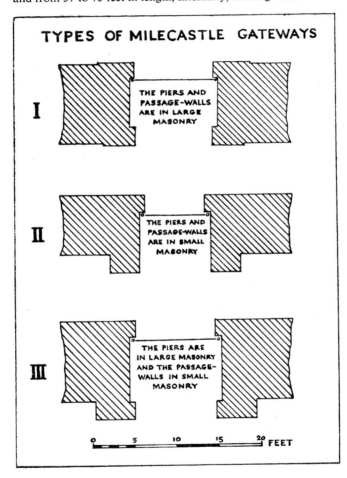

Turf Wall milecastles are larger. They were built so that the
Wall aligned with the milecastle's north face; but while the
foundations of the Wall and milecastle were usually laid simultaneously, the milecastle (or part of it) was normally erected

first and supplied with wing-walls ready to bond with the running work or curtain of the Wall, when this was built.

The milecastles have wide portals of massive masonry in the centre of their north and south sides. The northern gate was topped by a tower matching the turrets of the curtain Wall (see later). However, in Stone-Wall milecastles, as in the rebuilt Turf-Wall milecastle 79, the plans of the north and south gates are identical, even down to the projecting responds of massive masonry in type III gateways. Unless the south gates also had a tower it is difficult to see any purpose for this similarity of plan, which necessitated the building of much more solid and substantial structures than would have been required for simple unadorned gateways. The exception to this appears to be Turf-Wall milecastle 50, where the north gate has produced more post-holes than the south, suggesting that it was more elaborate. But the published plan makes it clear that the south gate was not so thoroughly excavated as the north, and it may well have had a larger number of post-holes than appears in the report.

Variations of gateway type occur, three of which are shown in the accompanying illustration.   Type II is only found in Narrow Wall construction, the equivalent (with only one pair of responds) found in Broad Wall milecastles is usually built of large masonry, and has been called type IV by some excavators. As this type appears to occur only east of the North Tyne, and type II only west of it, and both appear to be the work of the same legion they may be looked upon as a variation of the same basic type.

Internal structures consisted of two small buildings at most, flanking the road between the north and south gates. Little evidence for the size or purposes of these survives (and some of that which does relates to Wall Period II) but they are usually taken to have been barrack and storehouse provision for the patrol garrison. As the size of these buildings varies from milecastle to milecastle it seems likely that the garrisons varied too, from 8 to 64 men if the space allocation per man in normal fort barracks is any indication. However, as it has been estimated that a minimum force of 12 would be necessary to man the milecastle and guard its gates, either the space allocation per person in the milecastle barracks was less than in normal forts, or the buildings we now see represent a state of affairs when the patrol system had been heavily modified. Probably the surviving examples form too small a group to allow a clear picture of the orginal patrol garrison strength to be calculated. Finally, two barracks are the maximum provision, many milecastles possessed only one.

There are also differences in the overall shape of the milecastles, and some have their long axis from north to south, others from east to west; the general design, however, remains the same.

On the Turf Wall milecastles were built to the same design, with ramparts of turf and gateways and internal buildings of timber. Milecastle 50 TW (High House) has been completely excavated and remains of others have been found at Milecastles 49, 53, 54, 72 and 79.

Two points should be added concerning the later history of the milecastles. In the second Wall Period the milecastle gateways were normally reduced to posterns or foot-passages, by narrowing their width. If this action dates to the reign of Commodus it is possibly related to the apparent reduction or abandonment of the outpost forts which occurred then. But it has also been discovered that before this modification the original Stone-Wall milecastle gateways had in every case been supplied with new pivot-blocks in which to hang their doors, and these, unlike the alterations, are not associated with the rebuilding of the milecastles after a disaster. This can only mean that during the second century the doors of milecastles were for a time systematically dismantled, to be replaced later in the century. This dismantling, which shows that for a time the milecastles were disused and left open to passage unsupervised by any garrison, corresponds to an obliteration of the Vallum by the crossing system (described below p. 32), and to the reoccupation of Scotland in A.D. 140, when the frontier was moved northwards to the Antonine Wall between Forth and Clyde. The refitting of the doors represents the reoccupation of Hadrian's Wall later in the century (Period IB).

B. *Turrets*

Two turrets, regularly spaced at an average distance of about 540 yards, occur between each pair of milecastles. They measure some 14 feet square internally, and 20 feet square externally, and can best be understood as ordinary stone watch-towers built as an integral part of the Wall. On the Stone Wall they were built first, as were milecastles, and were provided with wing-walls for bonding: on the Turf Wall they were built as towers without wing-walls, and the turfwork of the Wall was then brought up to their east and west sides. They had an upper storey above the

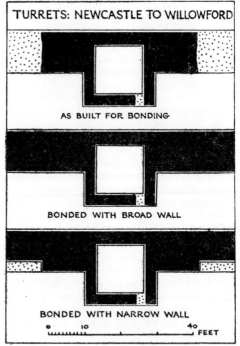

TURRETS: NEWCASTLE TO WILLOWFORD

AS BUILT FOR BONDING

BONDED WITH BROAD WALL

*Turrets as related
to the Stone Wall*

BONDED WITH NARROW WALL

0   10   40
                                      FEET

Wall top which was reached by an internal ladder. The usual
reconstructions show this, whether permanent or retractable,
with its feet resting on a little platform, or landing, in one
corner of the Stone-Wall turrets.

It is evident that the work of patrolling the Wall and sending
out relays of men to do duty in the adjacent turrets, was the
responsibility of the detachments quartered in the milecastles.
To discharge this task a force variously calculated from 650-
4,000 would be required. The forts as first designed, lying behind
the Wall, may have met this need; but the drain could have been
severe, as the fort garrisons cannot have exceeded about 12,000
in all. It is therefore thought that the Wall had two garrisons,
a fighting garrison of cohorts and *alae*, lodged in the forts, and
a patrol-garrison composed of units of other kinds, lodged in the
milecastles. Later, it was found that the work of patrolling and

signalling could be carried out by using fewer turrets, and many were dismantled in Wall Period II.

A local tradition already current in Camden's day credits the Romans with other means of communication than visible signals: speaking-trumpets or pipes, it was fabled, ran along the whole length of the Wall, as Michael Drayton states in his Poly-Olbion:

> And when I first decayd, Severus going on,
> What Adrian built of turfe, he builded new of stone;
> And after many a time, the Britans me repayr'd,
> To keepe me still in plight, nor cost they ever spar'd.
> Townes stood upon my length, where Garrisons were laid,
> Their limits to defend; and for my greater ayd,
> With Turrets I was built, where Sentinels were plac'd,
> To watch upon the Pict; so me my Makers grac'd,
> With hollow Pipes of Brasse, along me still that went,
> By which they in one Fort still to another sent,
> By speaking in the same, to tell them what to doe,
> And so from Sea to Sea could I be whispered through:
> Upon my thicknesse, three march'd eas'ly breast to breast,
> Twelve foot was I in height, such glory I possest.

In fact, however, there is no evidence whatever for such devices.

C. *The Forts*

The first system of garrison forts for the Wall consisted of the Trajanic posts lying along the Stanegate. Only a patrol force based on the turrets and milecastles seems to have been actually on the line of the barrier itself. The Stanegate sites, some cohort forts and other fortlets, are known at Corbridge, Chesterholm, Haltwhistle Burn, Throp, Nether Denton, Brampton Old Church and Carlisle, to which Carvoran and Castle Hill Boothby can probably be added, while another cohort fort has been argued to lie under the fourth-century fortlet at Newbrough. Whether there were more posts than these is uncertain. Some have proposed a regular system, consisting of alternating forts and fortlets, all the way from Corbridge to Carlisle, which would require additional posts at or near Wall, Grindon and High Crosby. But with the possible exception of a post at the crossing of the North Tyne, assumed on strategic grounds but not found, these others are doubtful. East of Corbridge and west of Carlisle next to nothing is known of the initial arrangement. At Kirkbride, south of Bowness, a site of the right date exists, but its true nature is not yet clear, while a newly discovered fort at Washing Well, between the Team Valley and Whickham, which could be part of the eastern end of the system, has not been put to the spade. Pre-Hadrianic samian ware has come from Benwell and Wallsend, and these two sites may yet have somehow to be fitted into the system. When Platorious Nepos decided to build forts actually on the Wall itself all these Stanegate posts were given up and their garrisons transferred to the Wall. At later dates Corbridge, Chesterholm and Carvoran, at least, were reoccupied, as part of the Wall system.

Of the initial Hadrianic Wall forts, some project beyond the line of the Wall so that their main north, east and west gates lie north of the barrier, permitting the garrison to deploy very rapidly, and intercept raiders or repel attack. These forts are at Wallsend, Benwell, Rudchester, Haltonchesters, Chesters, Birdoswald (Turf-Wall period) and Burgh-by-Sands. Forts in the same series which do not project are Housesteads, Greatchesters, Stanwix and Bowness, while Castlesteads actually lies to the rear of the Wall, owing to the nature of the ground. Other forts are later, or of unknown date: Carrawburgh, on the western rim of North Tynedale, was built before 133, and lay wholly to the south of the Wall, while Carvoran, in the Tipalt Gap, where inscriptions prove the fort wall to have been rebuilt in stone in 136-7, is free-standing. At Newcastle and Drumburgh we do not know the date of the fort, nor in the case of Newcastle, even its precise location. Considerable variation then, appears to exist; but tactically, at least, the arrangement of the forts shows that the fighting garrison was not intended to man the Wall and to fight from it, but to go out beyond it and deploy in the open.

The forts themselves are almost all rectangular with rounded corners. They are defended by a stone wall, about 5 feet thick, with an earth rampart piled against its inner face, the earth being derived from a ditch or ditches in front of the fort-wall. The gateways are at least four, and 6 if the fort projects beyond the Wall. The portals are often partly walled up, a practice once regarded as a symptom of declining morale in the army of the later Roman Empire, but now known to have been begun almost at once. In several cases it is clear that the masonry of the gates was quite new when they were blocked, a step which may be connected with the change of garrison in A.D. 140, when Scotland was reoccupied, but which might even more show that the forts were considered too vulnerable in the summer months when the majority of the garrison would be in the field.

The main street (*via praetoria*) from the front gate of the fort joins the principal cross-street (*via principalis*) at right angles near the centre of the fort. At this point stood the headquarters building (*principia*). This was planned with a fore-court surrounded by colonnades, giving access on to a large covered, colonnaded hall (*basilica*) and a series of small rooms, of which the central one was the regimental chapel (*aedes*) containing the standards, and dedicated to the worship of the Emperor or his Discipline. In some forts the chapel later contained the entrance to an underground strong-room designed to hold the chest for pay and regimental savings.

On one side of this central building stood the commanding-officer's house (*praetorium*), ranged in Mediterranean style about a courtyard, and often supplied with a private suite of baths. On the other side were the granaries (*horrea*), massive buttressed buildings with a raised damp-proof floor and fire-proof roof, to hold the grain and other supplies for the garrison, including a year's reserve. The annual replenishment of corn took the form of a tax in kind upon the province which the Wall defended (*annona militaris*).

In front of and behind this central range were rows of long narrow buildings mostly barracks for the men, but including stables, storehouses, and workshops. Each barrack building housed a "century" (*centuria*), actually 80 men, and its centurion; in a cavalry unit each block housed two *turmae* of 32 men apiece, each with a decurion. The men, whether infantry or cavalry, were grouped in mess-units of 8 (*contubernia*), each in their own room for living and sleeping, with an ante-room for kit.

Often forts also contained a hospital (*valetudinarium*), a courtyard building surrounded by individual rooms, each separated from its neighbours by a small passageway. A somewhat similar type of building consisting of a central corridor flanked by side rooms may have been a workshop/armoury (*fabrica*) rather than a hospital, although it has sometimes been mistaken for a hospital.

These internal arrangements can best be seen at Chesters (*principia, praetorium,* barracks) and Housesteads (*principia, praetorium, horrea, valetudinarium,* and late barracks).

A village (*vicus*), established with permission by veterans, camp followers, traders and locals, grew up outside most of the forts. Excellent examples of the shops and taverns which it contained are to be seen at Housesteads and Chesterholm. But the most notable external building was the regimental bath-house (*balneum*) of which a fine example can be seen at Chesters. Essentially it consisted of a suite of rooms graded in temperature from cold to hot: the bather began cold, went gradually from warm rooms to hot room, where he sweated profusely in a steamy atmosphere akin to that of a modern Turkish bath. After immersing himself in the hot bath he returned for a final cold douche.

In selecting a site for a fort, care was clearly taken that a copious supply of water should be available. The springs, rivulets, wells and aqueducts are still in many places to be traced, as at Benwell, Haltonchesters, Chesters, Chesterholm and Greatchesters. At Housesteads, situated on an outcrop of the Whin Sill, where the main source was the external Knag Burn, there is a very large number of collecting tanks supplied from roofs or surface drains.

After the collapse of Roman Britain, the forts and their villages ceased to be inhabited. Their names, once household words, were forgotten. The evidence of the *Notitia*, however, as Horsley discovered, fixes the names of 15, though the manuscripts do not always transmit a correct spelling: for example VINDOLANA should be VINDOLANDA; AMBOGLANNA should be CAMBOGLANNA, and BORCOVICIUM (not BORCOVICUS, a form for which there is no authority) is from BERCOVICIUM, the late-Roman spelling of VERCOVICIUM. In this book the modern names are employed for general use.

In spite of increasing numbers of modern visitors, some of the forts still present a scene of final desolation. The wayfarer may pass through some of them without knowing it: the sheep, cropping the grass-grown ruins, look listlessly upon the traveller, and the lap-wing, wheeling overhead, screams at the intruder.

III. THE VALLUM

The Vallum is an earthwork lying south of the Wall. The essential part of it is a ditch, normally 20 feet wide and 10 feet deep, with a flat bottom 8 feet wide, and thus quite unlike a Roman military ditch. Great care was taken by its original constructors to prevent this ditch from falling in or otherwise becoming obliterated at points of special engineering difficulty. Where it crossed a steep ravine its sides were revetted with stone, and where it crossed a marsh they were embanked like a canal. In sandy soil, as at Cawfields, its sides are artificially built in turfwork resting upon stone flagging, while in other places its sides are cut to a less steep slope to avoid revetment. Unlike the ditch of the Wall, it is never left undug.

The material taken out of the ditch is normally piled in two continuous mounds originally set 30 feet back from the ditch on either side of it. To make them stand sharply these mounds, 20 feet wide, are usually revetted with kerbs of turfwork. This gives the standard original section of the Vallum—mound, berm, ditch, berm, mound—the whole 120 feet across, the Roman surveyor's unit known as an *actus*. There is, however, often a third mound, on one or other lip of the ditch, known as the marginal mound; this is usually later in date, and is the result of cleaning out rather than re-cutting the ditch.

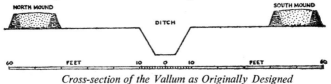

Cross-section of the Vallum as Originally Designed

The Vallum is laid out in truly Roman fashion, running straight from point to point, like a Roman road. Unlike the Wall, it is not placed upon ground with a good outlook or defensibility; it often runs at the foot of a slope equally useless for defence and for view. It normally runs close behind the Wall, so that when it approaches a fort attached to the Wall it usually deviates from a straight course and passes round it on the south; originally it was crossed at such points by a stone-faced causeway (discussed below), but later it was completely filled up in the immediate neighbourhood of the forts. It is not usually so close to milecastles as to compel its deviation from the straight course, and still less does it impinge upon the Wall itself. But in the Birdoswald sector it avoids the Turf-Wall milecastle at High House (50 TW) by a regularly-planned re-entrant, while east of that milecastle the north mound is omitted, as being too near the Turf Wall. This sector of the Turf Wall was, however, very soon replaced by a Stone Wall a little further north.

The discovery in 1935 of the relation between Wall and Vallum made their relative date a matter no longer of theory but of fact, while the discovery in 1950/1 of an original revetted causeway south of Greatchesters provided an even closer date for the Vallum's construction: Greatchesters cannot have been earlier than 128, while Carrawburgh, built across a filled-in portion of the Vallum ditch, was constructed by 133. In its purpose the Vallum falls into place as a rearward boundary strip demarcated by mounds and bisected by a deep, wide ditch which was an obstacle to all. At the forts, the causeways across the ditch were blocked in the middle by a great unfortified gateway, opened and controlled from the fort to the north of it.

At milecastles, also, causeways exist across the Vallum, but with the exception of milecastle 50 (TW) and apparently 51, all are of secondary date and it is very uncertain whether there was ever, normally, a primary causeway at milecastles. Primary gaps have been argued to have existed in the north mound to

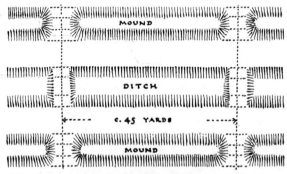

The obliteration of the Vallum by Crossings

allow the patrol troops to inspect the Vallum ditch: be this as it may, the original state of the barrier was soon radically altered as a result of the so-called "crossings". These are gaps made in the Vallum mounds, the resultant earth being used to throw causeways across the ditch. They are normally made at regular intervals of 45 yards, but in a few places they have been begun and not finished; and very occasionally they have not even been begun. Thirty-five of them go to every Roman mile, and the causeways south of the milecastles should be seen as part of the general arrangement. This systematic obliteration happened when the work had not been in use for long, and it is both dated and explained by the reoccupation of Scotland in A.D. 140. The Vallum thus functioned as a non-military boundary policed by military patrols: a demarcation as opposed to a defence. It was the southern boundary of a military zone.

Whether the Vallum was subsequently ever put back into full commission is unlikely, for both causeways and gaps in the mounds remain today visible for considerable lengths, and can be seen clearly, for example, from milecastle 29 to Carrawburgh fort, and in the neighbourhood of Cawfields. The date of the "marginal mound" is also uncertain: in many cases it comprises silty material cleared from the ditch, although near milecastle 42 it was mostly clean soil. It has been connected with the late clearing of the ditch, but it probably belongs much earlier in the history of the barrier, in fact at Limestone Bank it appears to be the result of an early cleaning-out of the ditch, which has been attributed to the result of frost action upon the newly rock-cut ditch. This phase in the upkeep of the work still needs much study.

IV. THE CUMBRIAN COAST

From Bowness to St. Bees' Head the Solway coast faces Scotland, exposing the western flank of the Wall to hostile attack from the north. Accordingly, the whole defensive system was extended approximately 40 Roman miles south to prevent this. In its essentials this extension was similar to the Wall itself, except that the linear features of Wall, ditch and Vallum were omitted, except for the first few miles, where two slight ditches were dug. Milecastles are represented by free-standing mile-fortlets, built of timber and turfwork, with a single gateway. Their size and shape varies, insofar as it has been ascertained, from 90 by 104 feet to 105 by 115 feet externally, but their internal arrangement appears to have been basically that of the mile-castles, with a barrack or barracks, facing a central street. The buildings were of timber. Cardurnock (5) is an exception in many ways: it is noticeably larger, measuring no less than 178 by 142 feet, which gives it an internal area of three times that of the next largest example known. As such it should probably be seen as a small fortlet rather than a normal milefortlet. Skinburness (9) may have been similar. Cardurnock also had a wooden tower, but in one corner and not over its gate, which may have been exceptional. Unlike milecastles, sometimes the milefortlets faced the sea and sometimes not: Brown Rigg (22) had a front entrance, Mawbray (16) and Low Mire (20) faced inland, while Cardurnock had a north entrance, although the coast lay to the west Too few examples, however, have been excavated for us to have any overall idea of size, shape and differences of type.

Wall turrets are replaced by free-standing towers, built of red sandstone and some 20 feet square, externally. Their height has recently been calculated to have been at least 25 feet, and in one case, tower 16*b*, half of a merlon cap-stone was found, implying a flat roof with crenellations. Platforms, or couches as they are sometimes called, are usually present, and the door is normally in the rear wall, at ground level.

This system of milefortlets and towers was regularly laid out (like the Wall) with two towers between each pair of milefortlets, the spacing between each feature being approximately 540 yards, or one-third of a Roman mile.

Present opinion is that the coastal system can be divided into two parts. First, the posts west of Bowness, as far as mile-fortlet 5 on the north shore of Moricambe Bay. Here, the position of most of the towers and milefortlets is known, and the system seems to be a continuation of the Wall milecastle spacing, but without the running barrier. In 1975, however, Professor Barri Jones discovered a pair of parallel ditches, generally 50 yards apart, but north of Cardurnock village 33 yards only, which contained the towers and milefortlets between them. At one point a slot for stakes was found beyond the north ditch. The light subsoil had necessitated frequent re-cutting, so that the ditches ranged from just over 3½ feet to 8½ feet in width, but the nature and purpose of the whole appeared clear: to provide a continuation of the Vallum and Wall ditch, enclosing the towers and milefortlets within a continuous barrier, either for defence or to prevent infiltration.

Milefortlets 1 and 5 are known to have continued in use through both Wall Periods IA and IB, suggesting that the turrets, too, in this sector were probably reoccupied on the return to Hadrian's Wall. At Cardurnock a fourth-century reoccupation is also attested.

Milefortlets 6, 7 and 8, once thought to have been removed by Moricambe, are now no longer considered to have existed: instead, the system is believed to begin again with milefortlet 9, which stood at the base of Grune Point, matching Cardurnock to the north. Re-numbering to remove this inconsistency might seem logical, but so much has already been published about posts under their traditional numbers that it would certainly lead to confusion.

The second part consists of the posts south of Moricambe, where the system was similar to that further north, except that no running ditches have yet been found. At Silloth, however, in 1976 Professor Jones located a pair of clay-filled trenches which had contained upright stakes. In the sandy subsoil of the region these are likely to have replaced the ditches located further north. Mr. Richard Bellhouse has recently shown that in this sector the positions of towers and milefortlets relate to Maryport fort, with those to the north laid out by measurement from its north-west angle-tower, and those to the south measured from its south-west angle. Maryport fort is now known to have been a Hadrianic foundation, but whether it is contemporary with the garrison-forts on the Wall itself, is still not certain. The most southerly known milefortlet and tower are 26 and 26*a*, at Risehow. Beyond here the sites, and the southern termination of the system, are as yet still unsubstantiated. But, as the coast changes direction at St. Bees' Head and thereafter faces the Irish Sea rather than Galloway, that point was the obvious one for the watch-system to end.

The southern sector was manned throughout Wall Period IA, and then, like the Wall itself, abandoned on the Antonine advance into Scotland. During Period IA, however, wind erosion had seriously affected many of the towers standing on the sandy coastal dunes, so that either then, or immediately after the beginning of Period IB, repairs had to be carried out. These were mostly crude and executed in inferior masonry. Whether a reoccupation of the whole system at the beginning of Period IB was ever contemplated, let alone carried out, is not known. In addition to the crude rebuilding, the slightest trace of Antonine pottery has been noted at two sites, suggesting, perhaps, a scheme for full or partial reoccupation, never implemented.

Just as on the Wall itself, the forts held the main garrisons. Maryport, as already said, is the key to the milefortlets south of Moricambe, and so must precede that part of the system. The other coastal forts, however, were probably a little later, for Beckfoot lies on the measured position of tower 14*b*, while Moresby, like Greatchesters, has produced an inscription of Hadrian as *Pater Patriae*, Father of his Country, which title he did not take until A.D. 128. The spacing of these forts is approximately equal: a little under 10 miles between Beckfoot and Maryport and about 11 miles between Maryport and Moresby. The distance from Bowness to Beckfoot is considerably greater, but Moricambe may have affected the arrangement. The remaining fort in this sector, Burrow Walls, is only 5 and 5¾ miles from Maryport and Moresby, respectively, suggesting that it was a later addition, which opinion is supported by the absence (to date) of pre-fourth-century pottery from the site.

Later, in the fourth century, some form of patrolling was re-introduced, for Cardurnock was rebuilt, and late sherds have occasionally been found on earlier sites, for instance at milefortlet 20, where they lay well above the earlier occupation levels.

If the towers and milefortlets ended at St. Bees' Head, the forts continued. A number of small finds made on various sites about the mouth of the river Ehen includes pottery and coins, and probably indicates the general location of the missing *Notitia* site of Tunnocelum, more correctly perhaps Itunocelum (Eden Head), which appears in the Ravenna List under the form Iuliocenon. The next fort south is Ravenglass. This is sometimes described as a staging post for shipping rather than the last of the coastal fort series, but it appears in the *Notitia*, like Moresby and Tunnocelum, as *per lineam valli* ("on the line of the Wall"), and as such it should be considered as the southernmost of the west-coast flank defence of the system.

v. THE OUTPOST FORTS TO THE NORTH

From Newcastle to the North Tyne, thence almost to milecastle 54, the outlook of the Wall to the north is everywhere so good that it would be possible to detect an approaching enemy in time to prepare an interception. In Cumbria, on the other hand, conditions are mostly different. North of Birdoswald an enemy could work round the shoulder of the fells which end in Gillalees Beacon; between Castlesteads and Stanwix he could lurk in the mosses and woodlands of the Cumberland plain; while beyond the Solway he could concentrate on the north shore, behind the screen of low hills. Accentuating this problem was the fact that part of the Brigantian tribal confederacy, which lay behind the Wall in the east, extended across its line in the west, into the northern Solway basin and south-eastern Dumfriesshire. That the north-western section of this great confederacy was cut in two by the Wall was unfortunate, but it was a geographical necessity which Rome attempted to rectify by control. In order to prevent a "Free Brigantia" movement, then, no less than to provide eyes and ears for a blind organism, outpost forts were provided in the west at Bewcastle, beyond Gillalees, at Netherby, beyond Stanwix, and at Birrens, beyond the Solway. The two first are known to be Hadrianic from inscriptions, the third from pottery associated with its defences (found in 1937 and in the 1960s), while the case for a possible Hadrianic inscription here too, has been argued by Professor Eric Birley.

In the Hadrianic period, little more is known of these sites than their existence, but the probable signal-post on Gillalees shows how one at least of the forts could be used in preparing a surprise interception of the enemy. All three of these forts continued in use during the Antonine reoccupation of Scotland, augmented by two new sites in the east, at Risingham and High Rochester. When Scotland was abandoned these 5 were retained as outpost forts of the Wall, with, most likely, Newstead, and, probably, Cappuck in addition. Together, all 7 ensured an effective control over a considerable buffer zone in advance of the Wall.

Just how long in the second century these forts were held is uncertain, but Birrens, Newstead, and presumably Cappuck, appear to have been given up about A.D. 180, and the end at Newstead is attested archaeologically to have been by fire. Risingham, too, appears to have been abandoned before the end of the century; and if Risingham then probably high Rochester. The trouble in the province under Ulpius Marcellus most probably provides the occasion for all of this.

Under Severus, Netherby, Bewcastle, Risingham and High Rochester were rebuilt and re-garrisoned, but neither Birrens nor Newstead, although third-century pottery has been recovered from the vicinity of the annexe at Birrens, while two inscriptions, now in Jedburgh, suggest that there was some post north of the Cheviots. Following the Caracallan peace, the four surviving posts took their place once more as outpost forts, making it clear that a wide zone beyond the Wall was again to be controlled, for each was strongly garrisoned with a part-mounted milliary cohort, supplemented by *exploratores* or Units of Scouts. Clearly, each served as a base for an extensive system of patrolling: far-ranging policing and the interception of enemy forces well beyond the Wall was thus made possible on an even greater scale than previously. In fact the Borders and the Southern Uplands, if not a much wider area, were turned into a huge protectorate in advance of the Wall, where the *Pax Romana* ran. The place of the *loca* in this has already been mentioned (see p. 7). The remarkable system so created lasted until well into the fourth century. It was then gradually given up, and that probably in the face of rising pressure. Although all the forts were reconstructed early in the fourth century, and both Bewcastle and Risingham were rebuilt again before 367 (possibly in 343), High Rochester received no such second fourth-century reoccupation. Everything, however, appears finally to have ended with Count Theodosius, who dismantled the system after convicting its garrisons of treason and complicity in the Barbarian Conspiracy of A.D. 367.

<h3 style="text-align:center">VI. THE MILITARY ROADS</h3>

For lateral communication, the Wall was at first dependent on either its own walk, or, more likely, a patrol path along the Vallum or the open trackless zone between them. Supplies reached the forts by branch-roads from the Stanegate. This road, situated to the south of both Wall and Vallum, afforded a direct line of communication between east and west. It ran from Corbridge via the North Tyne to Newbrough and Chesterholm, where a Roman milestone stands, and on to Carvoran and Nether Denton. It appears again at Irthington, running thence to High Crosby, east of Stanwix, and it has been traced at various points between. A feature of its western course is the engineering of deep cuttings in the face of natural obstacles. At four sites along this road, Corbridge, Chesterholm, Nether Denton and Carlisle, remains of the late first century A.D. have been found. It seems likely that the Stanegate began as one of Agricola's roads, initially constructed during his campaigns in north Britain of A.D. 79-84, with posts at Carlisle and Corbridge Red House. To these the other two sites were added after 87, about which time the Red House site was replaced by a new fort at Corbridge, lying a little further to the east. Under Trajan, after the destruction of A.D. 105, the forts were rebuilt and the line strengthened. Later, under Hadrian, it would be logical to expect the road to have been continued both eastwards and westwards behind the Wall (if in fact its extension had not already been carried out by Trajan). Little, however, is as yet known about this.

A through road from fort to fort along the Wall was thus not by any means the first element in the system. The Military Way, as this road is usually called, came later, after the obliteration of the Vallum; in fact, it is known in places to ride on top of the Vallum north mound. The actual date of construction is not certain: it is probably as early as Period IB, although the earliest milestones are of A.D. 213. The construction is that normal for Roman roads: it is usually some 20 feet wide, and the surface is cambered, the centre being elevated 1 foot or 18 inches above the adjoining ground. As a rule, it was metalled with small stone, chiefly trap, and surfaced with fine gravel, resting upon a heavy bottoming of large stones and edged with kerbs of large stones; but in some places, to bind it better, it had an axial rib of big stones as well as kerbs. Along the slope of the hills, the downhill side of the road was made up of unusually large kerbstones. In most places where the road still remains, it is completely grass-grown and a sheep-track generally runs along it.

For convenience of communication, the Military Way went from milecastle to milecastle, and so from fort to fort, sending off a branch path to each turret. In doing this it did not always keep close to the Wall, but took the easiest course between the required points. In negotiating the steep declivities between Sewingshields and Thirlwall the ingenuity of the engineer has been most successfully applied. While the Wall holds to its course over the highest and steepest summits, the road runs on the slope behind it, so as to serve the milecastles by the easiest possible gradients. It is a most instructive example of Roman road engineering.

Finally, in estimating the resources of Hadrian's Wall, we must recall that two great lines of communication serviced the Wall from the legionary bases; one from York crossed the Wall near Corbridge, with a branch road from Binchester to Newcastle; the other from Chester crossed it near Carlisle, with a branch from Kirkby Thore to Carvoran. The Sixth Legion, whose headquarters were at York, would have no difficulty at almost any season of the year in coming to the aid of the auxiliaries to whom the defence of the Wall was more immediately entrusted, at whatever point assistance might be required; while reinforcements could also be had from the Twentieth Legion at Chester.

VII. BRIDGES AND CULVERTS

At streams and rivers the Wall crossed by means of a bridge. The two best surviving examples are at Chesters on the North Tyne and Willowford on the Irthing, but others carried the Wall, or its attendant roads, across the Tyne at Newcastle and Corbridge and the Eden at Carlisle, as well as over numerous minor streams and small steep burns. In their first state both the Chesters and Willowford bridges seem to have been slight affairs, carrying only the curtain Wall over the rivers. Nevertheless, they had stone piers and abutments, and it has been argued that their upperwork was totally of stone. Later, each was enlarged to carry the Military Way as well, and there is some evidence for thinking that these wider bridges, although still based on stone piers and abutments, had timber upperworks. The road-bridges were probably of this type from the beginning.

At streams and small gullies the Wall was pierced by large culverts, of sufficient size to carry a full winter's spate. Numerous examples must once have existed, but comparatively few have survived, or been recorded. Bruce illustrated one example, west of Denton Burn, and the remains of another were recently, if briefly, seen on the Rudchester Burn.

VIII. TEMPORARY CAMPS

A group of earthworks exists in the vicinity of the Wall, and along Dere Street, which is without parallel in Britain, or beyond. This is a collection of ephemeral camps, erected by the Roman army when halting for the night, or when engaged in some such task as building the Wall. Some of the smallest camps are not large enough to have held more than a few men, and should probably be seen as practice camps, like the better known group of 18 on Llandrindod Common.

The normal marching camp consists of a shallow ditch backed by a low earth rampart of upcast, which was regularly constructed around the tents each night. On top of the rampart a palisade of sharpened stakes, *pila muralia*, was placed. The gateways were gaps in the rampart ditch and bank, defended by either a short traverse and a ditch placed in front of the gap (*titulum*), or a curved horn running internally or externally to cover the gap (*clavicula*). Occasionally, more sophisticated entrance arrangements occur, such as in the Glenwhelt Leazes and Chapel Rigg camps, but these are uncommon and seem to have been an early feature. Within this defence shelter was provided by tents, placed in regular lines, with the headquarters space and commanding-officer's tent in the centre.

Temporary camps were similar, but being occupied for a longer period of time they sometimes received metalled internal roads. Accommodation, however, was normally the same as in marching camps.

Practice camps were usually small in size, but have normal

corners and entrances. Clearly, it was practice in the construction of these rather than the comparatively simple rampart and ditch, which was considered important.

IX. QUARRIES AND METHODS OF BUILDING THE WALL

Both faces of the Wall are clad in carefully squared freestone blocks and the character of these facing-stones is distinctive and tolerably uniform. They measure on the face 6 or 7 inches high by 10 or 11 wide, and from front to back as much as 20 inches. The face of the stone exposed to the weather is cut across the "bait", or natural bedding of the stone, so as to avoid flakings, while the stone tapers towards the back so as to bond better with the core. The face is normally tooled with a smooth finish, but sometimes with distinctive patterns in the form of diagonal cross-broaching and diamond-broaching, as such tooling is called. The uniformity of their appearance enables

Inscribed Quarry Face, Fallowfield Fell
(*The stone is now at Chesters Museum*)

anyone, after a little practice, to recognize these stones at once in the churches, castles, farm-buildings and field-walls of the district through which the Wall runs.

But there are three exceptions. For gates of forts and mile-castles, larger stones were used, unless, as at certain milecastles, the steepness of the approach made it difficult to bring up a wagon. Examples include milecastle 39 (Castle Nick) and 40 (Win-shields). Here the whole structure is built of small stones that could be easily manhandled. Secondly, bridge piers and abut-ments and other such substantial pieces of engineering, which had to withstand great weight or lateral pressure, were con-constructed of monumental masonry often tied stone to stone, and course to course, with leaded iron cramps. Thirdly, larger stones are found in the lowest courses of the Wall, but not in its superstructure. They occur especially in the bottom course of what is now called "type A" construction, which obtains for 17 Roman miles westward from Newcastle. Conversely, stones

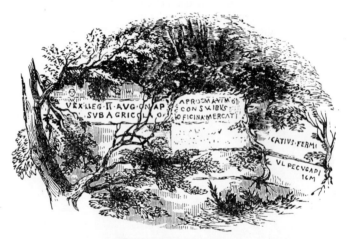

The Written Rock of Gelt

in the ramparts of some forts are smaller than those in the Wall; while the internal buildings of forts are also composed of comparatively small stones.

The stone used for the facing-blocks was normally a very carefully selected quartzose grit, which was not only hard but had a rough surface that bonded well with either mortar or clay.

The quarries from which the facing-stones came can be

identified. On Fallowfield Fell, not far from Chollerford, the face of one of these ancient quarries is inscribed with the words (P)ETRA FLAVI CARANTINI, "the rock of Flavius Carantinus". An old quarry on Barcombe, above Chesterholm, re-opened in 1839, yielded an arm-purse of bronze containing three gold and 60 silver coins, all current under Hadrian. North of Busy Gap wedge-holes still remain in exposures of rock. Just west of the Stanegate fortlet on the Haltwhistle Burn a Roman quarry once bore the inscription LEG. VI.V; and throughout the central sector numerous ancient quarries or worked outcrop faces, mostly without doubt Roman, are still to be seen up to half a mile south of the Wall.

In Cumberland, about two miles west of Birdoswald, and just over a quarter of a mile south of the Wall, Coombe Crag exhibits many Roman names inscribed by the men at work. Comparable inscriptions are recorded from Lanerton and seen at Wetheral, but the most remarkable group of such records is at the "Written Rock", on the Gelt, near Brampton, where the longest inscription records the presence of "a vexillation of the Second Legion under the *optio* Agricola, in the consulate of Aper and Maximus"; that is in A.D. 207.

East of the Glebe Farm at Irthington there are extensive ancient quarries, while excavations have revealed a quarry of considerable size at Bleatarn. There is another quarry at Grinsdale, on the river Eden, just north of the Wall, and a famous example once exhibited inscriptions at Shawk, south of Thursby. Generally, however, geological conditions in Cumbria render quarries both rarer and more distant from the Wall than in Northumberland, so that stone from north of the Solway was brought for use between Carlisle and Bowness.

Between the ashlar faces, the core of the Wall was packed with rubble, obtained close to the Wall, where the small pit-quarries from which it was taken can frequently be recognised. On the Broad Wall, the rubble was set either in mortar or a mass of tough puddled clay: only the ashlar faces were always set in mortar. The Narrow and Intermediate Walls, and reconstructions, were set wholly in mortar. The principal ingredient of the mortar is lime, which was also prepared close at hand, for limestone is abundant from Newcastle to the Red Rock Fault, west of the Irthing. An example of a limekiln has been excavated at Housesteads: and the small specks of charcoal sometimes found in the mortar came from burning in such kilns. The lime was next ground and mixed dry with sand and gravel. When about to be used, not before, water was added. Mortar thus prepared speedily hardens. In Cumbria, where limestone is scarce, the quality of mortar is less good.

Supposing the facing-stones to be quarried and trimmed and the lime burnt and mixed with sand and gravel, construction would begin. The foundation was laid directly upon the bared soft sub-soil where, below the line to be taken by the faces of the Wall, two rows of flags, from two to four inches thick and from 18 to 20 broad, were generally set, often in a spread of well-puddled clay. The middle space between the flags was filled with clay and cobbles or broken stone. On this foundation was laid the first course of facing-stones, which are usually the largest stones used in the structure. In the higher courses the facing-stones are uniformly freestone, but in the lowest courses whinstone is occasionally included. The flag-stones of the foundation usually project from one to two inches beyond the first course of facing-stones, and these again usually stand out an inch or two beyond the second course, after which the Wall is taken straight up. There are, however, variations in the treatment of the footing offsets which give the clue to work by different building-gangs. The foundation here described is that of the Broad Wall. The Narrow Wall, in the east, when not laid on broad foundations, had a foundation trench about 18 inches deep, packed with rubble and clay, upon which the footing-flags were laid. In the west the replacement of the Turf Wall had shallower foundations, whether narrow or intermediate. When one or two courses of facing-stones had been placed on their beds and carefully pointed, a mass of mortar in fluid state was poured into the interior of the Wall, and stones of any kind or shape that were of a convenient size were "puddled" in amongst it. Whinstones, as being most abundant in the district, were generally used for filling. Course after course was added, and one mass of grouting imposed upon another, as the work dried, until the Wall reached the required height. When the whole was finished it formed a solid, compact mass, firm as a rock.

At some points the rubble of the core has been first packed into its place, often laid slanting like herring-bone masonry, and the mortar has been laid on it with a trowel. In this case the mortar does not penetrate the interstices of the mass and makes a less solid structure. On undulating ground, and on some steep slopes, courses of the Wall follow the gentle wave of the surface; but on certain declivities, as at Peel Crag and on Walltown Crags, the stones are laid horizontally, stepping up the hill.

It is clear that the main part of the provincial army was engaged in the great task. Inscriptions record the legions at work on the milecastles, forts, Wall and Vallum, assisted by men of the Fleet and by auxiliary troops. All the mason's work was done by these troops, of whose training it formed part, but they were presumably assisted by native *corvées* for the rougher work, such as clearing, carting or puddling clay or road-making. The original building of the Wall itself was organised by centuries, each unit constructing a length of about 45 yards, and seems to have been almost entirely confined to the legions. The lengths so constructed were normally marked at each end by a small inscription mentioning the name of the century (sometimes cohort) which had done the work. These are the so-called centurial stones, of which over 200 are known, with up to 5 re-occurrences of the same century along the length of the Wall. Sometimes, as west of Housesteads, the lengths are shown by slight differences in thickness apparent at the back of the Wall. Stones also mention native communities, but these appear to belong to a later reconstruction, carried out by labour gangs contributed by the *civitates* which formed the provincial district governments. The Vallum also had centurial slabs, but of these much less is known. However, it does appear from stones of the First Cohort of Dacians found at Denton in 1936 that auxiliary cohorts were employed on the Vallum ditch and its mounds. Other stones from Newcastle, Carvoran and Wall-mile 58/9, all recording auxiliary cohorts, are possibly also to be associated with the Vallum.

X. ASSIGNMENT AND ORDER OF THE WORKS

It has been shown above that differences of plan and construction are visible in the curtain Wall, the milecastles and the turrets. Where inscriptions are associated with these it is possible to assign certain structures, and certain characteristics of construction, to particular legions. As the result of further study, and association, theoretical attributions have, in fact, been worked out for almost the whole undertaking. Starting with the building inscriptions of the Second Legion at milecastles 37, 38 and 42, these make it clear that this Legion constructed short axis milecastles with type I gateways, turrets with eastern doorways and broad side walls, and Standard A construction. Attribution in the case of the Twentieth and Sixth Legions is less certain, as problems remain unsolved. It is clear, however, that long axis milecastles with type III gateways go with west door turrets with narrow side walls, and Standard B construction. These are usually assigned to the Sixth Legion; and most of these characteristics do, in fact, occur with Sixth Legion inscriptions in the first, rebuilt, 5 miles of the Turf Wall.

This leaves the Twentieth Legion with long axis milecastles with type II/IV gateways, eastern door turrets with narrow side walls and Standard A construction. Unfortunately, however, milecastle 47, the only one with a Twentieth Legion inscription has, quite arguably, not type II gateways, but type III, while a Sixth Legion inscription was recently found reused in turret 33b, which was thought to have been built by the Twentieth. Further evidence, then, is clearly needed before a firm attribution can be made.

In the case of the forts, there is considerably less indication as to which legion built which, for Haltonchesters, alone, has produced an original legionary building inscription. Attributions in other cases have been made, but much additional evidence is needed here too.

It has been shown that the building of the Wall was subject to modification. The initial plan was to erect a broad Stone Wall from Newcastle to Willowford and a Turf Wall from Willowford to Bowness. When the foundation of the Stone Wall had been laid from Newcastle to the North Tyne, and intermittently beyond, the builders began the superstructure. Milecastles and turrets were built first: then the builders started the Wall itself, working east from Willowford to meet those coming west towards the North Tyne. The Turf Wall was probably also begun at this stage. But, after only part of the distance to the North Tyne had been covered, it was decided to build the Narrow Wall where the Broad Wall had not yet been erected. This decision was very likely the result of another: to move the forts on to the line of the Wall, and extend the whole to Wallsend.

Sometime after Greatchesters fort was built (not before 128) the Vallum was constructed behind the forts, an impossibility until after the decision to move the garrison-forts onto the Wall itself. Later still, Carrawburgh was added, and the Turf Wall rebuilt in stone as far as milecastle 54. All of this constituted well over 10 years' work. The Intermediate Wall, replacing the Turf Wall west of milecastle 54, came later, possibly in advance of the reoccupation of Hadrian's Wall, *c.* 163, on the abandonment of Scotland.

Less information is to hand for constructing a similar blueprint for the Cumbrian coastal system and the outpost forts.

CHAPTER III

LOCAL DESCRIPTION

SOUTH SHIELDS (ARBEIA)

ALTHOUGH it was not thought necessary to extend the Wall east of Wallsend, small posts may have occupied the south bank of the Tyne as far as South Shields, where a full-sized fort lay on the Lawe. The position is one of natural strength with a sea cliff to the east and the river to the north. Formerly the area now occupied by Ocean Road was liable to flood, and Bruce records local memories of occasions when the tide rose high enough to insulate the whole promontory.

South Shields is the ARBEIA of the *Notitia*, where its garrison is given as the *Numerus barcariorum Tigrisiensium*, or Unit of Tigris Lightermen—marines manning light, shallow-draught boats, rather than forerunners of the Tyne keelmen. An inscription attests the Fifth Cohort of Gauls, and a tombstone mentions the *Ala I Asturum*. The fort itself measured 622 by 361 feet over the ramparts, giving an area of 5.16 acres. It had a defensive wall 6 feet thick, backed by an earthen rampart 7 feet wide, and fronted by two ditches.

The history of the fort is exceptional. It was built under Hadrian, probably for a cavalry regiment 500 strong, perhaps the First *Ala* of Asturians. A Sixth Legion building stone from the east ditch tells us who carried out the actual construction. Modifications suggest a change of unit at the time of the Antonine retreat from Scotland (*c.* 163). Later, when Septimius Severus was campaigning in Scotland (209-11), the whole fort was converted into a defended stores-base, capable of holding supplies and grain for the entire army. For this most of the interior buildings were replaced by granary-storehouses. Lead sealings record the Fifth Cohort of Gauls, which is also attested at Cramond on the Firth of Forth. Probably the bulk of the unit lay there, with only a detachment at South Shields. A little later, however, an inscription tells us that the whole was at Shields; while after only a short period of use some of the granaries were altered into barrack units, which (if two are taken as accom-

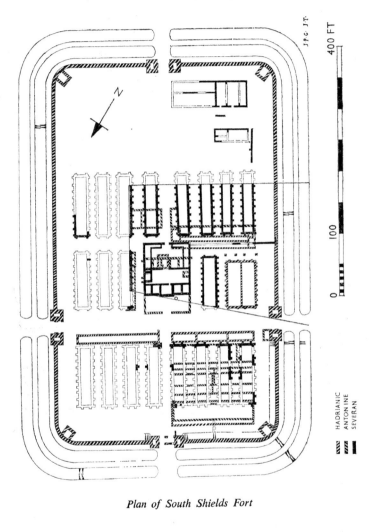

Plan of South Shields Fort

modation for one *centuria*) could have held the whole of the cohort, while the headquarters was swung through 180° and rebuilt. Alternatively, this conversion of the granaries may indicate some other and more specialized use. Later in the third century the fort fell into disrepair, particularly the northern portion, and rebuilding did not take place until some date well into the fourth century, when the whole area was again brought into commission, presumably for the *barcarii Tigrisienses*. The latest coins from the site are two of the Emperor Arcadius (A.D. 395-408).

Today, the fort lies in Roman Remains Park, and the visitor enters it by a wooden bridge across the western rampart. The first building on the left (I) is a double granary, with a colonnade along its southern side, and a loading platform to the north. This was the original granary of the Hadrianic fort, which continued in use until the late third century, after which a pair of tile-kilns was built within its western range. The eastern range still shows some of the supports for the raised floor. Beyond, lies the first single storehouse (II) 28 by over 80 feet in size. The flagged stone floor of this building was carried on dwarf walls to insulate the supplies.

To the south lie four single granaries (VI-IX), regularly spaced side by side. Each measured 28 by over 80 feet in size. The western pair (VIII and IX) were badly robbed, but each has a loading platform at its northern end. The other two (VI and VII) are similar, and enough survives of their internal arrangements to show that they had subsequently been divided into small two-roomed units, the inner with a flagged floor, most probably to accommodate the Fifth Cohort of Gauls, transferred here from Cramond. Below these granaries two earlier buildings are visible, running east-west. The more northern and complete is a cavalry barrack of Hadrianic date, with decurions' suites at each end. The southern is an Anto-nine infantry barrack. East of these four granaries is a main street of the fort (the original *via decumana*), and then parts of another two granaries (IV and V), which also overlie an Antonine barrack block. On

Altar for the Safety of Caracalla and Geta

the spacing of the granaries already described, a total of four can be expected in this second group, and a trace of the fourth was found in 1875-6.

North is the headquarters building. What we now see is the Severan rebuilding of the earlier *principia*, converted to face south. To do this the original cross-hall was retained, but the offices and courtyard were reversed. Today the visitor enters the building by its Severan entrance and sees the flagstones of the Severan courtyard, with guttering to carry off rainwater from the surrounding verandah. A re-erected pillar at the south-eastern corner originally stood on a low sill-wall, and supported the verandah roof: fragments of three others were found during the excavations. The line of the walls of the administrative range of the earlier *principiae* are marked out in white-coloured mortar for Hadrianic work, and pink for Antonine.

Beyond, lies the cross-hall with the Antonine dais to the left and its Severan successor to the right. Finally, just within the temporary fence, is the Severan office-range, with a sunken strongroom built of large blocks, once clamped together. This strongroom is so large that it must have held money in transit, needed for the great campaigns. To right and left lie the usual offices, while beyond the fence is the original Hadrianic fore-court, not now visible. A modification, usually dated to after A.D. 369, was the conversion of the cross-hall into a store- room by the addition of dwarf walls and raised floors, all now re-moved. Definitely of a late date are the shallow sockets cut into some of the wall stones of the *principia* to take the timber uprights of the final period walls.

Finally, in the central range, the wall of another granary (III) can be seen to the east. This is the only fragment now visible of a range of granaries which completely replaced the earlier commanding-officer's house.

Three other structures are visible in the excavated portion of the fort. The first is an east-west wall, most likely belonging to the time when the northern portion of the fort was in ruins and walled-off, while the rebuilt *principia* and the southern area were still retained. The second is the aqueduct filter-basin immediately south of granary IX. The third is the robbed-out stone foundations of the west wall and south guardchamber of the west gate, which, alone of the fort gates, was a single portal. Its south guardchamber is robbed, but the northern has survived better. These guardchambers projected 6 feet beyond the line of the fort wall: a feature difficult to parallel in Hadrianic forts. In Antonine times a small additional room was built against the rear of the north guardchamber.

The northern area of the fort was excavated in 1966-7, and the north-west angle tower and north gate are now on view. The excavation showed that the original northern buildings had been cavalry barracks or stables, 140 feet in length, running east-west. In Hadrianic times there had been a total of 8 buildings, of which the two fronting the *via principalis* were narrow store-houses, stone built, while the rest were barracks or stables constructed of timber. In later Antonine and Severan times modifications occurred, although no trace of burning or suggestion of hostile destruction accompanied either change. Under Severus the earlier buildings were replaced by 8 granary-storehouses, placed in two groups of four. All were of stone, 28 by 120 feet in size, with side buttresses for added strength, and loading bays at their southern ends. They faced on to the principal cross-road of the fort, which was widened to allow their loading. After a short life as granaries, they appear to have been first converted into barracks, and then deserted, so that by the end of

The Tombstones of Regina and Victor (*South Shields*)

the third century all had fallen into disuse, or were partly demolished.

The north gate was built as a double-portal entrace-way with projecting side towers. It was the principal gate of the fort in Hadrianic times, but in Severan times its western portal was blocked, and by the late third century the eastern passageway was in disrepair with its vault propped by a massive stone support. Partial demolition of the east guardchamber followed and some of its large stone blocks were left lying in the east passageway.

Of the other parts of the fort little can be said. The east gate also appears to have projected. At some date its south passageway was converted into a room, and a hypocaust inserted, while the original south guardchamber was coated inside with plaster. The south gate has also been located, and two buildings in the south-western part of the fort; but their plans are not readily intelligible.

The parade ground was discovered in 1959, on the northern side of Beacon Street, north-east of the fort. The possible remains of a stone dais were found, together with alter-bases and a small statue, perhaps of Mars. Other finds include an altar to the goddess Brigantia by one Congennicus, and another to Mars Alator. South of the fort lay the cemetery, which has yielded two of the finest tombstones found on the Wall. One is to Victor, aged 20, the Moorish freedman of Numerianus, trooper of the First *Ala* of Asturians. The other is to Regina, aged 30, the Catuvellaunian freedwoman and wife of Barates of Palmyra. Regina is shown seated on a chair in the manner of Palmyrene women, and the stone must have been carved by a Palmyrene craftsman. Her husband is commemorated at Corbridge (see p. 99). Another stone records the son of Lucius Arruntius Sulvianus, aged $9\frac{3}{4}$ years.

These are to be seen in the site museum, together with inscriptions, models, photographs and plans. Small finds include the remains of an inlaid sword-blade found, together with a series of elaborately enamelled bronze belt-plates, below the Hadrianic rampart backing; and leaden sealings, as attached to the fastenings of official stores. Many of these bear the heads of Severus and his sons, and indicate preparations for the great Scottish campaigns. Further objects are in the Museum of Antiquities at Newcastle; but one interesting altar is in the Ashmolean, Oxford. This was dedicated to the Preserving Gods,

for the welfare of the Emperors Caracalla, the Most Great
Conqueror of Britain, and Geta, Conqueror of Britain . . . for
their return, in fulfilment of a vow. The stone dates to 211 or
212 and was set up for the safe return of the Emperors, either
after campaigning in Scotland, or on their departure from
Britain for Rome, possibly from South Shields itself. Later the
name of Geta was erased.

Few records, only, of the *vicus* have survived, although it was
probably of considerable size, while the harbour is thought to
have lain to the south-west, close to the mouth of the old
Milldam.

THE TYNE TO WALLSEND

The rocky promontory, which is now graced by the ruins of
TYNEMOUTH Priory, is a peculiarly strong position. Two Roman
stones, an altar of the Fourth Cohort of Lingones and part of a
dedicatory inscription from a temple, were found here in the
eighteenth century, but they are perhaps best seen as re-used
material transported from Wallsend fort. Recorded finds of a
tile inscribed LEG VI V and single coins of Constantius II (324-
361) and Magnentius (350-353) appear to be chance discoveries,
for as yet no structural evidence for a military site has been
found on the headland.

Two Fragments of Monumental Inscriptions from Jarrow (Newcastle)

Across the river, JARROW, at the mouth of the Don, may have
been the DANUM of the *Notitia*, but the equation is at best uncertain. Tradition mentions a rectangular area of about 3 acres

enclosing the church, but excavation of the monastery has failed to produce more than a handful of Roman material. Any site is more likely to have lain farther north, on the higher ground overlooking the Tyne, now occupied by storage tanks. The church and the ruins of the monastery contained Roman stones, including a much-weathered sculpture, and two fragments of inscriptions, now in Newcastle, which are usually interpreted as part of a triumphal monument of Hadrianic date. One fragment is early Hadrianic, and could be from such a monument, the other is later and records the driving-out of barbarians, the recovery of the province and the provincial army. One or more trophies may well have stood somewhere in the vicinity in Roman times.

It has been suggested that a series of fortlets continued the Roman chain of control along the south bank of the Tyne to South Shields, but no evidence has materialised for this.

WALLSEND (SEGEDUNUM)

Wallsend, once famous for its coal, owes its name to its position at the east end of the Roman Wall. Here was planned the fort of SEGEDUNUM, the first of those listed in that section of the *Notitia* headed *per lineam Valli*. The site of the fort is good and its ancient name means "Strong Fort". It possessed an extensive view in every direction and commanded an angle of the river formed by two of its reaches: the Long Reach which extends downstream to the west end of South Shields, and the Bill Reach which stretches nearly two miles up water. In either direction, therefore, any attempt to slip across the river could easily be observed by the Roman garrison.

The site of Wallsend fort and *vicus* is now almost completely covered by streets, houses and shipyards. In Horsley's day the ruins were clearly discernible and the ramparts could be traced, including two turrets at the western and eastern gates of the fort, and another at the south-western corner. In 1778 a colliery shaft was sunk just outside the west rampart, and 5 years later Brand remarked that inscribed stones had been found, "but incurious masons built them up again in the new works of the colliery." By the early nineteenth century the whole area of the fort had become a busy pit village, a state of affairs which continued until 1853. In 1884 streets were laid out over the area, which today is being rebuilt.

C

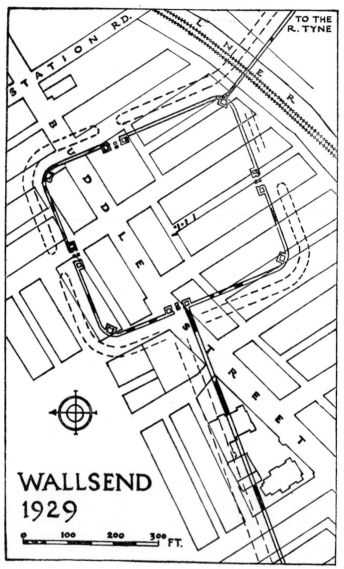

STATION RD.

B

C

D

D

L

E

STREET

L   N   E   R

TO THE
R. TYNE

WALLSEND
1929

0   100   200   300 FT.

Plan of Wallsend Fort

Excavation in 1929 recorded the outline plan of the fort, which Wallsend Corporation with commendable and enlightened interest in the history of their town, marked in the streets by means of white paving-stones.

The fort measures 453 by 393 feet over the ramparts, giving an area of 4.1 acres; it had four double gates, and was surrounded by a single ditch 21 feet wide. Its garrison in the second century was the Second Cohort of Nervians, although it may originally have been built for another unit, and in the third and fourth centuries it held the Fourth Cohort of Lingones; both units were normally 500 strong and the Lingones were part-mounted.

The most important discovery made in the 1929 excavations was that the Wall, where it joined the fort on the west, is not

Altar of the Fourth Cohort of Lingones, Wallsend

only of one build with the fort gateway, but is built to the narrow gauge. This means that Wallsend fort is associated with the Wall's second phase, the Narrow Wall as distinct from the Broad. This, the fort's regular spacing from Benwell, and the fact that three of its gates open north of the Wall, suggest that the extension took place at the same time as the decision to move the garrison forts on to the line of the Wall. Consideration had probably shown that marauders could slip down to the river between Newcastle and Wallsend by the deep denes, which provided good cover for a surreptitious approach to the crossing, and we know that as late as 1813 the river hereabouts was only 130 feet wide and 10 feet deep at low water.

In order to prevent an enemy passing between the fort and the Tyne, the Wall went down from the south-east angle of the fort into the river. Some traces have been noted in the past before the river was contracted and its new-made banks covered by the shipbuilding yard of Messrs. Swan Hunter. Bruce records that John Buddle the younger, when bathing in the river as a boy, had often seen the Wall foundations extending far into the stream. In 1903 a portion of it was uncovered and found to be 6 feet 6 inches thick, horizontally coursed and standing on a flagstone-and-clay foundation-course 7 feet wide, sloping downhill with the ground. It was removed and re-erected in Wallsend Public Park as the site, marked by a commemorative tablet, was required for the extension of slipways from the *S.S. Mauretania*. Also re-erected in the Park are the remains of the east gate, found in the summer of 1912 when the ground was being cleared for the building of Simpson's Hotel, which bears another commemorative tablet.

In 1975-6 excavation on the north side of Buddle Street showed that the northern portion of the Hadrianic fort had contained four cavalry barracks and at least two other buildings. Each barrack was 150 feet by 26 feet in size and divided into a 40 foot decurions' suite and 9, 12 foot *contubernia* for the troopers. The Antonine arrangement was similar, but alterations occurred after A.D. 180, which included the rebuilding of one barrack block apparently as a stable, 21 feet in width. Later, either at the end of the third or early in the fourth century the most northerly two buildings were completely demolished, while the next pair to the south were replaced by small, detached buildings, narrower than the earlier barracks. These faced across a new east-west street, on the south side of which were more, smaller, assorted, detached structures. The appearance of the *praetentura* of the fort at this date must have been extremely irregular. Finally, further alterations occurred, but pottery types show that some form of occupation continued into the period A.D. 370-400. The north gate, which was uncovered, did not appear to have had any form of blocking; a most unusual absence. The excavation also produced evidence suggesting pre-Hadrianic timber buildings, together with abundant traces of pre-fort cultivation, including three sets of plough marks cut into the subsoil.

Numerous Roman relics have been found at the site, including coins going down to Gratian (A.D. 383); but few inscriptions have been recovered. In a cellar under the dining-room of Wallsend House, near Horsley's Cousins House, a well was come upon. Inscribed stones are now in Newcastle, but there is also a collection of earlier finds, mostly coins, at Wallsend library.

A considerable settlement, *vicus*, extended along the north bank of the river, Horsley noting buildings on the slope between the south rampart and the Tyne, and also south-west of the fort. One, in particular, was a "remarkable numerous heap in the south-west corner of the western close, which is supposed

to have been an ancient building, perhaps a temple". The bath-
house was discovered in 1814, "a little above high water mark",
and destroyed when the Fawdon (Coxlodge) Staith was constructed. Hodgson noted "a very curious cauldron for heating
water", apparently an oval bath 5 by 6 feet in size and 3 feet
deep, lined with a fine smooth and hard cement. "It was, however,
only the last part of a considerable building that was remaining
when I visited the spot, all the rest having been removed before
I heard of the discovery." Many coins were found at the same
time, but are now lost. Lingard described "a brick-arched cavity,
in which were many broken urns", which has been seen as a
potter's kiln, while others noted remains which they took to be
a Roman quay on the river bank below the fort. The whole of
this area was drastically altered, however, starting in the 1840s,
by the dumping of ballast on the tidal foreshore to narrow the
river channel.

FROM WALLSEND TO NEWCASTLE

The Wall started upon its westward course from the south
jamb of the west gateway of Wallsend fort. It was the Narrow
Wall, some 7 feet 6 inches thick, on a foundation 8 feet wide,
and it is marked as a path in the east enclosure of Carville
Methodist Chapel. Thereafter, it runs via the Salvation Army
Citadel to The Avenue, where it was noted still standing several
feet high during alterations to the road in 1973. Beyond, is
George Road (Philiphaugh) on the west side of which two
altars dedicated to Jupiter Optimus Maximus were found in
1892-3, together with fragments of two carved stone plaques
dedicated to Mercury.

The sites of turrets and milecastles between Wallsend fort and
milecastle 3 are variously located by different antiquaries, but
none has been seen in recent times, so that uncertainty remains.
While digging the foundations of "The Grange", the remains
of the Wall were come upon, and a square building, which the
workmen called a cellar. At the time this was thought to have
been a turret, but it could equally have been the north gate of
milecastle 1 (The Grange). The site is now the presbytery of St.
Francis Catholic church. Just south-east of the milecastle the
Military Way was found in 1964, overlying earlier ploughmarks,
while a little to the west, where the Wall crossed Stott's Pow,
the remains of a culvert were once visible in the streamlet.

Early in the nineteenth century the Wall in this vicinity still stood between 3 and 4 feet high, covered with brushwood; the whole district, however, was developed for housing in 1939. The new Fossway, which connects Wallsend with Byker Hill, converges with the line of the Wall and passes obliquely on to it at Coutts Road, near the presumed site of turret 1*b*. West of Sutton Street the same road occupies the site of the Wall ditch and has obliterated all trace of the Roman works up to Newcastle.

Milecastle 2 (Walker) was placed by Horsley half a mile east of the summit of Byker Hill, approximately on the site now occupied by "The Foss" public house, although the Ordnance Survey Map of Hardian's Wall places it further west, and MacLauchlan thought hc had identified it in the vicinity of the present Tunstall Avenue. The whole area is now built over, and destroyed by quarrying or modern development, but in 1725 the Wall was here standing in good order, as appears from the "View of the Tract of the Picts' Wall, Newcastleward, from Byker Mill Hill, 4 Septr., 1725" which Stukeley gives in his *Iter Boreale:* and it must have remained so until 1800, when the *Monthly Magazine* noted that "At this period a portion of the foundation of the Roman Wall was taken up at Byker Hill, for the purpose of repairing the highways."

From Byker Hill the Wall turned slightly towards the north and ran down to the Ouseburn on a line parallel with Shields Road, which occupies the site of the berm and ditch. Milecastle 3 (Ouseburn) stood to the east of Byker Bridge, at the north end of Stephen Street, where a small altar was found, and where Bruce noted two of the milecastle's massive gate-way stones. Several trenches cut mechanically on the supposed site in 1974, however, failed to locate anything but industrial debris from local potteries.

From here the Wall ran steeply down into the ravine of the burn, and up the other side, but its course is not exactly known until a little east of Crawhall Road. It passes under the south end of St. Dominic's Church, to run thence almost straight to the Sallyport Gate, its foundations being last found in Grenville Terrace, 8 feet 5 inches in width. Thereafter, it is only from the ditch that the Wall line has been deduced, turning northwards in a gentle curve and passing under the northern end of All Saints' Church, to the presumed site of milecastle 4 (Pilgrim Street), on the Tyne Bridge approach, where deposits of Roman pottery have been found. This much was postulated in 1928, but an excavation in Silver Street in 1973 produced no sign of the Wall ditch at all, making the Wall alignment hereabouts less certain than previously thought.

In central Newcastle there is even more uncertainty. Again, from ditch sections, the Wall is thought to have run as far as Painter Heugh, behind Pilgrim Street, aiming as if to pass a little north of St. Nicholas's Cathedral; but tradition suggests that it turned southwards and it is said to have been found just south of the Cathedral. Alternatively, Stukeley, who visited Newcastle in 1725, claimed that it ran from Painter Heugh to join the Castle where the Dog Leap Stairs are. Its line in this heavily rebuilt area may now never be known.

The milecastles between Wallsend and Newcastle are abnormally spaced. Normally, milecastles occur with very fair regularity at the distance of a Roman mile (1,620 yards); but here it seems the intervals are not so regular. Furthermore, milecastle 1 is apparently only some 800 yards from Wallsend fort and about 1,200 yards from the terminal point of the Wall in the river, which suggests that this sector was laid out from Newcastle. In addition, there is no doubt that, since the Wallsend-Newcastle length is built to the narrow gauge, not only Wallsend fort but the Wall itself from Newcastle to Wallsend were additions to the original scheme.

NEWCASTLE UPON TYNE (PONS AELIUS)

It is clear from the *Notitia* that a fort called PONS AELIUS stood at Newcastle, with the function of guarding the bridgehead, but its outline and details remain unknown. In 1929, trenches dug immediately south and west of the Castle Keep revealed Roman buildings, one with a hypocaust added after its original construction and still showing the sills of doors and windows; but whether the building lay inside or outside the fort is obscure. Walls, pottery, coins and two altars (one illegible, the other uninscribed) were found on the site of the Moot Hall in 1810; however, the Wall is said to have been encountered below Amen corner in 1788, that is, south of the cathedral's south porch, so possibly the fort lay thereabouts, with a *mansio* under the Keep, and the *vicus* crowning the bank top, from the Moot Hall westwards. The cemetery, to judge by Roman burials found near Clavering Place, lay south-west of the fort, while the mouth of the Lort Burn could have been used as a harbour by river craft.

In the early fourth century, the garrison of the fort was the First Cohort of Cornovians, the British tribe whose capital was Wroxeter on Severn. This is one of the rare cases of an auxiliary unit serving in its own province, though most regiments brought to Britain or any other province, came to have more and more local recruits, even during the second century.

Inscription of Julius Verus from the Tyne Bridge (Newcastle)

PONS AELIUS took its name from the bridge which Hadrian, whose family name was Aelius, built over the Tyne. The Roman bridge lay on the site of the present Swing Bridge and seems to have served, with renovations, until a new bridge was built about 1248. This bridge, destroyed by the great flood of 1771, stood on the piers of the Roman Bridge, as did its successor of 1775. When the Swing Bridge was built, in 1866-75, the wooden piles and framework of the foundations of one of the Roman piers were carefully observed and recorded during removal. Both in 1775 and 1875 Roman coins were found, while many others, thrown from the bridge as votive offerings to the river-god, have been recovered from near the site during subsequent dredging. It is known, then, that the Roman bridge had stone piers, each founded on a raft set on massive iron-shod oak piles, with cutwaters up and down stream. The roadway was about 18 feet wide and, to judge by analogy, rested on segmental arches of timber. Twin altars, dedicated respectively to Oceanus and Neptune were dredged from the river in 1875 and 1903. They came from a bridge-shrine erected by the Sixth Legion and intended to protect the structure against tides and floods. In this shrine, too, reinforcements from the German provinces for the three British legions set up an inscription on their arrival in or before A.D. 158.

Hadrian's Bridge is important for another reason. Since only the Narrow Wall exists between Wallsend and Newcastle, while the Broad Wall is known in the western suburbs of Newcastle, and its milecastle sites are exactly spaced from the bridge,

Altars from a Shrine on Hadrian's Tyne Bridge
(Newcastle)

it must be assumed that the Wall was originally planned to begin at *Pons Aelius*, that is, at Hadrian's new river-crossing.

No visitor should leave Newcastle without seeing the very important collection of inscribed and sculptured stones and other material illustrating the Wall and its works, housed in the Joint Museum of the University and Society of Antiquaries of Newcastle upon Tyne, situated in the University Quadrangle.

FROM NEWCASTLE TO BENWELL

The Wall runs along the southern frontage of Westgate Road. Its south face, found within the railings of the Mining Institute in 1951, is marked by a strip of red concrete and an inscribed plaque. The ditch was found both there and, in 1934, just north of the Stephenson monument. From this point almost to Benwell the modern road lies, as Stukely records, partly north of the ditch and partly over it. No foundations of the Wall have been recovered in this sector, despite careful search. Here, however, if the Wall was built to the broad gauge, it will have had a shallow foundation-course of flagstones only, which could have been completely removed by persons in search of stone. Had it been the Narrow Wall, its deeper foundations of clay and broken stone would have survived, as throughout east Newcastle, since they did not invite stone-robbers.

Milecastle 5 (Quarry House) stood at the junction of Westgate Road and Corporation Street. The site, where Horsley recorded vestiges of the milecastle, is exactly one Roman mile from the north abutment of Hadrian's Bridge, that is, in the right position the first milecastle of the Broad Wall.

Milecastle 6 must have been at Benwell Grove, but no remains of it are recorded, nor is any turret known in this sector, so densely covered by modern buildings.

The Wall is now accompanied by the Vallum. Horsley states emphatically that "there is not, in all the space between Cousins House and Newcastle, the least vestige or appearance of Hadrian's Vallum, or anything belonging to it". Subsequent research confirms this. The farthest eastward point at which the Vallum is credibly recorded is close to the site of milecastle 5, about Elswick Row: and excavations undertaken in 1929 to discover whether it continued eastward in the same line, as Bruce and others had supposed, yielded clear evidence that it did not. Likewise, trenching in the Cromwell Street area in 1974 failed to produce any trace of it. What happened to it after reaching Elswick Row is not certain, but it has been suggested that it here turned southward and ran down to the river.

The mounds and ditch of the Vallum used to be seen at the back of the houses on the south side of Westgate Road, opposite the General Hospital, while to the north of the road the ditch of the Wall was visible, together with the upcast mound on its north edge. But all has now vanished. The Vallum ditch can be traced, however, by the subsidences causing cracks in houses or walls that have been built over its softer filling. The effect is well seen in Campbell Street, Cromwell Street, Kingsley Terrace, Ladykirk Road and Condercum Road, and less well at other points on the course.

BENWELL (CONDERCUM)

The third fort on the Wall is Benwell, the CONDERCUM of the Romans, which lies a little over two miles from Newcastle. It occupies a magnificent natural position, on a level hill-top about 415 feet above the sea, from which the ground falls away gently to the north and more steeply on the other sides. Its ancient name, in fact, means "The Place with the Fine Outlook". The site was chosen to guard the gap formed by the valley of Denton Burn, immediately to the west.

The fort measured 581 by 417 feet over its rampart and covered 5·64 acres. It was garrisoned in the second century first by cavalry and then by the First Cohort of Vangiones and in the third century by the First *Ala* of Asturians, mentioned in the *Notitia*.

Inscription of the British Fleet at Benwell
(*Newcastle*)

Its northern third was finally destroyed when the high-level reservoir of the Newcastle and Gateshead Water Company was enlarged in 1957. Earlier, Bruce had recorded "the roots of buildings" in the whole area, one of which was standing tolerably high, while the north gate was noted when the original reservoir was being built. The southern two-thirds, now covered by the Denhill Park housing estate, were examined in 1926 and 1937.

The north front of the principal buildings is covered by West-gate Road (A69). Running from east to west they comprise the commanding officer's house, a large headquarters building, twin granaries and a workshop or forge. Little remained of the commanding-officer's house, though hypocausts for heating were observed both in 1751 and 1926, while a well was found in its courtyard in 1959. The headquarters is remarkable for two features. An underground strong-room for pay and savings, located in 1929 east of the *aedes*, was cut in the rock, decorated with wall-plaster and lit by a splayed window in its south wall. Secondly, the front court contained a remarkable settling-tank divided into aeration chambers by pierced partitions of strong masonry: this received water from an underground pipe-line,

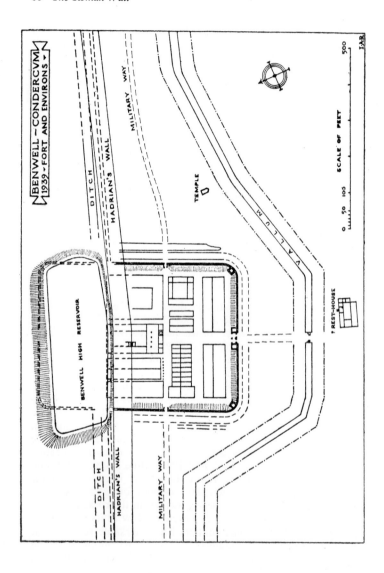

the natural water-table here lying too deep for wells. The granaries were loaded from platforms sheltered by a portico on the *via quintana*, and their dedication-tablet, now in the Museum of Antiquities at Newcastle University, can be translated as "For the Emperor Caesar Trajan Hadrian Augustus, under Aulus Platorius Nepos, the Emperor's propraetorian legate, a detachment of British Fleet (erected this building)". It dates the building and the fort to the governorship of Nepos, which began in 122 and lasted beyond 124. The workshop yielded a mass of forge-sweepings, including local coal, heaped against its east wall.

The road behind these buildings, the *via quintana*, ran between the minor east and west gates, the latter located in 1937. South of it, and east of the axial street, lay a courtyard building, probably a hospital, and another smaller building of uncertain purpose. West lay two barracks, back to back, accommodating four *turmae* or 128 men in all, one quarter of the garrison. Behind this lay what was apparently two double stable-buildings and the south rampart, with twin-portalled gateway, angle-towers and single ditch.

Behind the fort the military zone is enclosed by the Vallum, which made an almost regular diversion from its straight course to enclose the site, its ditch being somewhat reduced in width, as a rock-cut section revealed. The causeway across this ditch lay opposite the south gateway of the fort and is seen at the foot of Denhill Park Avenue. It is a natural causeway of undisturbed subsoil, with revetted vertical sides of masonry and covered by a heavily metalled road. On the axis of the ditch the causeway was crowned by a monumental gateway, non-defensive in character, with double doors opened from the north, that is, controlled from the fort. In this way access to the military zone from the south was carefully regulated. The long life of the gateway is attested by renewal of its pivot-holes in association with a new road-surface. The ditch had very steep sides, as seen in the adjacent sectors, now cleared of their silt filling. It was drained from the east when the water in it rose too high, by an overflow drain set in the upper part of the causeway. The visitor should on no account miss this Vallum causeway, since it is the only example now seen of the kind with which most forts were once furnished. The site, as the temple described below, is in the keeping of the Department of the Environment.[1]

---

[1]Hereafter abbreviated to D.O.E.

BENWELL : VALLUM CAUSEWAY

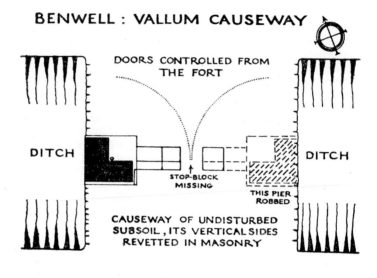

DOORS CONTROLLED FROM THE FORT

DITCH

STOP-BLOCK MISSING

THIS PIER ROBBED

DITCH

CAUSEWAY OF UNDISTURBED SUBSOIL, ITS VERTICAL SIDES REVETTED IN MASONRY

0   10   50 FEET

The village, or *vicus*, that grew up round the fort lay both north and south of the Vallum and in the later second century obliterated it. Of its buildings three are notable. The temple of Antenociticus, a deity either local or imported by the Vangiones, is still to be seen in Broomridge Avenue, opening west out of Weidner Road. It is rectangular, 16 feet by 10 feet internally, with an apse at the south end for the stone cult-statue of which the head, ovoid in shape, with wild hair and Celtic neck-torque, is now in the Museum of Antiquities at Newcastle University. The apse is now flanked by casts of two original altars in the same Museum. One, gracefully carved, is dedicated to Antenociticus and the deities of the Emperors by Aelius Vibius, centurion of the Twentieth Legion. The other has an inscription referring to the promotion of its dedicator, which may be translated "To the god Anociticus, Tineius Longus, given senatorial rank and chosen as quaestor designate while cavalry prefect, by decrees of our best and greatest Emperors, under Ulpius Marcellus, consular!"

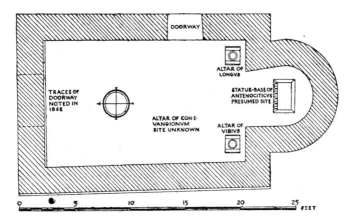

Temple of Antenociticus, Broomridge Avenue, Benwell

Anociticus is a blunder in the draft for Antenocitus, and the altar probably belongs to the year A.D. 180, or even 179.

The second remarkable building was the bath-house of the fort, found some 300 yards south-west in 1751, and carefully planned by Robert Shafto before destruction. It had more than 8 rooms, whether original or not, and was of the normal Wall type, today best seen at Chesters (see p. 117).

The third building lay not far south of the Vallum causeway. It was a large domestic building, clearly resembling that overlooking the bridgehead at Corbridge, and explicable as a *mansio* or rest-house for official travellers. Between these buildings of some pretensions there huddled shops and taverns, the 'snake basking beside a warm wall,' as Kipling called them. These are not much known in detail: but both excavation and chance finds show that they existed. West of the *vicus*, on Denton Bank, seams of coal once came to the surface, and these have been shown by analysis of the coal found in the fort workshop, to have been exploited by the Romans. Such open-cast working is not to be confused with the more recent bell-pit workings, on the site of the lower reservoir, which Bruce thought to be of Roman origin.

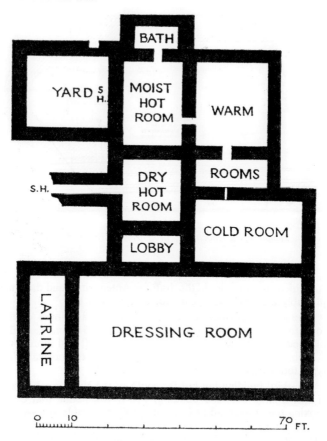

Bath-house at Benwell, 1751

FROM BENWELL TO RUDCHESTER

The Wall runs across to the south side of the road as it descends Denton Bank and was there found in 1953, in the garden of the Methodist chapel. The site of turret 6*b*, found in 1751, is 308 yards beyond the fort, just east of Two Ball Lonnen, the wide road running north. Milecastle 7 (Benwell Hill) is presumed to have stood at the quarry, where the lodge of St. Cuthbert's School now stands; but all trace of it has long been obliterated by the quarry. The surface of the road hereabouts was lowered in 1927-28, and the Wall ditch, once visible beside it, no longer appears.

Descending Denton Bank, the Wall was found in 1953 in the garden of the Methodist chapel, on the south side of the Road. At Denton Burn, south of the road and east of the stream, occurs the first fragment of the Wall now to be seen above ground. The illustration on the following page was made in 1867; and a comparison with the visible remains shows that the structure has suffered little since. In 1927 it was excavated and found to be a typical piece of Broad Wall, 9 feet 1 inch to 9 feet 5 inches thick, laid on a foundation of flagstones and clay. The courses follow the slope, at a gradient of about one in twenty.

Altar from the Shrine of Antenociticus, Benwell (Newcastle)

In 1866 Bruce noted the culvert by which the Denton Burn passed through the Wall, but it has long since vanished. A little further west, and south of the road, is turret 7*b*, excavated in 1929, and now in D.O.E. guardianship. It measures 13 feet by 13 feet 9 inches internally, and is recessed 5 feet into the Wall. It showed traces of three occupations, stretching from A.D. 122-367. The Wall here is again typical Broard Wall, with very massive stones in the lowest course, many weighing over a ton each. Denton Hall itself is a 17th-century building, associated with Lady Mary Wortley Montague, Dr. Johnson and the ghost known as Silky. In the stable a few inscribed and sculptured stones from the Wall are preserved. West of Copperas Lane a short length of Wall foundation is visible on the strip alongside the Carlisle Road. The southern track of the road occupies the site of milecastle 8 (West Denton), which in 1928 yielded pottery and other relics.

*The first Fragment of the Wall West of Newcastle, at Denton Burn,
as in 1848*

The interval between the seventh and eighth milecastles is probably longer than the normal 1,620 yards, but until milecastle 7 has been precisely located the true state of affairs must remain obscure. It is, however, certain that the western third is widely spaced and that Vallum crossings, once visible south of Denton Hall, were spaced wider than usual, presumably to retain the standard number of 35 crossings between one milecastle and the next.

The Vallum between Denton Burn and Copperas Lane was destroyed in 1938. Its mounds, boldly kerbed in turf, yielded six inscribed slabs, set into the faces looking on to the berms. This was the first discovery of the fact that the Vallum, like the Wall, had centurial stones. The sector had been built by centuries of the Second Legion and by the First Cohort of Dacians, each placing a slab at each end of the length it built. A centurion of the Dacians recorded his name, Aelius Dida, the second element of which is considered to be Dacian, reminding us that when this regiment was first engaged on Hadrian's Wall it probably still contained a good number of its

*Inscription of the First Cohort
of Dacians, from the Vallum at
Denton (Newcastle)*

original Dacian recruits. Between Southway and West Denton Hall, now St. Vincent's Home, the Vallum is well preserved, with crossings still visible, as an unbuilt strip on the south side of Wallington Drive.

On the site of West Denton School the Vallum ditch was found in 1961 to be rock-cut, almost 11 feet wide across the top and 7 feet 9 inches wide across the flat bottom: it was 12 feet deep with sides standing at 70 degrees. The berms were 35 feet wide and the mounds turf-revetted. Between Wall and Vallum was found the Military Way, 24 feet wide with a large stone bottoming.

After passing West Denton, the Wall crossed Sugley Burn, where once was seen a culvert two feet square. Here the Wall and Vallum are about 200 yards apart; they then slowly converge, until at Walbottle Dene they are only 60 yards apart, and thereafter keep nearly parallel until they approach Rudchester. Ascending the hill from West Denton, the road falls into line with the Wall and so continues for $3\frac{1}{4}$ miles, as far as Great Hill. To the north of the road, the ditch of the Wall was bold, but modern development has obliterated more and more of it until it now only survives in short stretches, between here and the summit of Great Hill. The Vallum, to the south, is much ploughed and relatively faint, but crossings can be detected between Walbottle School and Walbottle Dene.

Turrets 8*a* and 8*b* (West Denton and Union Hall), located in their expected positions, have since been destroyed by the dual carriageway. They trisected the distance between milecastle 8 and milecastle 9 (Chapel House), which lies just before the entrance to Blucher village, on the old road. Excavated in 1929, it measures internally 48 feet 10 inches wide and 60 feet long, and its walls were found to be of the same thickness and construction as the Broad Wall hereabouts. Its north gate, which is of type IV, was recorded in 1951. This milecastle had been occupied for as long as the Wall was in use and yielded a coin of Valentinian I (364-375), while confused fragments of skeletons suggested that it had come to a violent end. In the next mile, the ditch of the Wall is visible more than once on the north. Turret 9*b* has been located in Walbottle village, opposite Hawthorn Terrace.

At Walbottle Dene House comes milecastle 10 (Walbottle Dene). It was first noted by Bruce in 1864, and partly excavated in 1928, when it was found to measure 58 by 47 feet internally. Both gates have been recorded: constructed of massive masonry, they appear to have been of type IV. The northern lies at the south-eastern corner of Dene House front garden. Just before crossing the dene, both Wall and Vallum turn about 20 degrees south, to aim for Great Hill. Here, in 1864, a long stretch of the Wall was removed when the approach to the burn was recut on the east side.

The site of turret 10*a* lies east of Callerton cross-road, in Throckley. The southward cross-road leads to Newburn, where the Tyne is for the first time fordable. In 1346 David, King of Scotland, crossed this ford on the way to defeat at Neville's Cross, and in 1640 the Scots under General Leslie broke the troops of Charles I at Newburn, causing them to retreat and to leave Newcastle undefended and open to occupation. At the ford there is an ancient framework of stone across the bed of the river.

Throckley Bank Top is the computed site of milecastle 11, but no structure or other relics were found in 1928. Near this point a hoard of over 5,000 silvered coins of A.D. 244-275 was found in 1879, just behind the Wall and below the main road. Further west the facing-stones of the Wall were once seen in the road, at a width of 8 feet 6 inches only, suggesting that variations in thickness may have occurred much further east than generally accepted, although some could have been the result of wholesale rebuilding at a later date. Set back from the Royal French Arms public house, on the north of the road, is Frenchmen's Row, originally built for workmen employed in Heddon colliery, but afterwards given to house refugees from the French Revolution of 1789. Sadly, the cottages now to be seen are modern replacements. On the south of the road the Vallum is clearly visible.

Turret 11*b* lay beyond Frenchmen's Row, almost on the summit of Great Hill. When the road was remade here in 1926 the Broad Wall was exposed and removed with great difficulty, owing to the hardness of its tough white mortar. On the north of the road, after the houses end, the Wall ditch is seen notably deep. Both it and the Vallum are here cut through fireclay. On the south side of the Vallum ditch the tool-marks of the Roman workers are visible and the sides are revetted in masonry where the rock exhibits gaps. The first archaeological sections ever cut through the Vallum were made here in 1893.

After Great Hill the Wall diverges from the modern road and a length of about 100 yards is preserved by D.O.E. in the field to the south. The north face stands four courses high and the south face 7; the flag foundation is 10 feet 7 inches wide and the Wall 9 feet 7 inches thick. At the west end of the stretch a circular structure built into the back of the Wall is not Roman, but a much later kiln. The stones are now all reset in mortar, to preserve the work: when first examined the core was set in tough puddled clay.

The ditch of the Vallum is seen in the hamlet of Heddon-on-the-Wall as a sunk lane parallel with the main road. Milecastle 12 (Heddon) lay at the west end of Town Farm but has been entirely destroyed, although its north gate was thought to have been found in 1926. A large hoard of Roman coins in wooden boxes was found here in 1752, but its composition was not recorded. Another hoard, discovered at or near Heddon about 1820, comprised coins of Emperors from Maximian to Arcadius. The latest coin dated to 394, and is a precious indication that some form of habitation of the area continued into the closing years of the fourth century, and later. The Saxon church of Heddon has a Norman chancel: in it a partly legible centurial stone occupies a window-sill in the south aisle.

The A69 now branches south, to Horsley, Corbridge and Hexham; the minor road (B6318) which occupies the site of the Wall goes straight forward. Its history is as follows. When the Pretender's forces appeared before Carlisle in 1745, the Royal troops were lying at Newcastle, where the enemy had been expected. At that time no road fit to carry artillery existed between Newcastle and Carlisle, so that General Wade was obliged to abandon Carlisle and to seek his enemy by a more southerly route. After this, the road now known throughout the district as "the Military Road" was made. For miles together the tumbled ruins of the Wall were levelled flat to form it, despite the antiquary Stukeley's pro-test. Formerly the facing-stones were often seen pro-truding through the mac-adam, but are now hidden by the bitumenised surface. Finally, two stones found in the construction of the road, and presumed to come from the vicinity of Heddon, should

Sixth Legion rebuilding stone of A.D. 158, Heddon (Newcastle)

be noted. Both record the Sixth Legion engaged on rebuilding work (*Leg. VI V.P.F. ref.*), and one bears the names of Tertullus and Sacerdos, Consuls for A.D. 158.

From Heddon, the Wall and the Vallum run straight and parallel towards Rudchester, with the south mound of the Vallum visible for most of the distance as an imposing ridge in the fields south of the road. The Wall ditch is finely preserved and, 210 yards east of turret 12*b*, was found in 1956 to be 27 feet wide and 7 feet deep, with an upcast mound 30 feet wide. Turrets 12*a* and 12*b* were found in the expected positions on the south side of the road, and were excavated in 1930. Turret 12*a* (Heddon West) produced third-century pottery. Sections cut west of 12*b* (North Lodge) in 1975, showed the Wall to be standing in places up to 5 courses high, and resting upon a sandy clay and stone foundation 2½ feet deep. Its core is set in similar sandy clay.

Just before milecastle 13, where the Heddon bypass crosses the Military Road, is the Rudchester Burn. Here, parts of the Roman culvert carrying the burn through the Wall were seen in 1974, very similar to the culvert illustrated by Bruce at Denton Burn. Milecastle 13 is visible as a low platform south of the road, 170 yards beyond Rudchester Burn. A very large hoard of gold and silver coins, the latest dating to A.D. 168, was found here in 1776. The milecastle measures internally 58 feet 9 inches from east to west by 50 feet from north to south; it is thus of short-axis type, with its east and west walls of narrow-gauge, 7 feet 8 inches thick and its gates of type I. Turret 13*a*, also dug in 1930, has walls four feet thick, like Nos. 12*a* and 12*b*. Beyond this point facing-stones formerly visible in the road proved, as was confirmed in 1930 at milecastle 13, that the Wall hereabouts was the Broad Wall, 9 feet 3 inches thick. The next cross-roads lies just outside the east rampart of the fort of Rudchester.

RUDCHESTER (VINDOVALA)

Rudchester, the ancient VINDOVALA ("White Strength") and the fourth fort on the Wall, lies 6¾ miles from Benwell. It was garrisoned in the fourth century by the First Cohort of Frisiavones, rendered in the *Notitia* as *Frixagorum*, troops recruited from a coastal tribe of Lower Germany. The same unit was probably in garrison in the third century, and the fort was most likely initially built for a cohort, 500 strong and part-mounted.

The fort guards the valley of the March Burn to the west, an ancient route southwards to the Tyne ford at Newburn, while

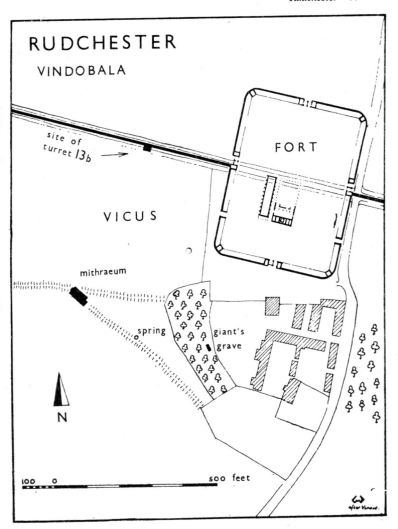

RUDCHESTER

VINDOBALA

site of
turret *13b* →

FORT

VICUS

mithraeum

spring

giant's
grave

N

100   0   500 feet

Plan of Rudchester Fort

78 *The Roman Wall*

to the east the ground drops away to the Rudchester Burn. It measured 515 by 385 feet over its rampart, covering about 4·5 acres. To the north of the road a platform and slight traces of its ditch mark its position. South of the road, the west and south ramparts are clearer. The farm-buildings lie to the south, beyond them.

The Wall joined the fort at its main east gate, leaving rather less than half of it projecting to the north. As at Haltonchesters, Chesters and Birdoswald, the Wall ditch already existed before the fort, and Haverfield's excavation of 1902 made contact with the massive foundations laid to carry the main west gate across its line.

Altar to Mithras from Rudchester (Newcastle)

Excavations in 1924 were directed to gates and principal buildings. Four gates were of the usual double-portal type and two, at the ends of the *via quintana*, single portals. But the south gate had been reduced to a single opening about the middle of the second century, by converting its west portal into a guard-room and fitting the east portal with inner doors. The main west gate, as at Haltonchesters, had been totally blocked, so soon after its erection that the threshold remained unworn by traffic. Inside the fort, the headquarters building and its underground strong-room were examined; a granary was identified and a hypocaust in the commanding-officer's house was partly revealed.

In 1972 an area was excavated partly on and partly south of the *via quintana*, in the south-eastern area of the fort. It yielded the northern end of a stone barrack-block of Hadrianic date, which had been burnt down, to be replaced in the late second or early third century, by another barrack of similar design. This had eventually fallen into ruin, probably at the end of the third century, and had never been rebuilt, so that its ruined walls became covered by a layer of humus, matching the state of affairs found at Haltonchesters during recent excavation and known at Birdoswald from an early fourth-century inscription (see p. 205). In the late fourth century, possibly about A.D. 370, a final period of occupation occurred, attested by Crambeck and Huntcliff pottery and a stone sill-beam with socket-holes for wooden uprights cut into its upper surface; this was not dissimilar to the last period stonework found at Haltonchesters.

Another piece of evidence recovered during this excavation was a series of plough-marks cut into the subsoil below the earliest Roman level. Similar plough-marks have been found underlying Wallsend, Haltonchesters and Carrawburgh in recent years, indicating much greater cultivation of the heavier clays in the pre- or early-Roman period than had hitherto been thought.

The Wall, where it leaves the west gate of the fort had a first-course offset of 14 inches, topped by a cavetto-moulded plinth. This elaborate treatment is not known elsewhere on the Wall. The Vallum makes a slight southward turn some 700 yards east of the axis of the fort and passes it some 240 feet to the south; no deviation in its line comparable with that at Benwell was therefore required.

South and south-west of the fort lay the usual village (*vicus*). The sole visible structural relic lies west of the farm, on the brow of the hill. It is a cistern 12 feet long, $4\frac{1}{2}$ broad and 2 feet deep, with an outlet-hole close to the bottom at one end, and was once popularly called the "Giant's Grave". Another folk-tradition is recorded in Sir David Smith's manuscript, now preserved in Alnwick Castle: "The old peasants here have a tradition that the Romans made a beverage somewhat like beer of the bells of heather, which art is now supposed to be lost; and those who do not admit the conjecture that the excavation was for funeral rites seem to think it might have been for the process of making such drink." When discovered, in 1766, it had a masonry partition across it, and contained many bones and an iron implement, described as being like a three-footed candlestick. Its purpose remains obscure.

The place was rich in shrines. About 1760, a life-size statue of Hercules was found and is now at Newcastle. In 1844, 5 altars dedicated to Mithras were discovered, and his temple was excavated in 1953. It had been built during the third century and seems to have lasted into the fourth, when it was deliberately destroyed. The first building was 43 feet long by 22 feet wide, with a segmental apse for a sanctuary, and any irregular vestibule, or *narthex*, attached to its front. It was built on the site of earlier but different structures, destroyed towards the end of the second century. Later the *narthex* collapsed, after which the shrine was renovated, receiving larger benches and wooden pillars supporting its roof. Small altars for offerings and a thurible were ranged along the benches. Four of the 5 altars, discovered

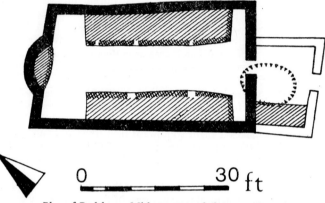

0 _____ 30 ft

Plan of Rudchester Mithraeum, *with first-period porch*

in 1844, had occupied the sanctuary. One of the altars is shown; the sculpture on its face and sides, a wreath and other symbols, leaves no doubt that the unnamed god is Mithras. The inscription means in English: "To the God (Mithras) Lucius Sentius Castus, (centurion) of the Sixth Legion, set up this gift." Two of the other altars are dedicated by prefects to the Unconquered God and the Unconquered Sun, one recording a restoration of the shrine. The fourth is dedicated to the Unconquered Sun-god Apollo. A fifth is uninscribed, and probably stood against a bench-side in the temple.

Centurial Stone at Rudchester

Many of the stones of the old farm-buildings and adjacent field-walls are Roman. A few fragments of inscriptions, built up in the walls, include part of a gravestone, with some such text as [D(IS) M(ANIBVS)] AVR(ELI) [. .]RINI [VI]XIT[AN]NIS [. .]: "To the spirits of the dep-

arted and of Aurelius . . . rinus, he lived . . . years . . ." At the
house are millstones and a centurial stone that reads [CO]H IIII >
PEDI QVI, "the century of Pedius Quintus of the fourth cohort."

FROM RUDCHESTER TO HALTONCHESTERS

Turret 13*b* lay some 80 yards west of the fort. Milecastle 14
(March Burn) is seen as a low platform crowning a slight knoll
east of the stream and south of the road. On the south of the
road, also, a former public house, known as "The Iron Sign",
existed until 1965, when it was demolished. The inscriptions
built into it are now in Newcastle, and can be read under favourable conditions as: > .ISI VERI, COH VIII > FL.LATINI and >
HOS[IDI]LVPI respectively. Next comes a knoll called Eppies Hill,
the Vallum skirting its south side and the Wall seizing its rocky
top, upon which Horsley saw remains of turret 14*a*. The Wall
ditch is very distinct here, forming a deep hollow on the north
side of the road all the way to Harlow Hill. The Wall and the
Vallum on the summit are within 30 yards of each other, but
soon draw apart; for while the Wall inclines to the north, aiming
for the next high point, the Vallum continues in a straight line.

A little more than half a mile beyond Eppies Hill, milecastle 15
(Whitchester) is marked by a bold platform and hollows where
its walls have been robbed. The Vallum is here 400 yards from
the Wall and, after a slight turn, runs quite straight for 5 miles
to Carr Hill. The ditch of the Wall is again in fine order on the
forward slope. Turrets 15*a* and 15*b* were located in 1931 to the
east of Harlow Hill, at the normal spacing, while in the village
the Wall passed through yards south of the road. Several antiquaries, including Horsley, Brand and Skinner, record its width
here as 7 feet 4 inches, and 8 feet, although further east excavation
in 1929 produced a section 9 feet 2 inches wide. Milecastle 16
stood here, but, as at Heddon, no trace now exists. At the bottom
of the hill to the west lie the Whittledean reservoirs of the
Newcastle and Gateshead Water Company.

The village of Welton, about half a mile south of the cross-
roads, contains the ancient pele-tower called Walton Hall,
built almost entirely of Roman stones. Over the door the inscription "W.W. 1614" commemorates Will of Welton, of whose
enormous strength strange tales were told. Nearly opposite
Welton Hall and close behind the Wall, was found a Roman
milestone of the Military Way, set up by the Emperor Antoninus,
known as Caracalla, in A.D. 213.

On ascending the hill, 200 yards beyond the reservoirs, mile-castle 17 (Welton) is seen on the south as a bold hump. Excavation in 1931 showed that, like milecastle 13, it had narrow side-walls, 7 feet 11 inches thick, and measured internally 58 feet east and west by 49 feet north and south, with gates of type I. The Vallum converges upon the Wall without deviating from its straight course, until, at a point 300 yards beyond the milecastle, the two almost make contact.

Turrets 17*a* and 17*b*, in normal positions, were excavated in 1931. All known turrets east of milecastle 17 have a door in the south-east corner and a ladder-platform in the south-west; in turrets 17*a* and 17*b* the positions are reversed, a variation which seems to correspond to one in the Wall's construction. Hitherto there has been one course of large stones above the flag founda-tion and then a single offset, which reduces the Wall to its standard thickness (type A): henceforward, instead of one course of large stones, there are three courses of small stones between foundation and offset (type B). The transition occurs about 190 yards west of milecastle 17.

Milecastle 18 (East Wallhouses) lies about a furlong west of the Robin Hood Inn, where an accommodation-road turns south to a farmhouse. It was found in 1931 to measure 53 feet 8 inches from east to west by 59½ feet from north to south, and its side walls are 7 feet 9 inches thick. Its gates are of type I.

Between this point and the fourteenth milestone all the earth-works of the system are very well preserved. The Wall ditch is in excellent order; while the Vallum is not only in very good condition, but also shows gaps in its mounds and causeways in its ditch; in other words, complete crossings unremoved by any subsequent cleaning-out of the ditch. These can be seen best immediately east of the southward lane at Wallhouses, and again a quarter of a mile beyond Matfen Piers, where a unique additional feature appears, namely, a small mound like a traverse, obstructing the south approach to each crossing. It will be noted that the marginal mound is absent. Air-photographs show ploughed-out crossings all the way between these two points.

Turret 18*a* (Wallhouses East), partly excavated in 1931, was found to be exceptionally well preserved and its ladder-platform was standing to full height, with 6 stone steps. Turret 18*b* (Wallhouses West), for long covered by an eighteenth-century turnpike gate toll-house, was partly excavated in 1959, when it was found that it had been used as a workshop in Period

IA. Ample deposits of animal bones and pottery were found, but nothing later in date than the second century. A short distance further west a road runs south to Corbridge, about four miles away, and Hexham, some three miles further.

Where the piers of the old gateway of Matfen estate mark a by-road to the North, milecastle 19 (Matfen Piers) occurs. It measured internally 56 feet 5 inches from north to south by 53 feet 4 inches from east to west. Its gates are of type III. In 1931, an altar dedicating "a shrine, with altar to the Mothers, by a detachment of the First Cohort of Vardullians, under the direction of Publius D.V.", was found just outside the south gate of the milecastle, associated with the second-century road surface. It is now in the University museum at Durham. Bruce recorded that facing-stones visible in the road here gave a width of under 8 feet for the Wall, but found it over 9 feet wide a mile farther on.

Turret 19*a* (East Clarewood), found in the normal position in 1932, was disused, its walls largely demolished and the recess built up, in Period II. Turret 19*b* (West Clarewood), was built mainly with clay instead of mortar. A recent study of its pottery shows that it too was abandoned by the end of the second century. The doors of both turrets are in the south-west corner.

Milecastle 20 (Halton Shields) was examined in 1935, and found to be about 59 feet long and 54 feet 4 inches from east to west, with gates of type III. The Vallum here runs so close to the Wall that its north mound will have lain only 5 feet away from the milecastle's south gate, if it was not omitted, as at Harrows Scar and High House milecastles (49 and 50 TW). The Military Way accordingly runs on the north berm of the Vallum and remains there as far as Down Hill. Hereabouts, the Vallum is better preserved than anywhere so far seen.

The modern road avoids the summit of Carr Hill, where facing-stones of the Wall, 9 feet 6 inches wide, used to show through the nineteenth-century surface and a southward bend could be observed. The Wall and Vallum, now 55 yards apart, run virtually parallel for some distance, until the Vallum bends sharply south to avoid the rocky hummock of Down Hill. It then returns as sharply to something like its former direction. The Wall, on the other hand, runs straight across the hill and its ditch is cut in the solid rock. This relationship of Vallum and Wall led Bruce to observe justly that "If the Vallum had been constructed as an independent defence against a northern foe, and nearly a century before the Wall, an elevation which so entirely commands the Vallum would surely not have been left open to the enemy, especially as it would be just as easy to take the Vallum along the north flank of the hill as the south". But the siting of the Vallum elsewhere, as at Heddon-on-the-Wall, tells with equal decisiveness against Bruce's own explanation of it as a southward defence.

Excavation in 1893 showed that the Vallum mounds had here been revetted in stone instead of turf. The gaps in the mounds are very plain, and amongst the best to be seen, but the causeways in the ditch have been removed, and there is a marginal mound on its lip.

Down Hill is pitted with hollows, no doubt marking Roman quarries. The modern lime quarry and kiln on its west edge lie close to the site of milecastle 21. West of Halton Red House turret 21*a* was found in 1935, in the normal position, 80 yards east of the fort of Haltonchesters.

HALTONCHESTERS (ONNUM)

Haltonchesters fort was initially garrisoned, perhaps, by a cohort of 500, part-mounted. In the third century it held a regiment of cavalry, the *Ala I Pannoniorum Sabiniana*, named after Sabinus who first raised it, and called *Ala Sabiniana* in the

Fragmentary Tombstone from Haltonchesters, mentioning the Ala Sabiniana (Trinity College, Cambridge)

Notitia. An inscription confirming the *Notitia* was first observed by Camden, and is now at Trinity College, Cambridge. It is from a monumental tomb erected to a native of Noricum, who died at 30, by his brother Messorius Magnus, himself a trooper of the *Ala Sabiniana*, on double pay (*duplicarius*).

The fort lies on the east bank of the Fence Burn, 7½ miles west of Rudchester. Its ancient name ONNUM, "The Rock", probably refers to Down Hill, just to the east. The choice of the site is unexpected as it does not make close contact with Dere Street, which passes through the Wall at Portgate, three-quarters of a mile to the west; nor is its northward outlook the best to be had. But a water-supply is assured by an aqueduct from the source of the Fence Burn, while the site commands both the deep ravine of that burn to the west and a ridge by which men could steal round the marshy headwaters of the Pont, north of the Wall.

The Wall, running below the south verge of the Military road, joined the fort at the south towers of its main east and west gates; and originally had run right across the site before the building of the fort. The ditch, too, had been already dug before the fort was built and when the fort came, it was filled up to carry the north portal and north tower of both gates and the north half of the main street connecting them. The Vallum, its ditch contracted in size as at Benwell, made a diversion, presumably symmetrical, round the fort but only its east arm has been traced. The planning of the site, however, was complicated by a westward extension in Period II, which enlarged the fort on the south side of the Wall only, thus creating a unique L-shaped plan. The original fort measured approximately 460 by 410 feet over the ramparts, the extension gave to the rearward portion a total width of some 570 feet, the two areas being 4·3 and 4·8 acres respectively.

The northern third of the fort, significantly called by those who first tilled it in 1827 the "Brunt-ha'penny field", was examined in 1936. Agriculture had removed the late fourth-century layer: only the superimposed buildings of Periods I and II were left. In each of these Sir Ian Richmond, the excavator, considered that he had found stables—the first time that they had been identified on the Wall. It is clear, however, that the buildings and the street-plan had differed between the two periods. The Period II fort had been focused upon a monumental fore-hall, 160 feet long, which spanned the 30 foot street in front of the headquarters building. Hadrian's architects had been less ambitious. Their most massive masonry, carrying the main east and west gates across the obliterated Wall ditch, had been hidden from view. These gates had twin portals and towers containing guardchambers, and in Period II the south portal of the east gate had been blocked. At the west gate, where the fort was terraced high above the obliterated Wall ditch, both portals had been blocked almost at once, before an external road was provided. Little remained of the north gate, but its west portal was reduced in size in Period II, the east portal being presumably

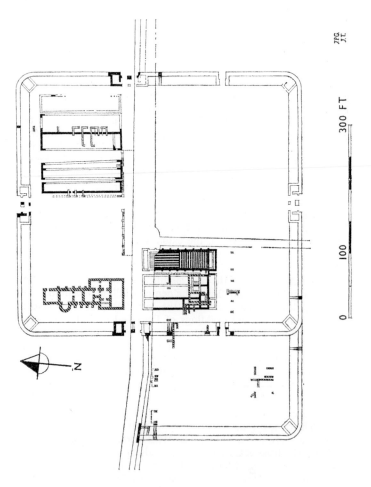

Plan of Haltonchesters Fort

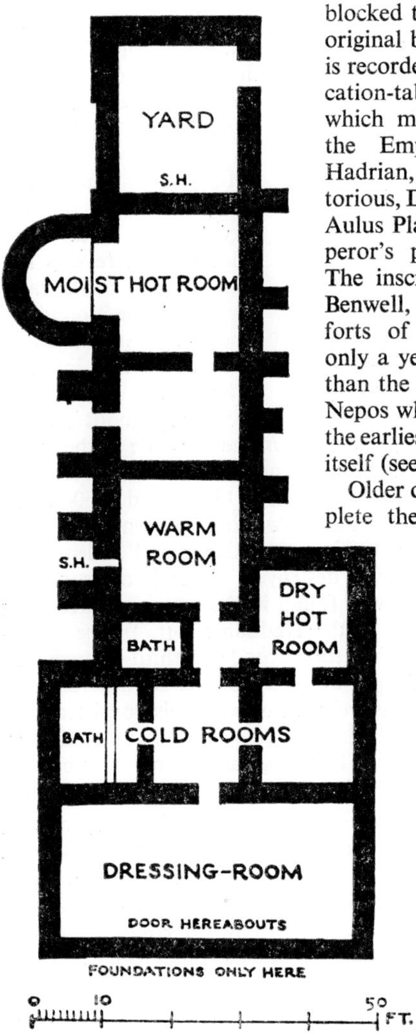

YARD

S.H.

MOIST HOT ROOM

WARM
ROOM

S.H.

DRY
HOT
ROOM

BATH

BATH | COLD ROOMS

DRESSING-ROOM

DOOR HEREABOUTS

FOUNDATIONS ONLY HERE

0   10   50
|ɪɪɪɪɪɪɪ|————|————|————|————| FT.

blocked then, if not earlier. The original building of the defences is recorded by a weathered dedication-tablet from the west gate, which may be translated "For the Emperor Caesar Trajan Hadrian, the Sixth Legion, Victorious, Dutiful and Loyal, under Aulus Platorius Nepos, the Emperor's propraetorian Legate". The inscription, like that from Benwell, shows that the eastern forts of Hadrian's Wall were only a year or two later in date than the curtain wall, for it was Nepos who built the milecastles, the earliest structures on the Wall itself (see below pp. 166-8).

Older discoveries help to complete the picture of this area. When the portion of the fort north of the road was first ploughed in 1827, one of the buildings found was an elaborate bath-house, now known to belong to the late fourth century. It consisted of a row of cold and heated rooms entered from a changing-room 34 by 40 feet in size. The plan of this building, the outline of which can still be seen in air-photographs, was made by John Dobson, the architect, who supplied the details for a description by John Hodgson. So large an internal bath-house, a rarity on the Wall, is not uncommon in late-Roman forts of the Continent.

D

Horsley knew the southern portion of the fort as "Silver Hill", no doubt from the discovery of *denarii* in it. An elaborately carved slab of Antonine date, commemorating work done by the

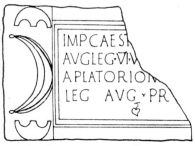

Hadrianic Building Inscription from Haltonchesters (Newcastle)

Second Legion, was found here in 1769, and is preserved in the Museum of Antiquities in Newcastle. As the ground has not been ploughed, it reveals not only the line of the ramparts, but the mounds of the ruined buildings and streets of the interior. The road to Halton runs across it, about 50 feet west of the *via decumana*, leading from the *principia* to the south gate. Excavation was carried out in a portion of the south-western quarter of the fort, and the extension, in 1956-8 and 1960-1. The original west wall of the fort was shown to have been demolished in Period II, when the extension was added; and at least one earlier external building was destroyed. Several traces of late fourth-century structures were found in the extension, overlying the demolished west wall of the Hadrianic fort. In the south-western quarter of the original fort second and third-century barracks or stables were found, and part of the central range of buildings was more exhaustively excavated. This consisted of a large granary, which had flanked the *principia*, as at Rudchester, and a courtyard house which had originally been partly built in timber, and was rebuilt in Period II to a slightly different plan.

There was no Constantian re-occupation of the fort; instead, the buildings fell into ruin and became covered by humus, as at neighbouring Rudchester and, on epigraphic evidence, Birdoswald. The only later occupation began in A.D. 369, and consisted of timber-framed buildings resting on either stone sill-blocks, pecked to take the uprights, or small-sized ashlar.

Tombstones tell of Aurelia Victorina, mourned by her father, and a slave of Hardalio, whose stone was set up by the guild of his fellow-slaves. Another records that "Virilis and . . . in their lifetime set up this tombstone, to themselves and to . . .". The stone, of rough workmanship and late third-century date, shows father, mother and young child, whose death was possibly the reason for the monument. Apart from sculptures and inscriptions, the most spectacular small-find from the fort was a massive gold signet-ring discovered in the northern area in 1803, and long since lost. For its bezel it contained a small artificial stone on which was

Inscription of the Second Legion from Haltonchesters (Newcastle)

engraved a female figure. No doubt it was the possession of some prefect of the *Ala* who, as an equestrian, was entitled to wear it.

The *vicus* now lies below the pasture south of the fort, while still further south Halton Tower and church are chiefly composed of Roman stones. The churchyard contains a Roman altar, placed upside down, but its inscription is obliterated. At the door of the house there is a small altar with a carved sacrificial dish and a jug on its sides, and in the garden wall a weathered gravestone, on which is carved a man on a couch—part of a traditional funeral-banquet scene. A much defaced male figure on the wall of the back buildings is probably not Roman.

FROM HALTONCHESTERS TO PORTGATE

On leaving Haltonchesters we cross the Fence Burn, and the road then cuts through a prominent hummock, the site of turret 21*b*. Ascending the hill past a trace of the Military Way we come to the site of milecastle 22 (Portgate, or, better, Errington Arms) faintly visible. Excavation in 1930 showed that the side walls of this milecastle were 8 feet thick, while the Wall had the normal thickness of 9 feet 3 inches. The internal width of the milecastle was 55 feet and its north gate, of type III, had been blocked in Wall Period II, doubtless because the adjacent gateway carrying Dere Street through the line of the Wall was near enough to serve all purposes for which a milecastle gate could be needed.

Dere Street, running northwards, crosses the Wall at right angles 263 yards ahead. Just before the roundabout, the Wall, below the old road line, is 10 feet wide. At the crossing Horsley observed traces of a guard-house or gate, "half within the Wall and half without", and the ditch indeed once appeared to turn northwards round such a structure. The presence of this gateway was confirmed by excavation in 1966 when the massive masonry blocks of the north face of its western side were revealed, showing that it projected 10-12 feet north of the Wall. It now lies immediately to the south-west of the Errington Arms roundabout, on the north side of the old road line.

Dere Street, now the A68, was no doubt built by Agricola on his advance into Scotland. To the south it links the Wall with York, the legionary headquarters, by way of the forts at Corbridge, Ebchester, Lanchester, Binchester and Catterick. Crossing the Wall it proceeds to Risingham, High Rochester and beyond (see p. 287).

CORBRIDGE, RED HOUSE AND THE STANEGATE

Dere Street runs south from the Wall via Stagshaw, to reach Corchester, 2¼ miles way (for the road see p. 287). Here, on a level stretch of the river terrace, just to the east of the confluence of the Tyne and the Cor Burn, and half a mile west of modern Corbridge, lies the Roman site traditionally known as CORSTOPITUM. This is the name listed in the *Antonine Itinerary*; however, long ago it was pointed out that it is probably corrupt, as it would not give the modern names Corbridge and Cor Burn; accordingly it is not used here. A much better name is COR-CHESTER, but as this has never achieved popularity, Corbridge is

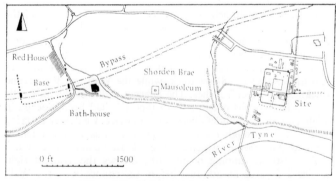

Plan of Corbridge and Red House Sites

used in its stead. Of alternatives, the *Ravenna List* provides Corielopocarium, which may be more correct, though it itself presents problems. The initial *corie-* element is similar to *curia*, meaning host or tribe.

Systematic excavation from 1906 to 1973 has shown the site to be a key one in Wall studies. It began as a normal bridge-head fort, becoming a depot during the second century and then developing into a market town with a vigorous life of its own; but one with a military presence, as witnessed by works-compounds and stores buildings. A small museum contains many of the stones from the site, in addition to a selection of the pottery, glass, jewellery and general small finds. The late first century hoard, described below, is now in Newcastle, and further stones can be seen in Hexham Abbey. The site is in D.O.E. guardianship.

The earliest Roman occupation, long thought to have begun under the governor Julius Agricola (79/80), or even Petilius Cerealis (71/73), is now known to be no older than the occasion of the withdrawal from northern Scotland (87/90), a discovery confirmed by the location in 1974, of the true Agricolan site some mile to the west, at Red House. The first fort at Corbridge, built of turf and timber, was probably to house the *Ala Petriana*, then 500 strong. The tombstone of Flavinus, a standard-bearer of this regiment, is now to be seen in Hexham Abbey. At some stage during the fort's life alterations to its barracks occurred, probably indicating a change of garrison. About the year 105 the whole was

Tombstone of the Standard-bearer Flavinus (Hexham Abbey)

destroyed, almost certainly by enemy action. Sealed below the floor of a workshop (*fabrica*) in the central range of buildings, where it had been buried, were the remains of a wooden chest containing fragments of leather, cushions and writing tablets, scraps of lead and bronze, iron nails, bars and struts, bundles and loose spearheads, knives, saws, a pick-axe, shears, gouges, a jemmy, two blocks and tackles, a scabbard, pieces of furniture fittings, a set of gaming-counters and three almost complete segmented legionary cuirasses (*loricae*). These are the first complete portions of

Pediment showing Romulus and Remus from shrine of Dea Roma (Corbridge)

such armour ever to have been recovered, and form the basis of all recent reconstructions. The contents of this "hoard", together with full-scale reconstructions of the armour, made from it by Mr. Russell Robinson, are on view in Newcastle.

The second fort was built under Trajan, as part of the Stanegate system of posts, and continued in use into the reign of Hadrian. What evidence we have suggests that it may have held a part-mounted cohort, 1,000 strong. The third fort was a fullscale rebuilding in which much of the central range was totally reconstructed, and a stone *aedes* was incorporated in the *principia*. Its garrison may have been an infantry cohort of 1,000. The third fort was later given up, and a gap in the occupation of the site followed. In the light of this it is not unreasonable to see the abandonment as part of the general movement of garrisons onto the Wall carried out under Hadrian.

The fourth fort was the first on the site to show the widespread use of stone, but even then most of the buildings consisted of timber-framed walls resting on stone sills. Two inscriptions (in the site museum) link this period with the governorship of Lollius Urbicus and the years 139/140. The garrison seems now to have been either a part-mounted cohort, 1,000 strong, on an *ala* of

500. Possibly some alterations occurred under Julius Verus (?155-158), when the unit seems to have been the First Cohort of Loyal Vandullians, part-mounted and 1,000 strong. Those buildings still without stone sill-walls now received them.

Not only was this the first fort built of stone, it is the first of which any appreciable portion can be seen on the site. Its two granaries lie below the visible structures, but part of the *fabrica* (usually called a hospital) is exposed in front of the fountain-house on the north side of the Stanegate, which lies on the *via principalis* of the successive forts. Next to the east, lies the

Inscription of Lollius Urbicus
(Corbridge)

office range of the headquarters building, and east again part of the commanding-officer's house is conspicuous. These last two occupy the central area of the later, large courtyard building.

The next change was radical, and saw the end of a regular fort layout. The defences, *principia*, *praetorium* and granaries remained standing (the granaries even receiving an enclosing wall), but the barracks of the *praetentura* and *retentura* were demolished and replaced by new, original stone structures. Hearth debris, scattered about the *retentura*, suggests workshops in that area. Again, inscriptions give a date for this alteration, recording the governorship of Calpurnius Agricola, about the year 163. One inscription, dedicated to *Sol Invictus*, the Unconquered Sun, strongly suggests a temple, and from its dimensions a building of some size.

At some later, but still unknown date, preparations began for a second drastic alteration of the site. This time the surviving headquarters building and commanding-officer's house of the previous period were demolished, and the fort defences were levelled (if they had not been in fact been removed earlier). Likewise, the earlier granaries were demolished and new, larger and totally stone replacements were begun on the same site. Immediately east of the granaries an aqueduct channel was brought into the centre of the site and a fountain-house with aeration basin and water tanks was built. East again, a great square courtyard-building 220 by 215 feet in size was laid out and its construction in large ashlar blocks was begun.

It is often said that this courtyard-building was constructed of rusticated masonry, that is, with rough central bosses still left on the blocks. Inspection of it, however, makes it abundantly clear that the intention was to strike these off at a later stage in the operation, and leave clean, dressed masonry everywhere. When no more than a portion of the granaries and courtyard-building were completed, however, work was drastically halted, never to recommence. The half-worked state of some of the wall-stones laid in the west range of the courtyard-building, makes this halt abundantly clear. Violent destruction of (temporary) timber buildings standing on the site occurred at the same time as the cessation of work.

Inscription of Calpurnius Agricola (Corbridge)

The true purpose of the square building is uncertain. A storehouse and a legionary headquarters have both been suggested, but perhaps a third possibility is more likely: that it was the forum of a *civitas* capital forum-basilica complex. Eighty years later Carlisle is attested as a *civitas* capital in the west. A plan for a tribal *civitas* in the east, based on Corbridge, is by no means an impossibility under the Emperor Marcus, who is known to have fostered civil development in other provinces of the Empire, and to whose reign this building must date. Construction must have begun in the late 170s for the destruction of 180 to have provided the occasion for its abandonment, with its ground plan barely completed.

As with other sites on the Wall and beyond, the next 25 years were something of a period of stagnation at Corbridge. The front

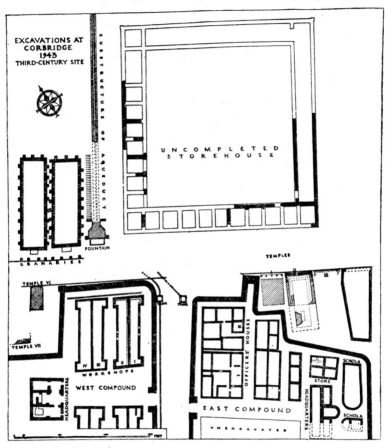

range of the "forum" was converted now (or later) into shops, and two groups of small stone-built temples grew up along the south side of the Stanegate; but little else can definitely be attributed to the reign of Commodus, or the governorship of Clodius Albinus.

With Septimius Severus came new building. A fragmentary

inscription records the completion of one of the granaries, abandoned in 180; the fountain-house and water-basin were rebuilt, while to the south of the cross-road two military compounds were now constructed, each enclosed by a wall which carefully omitted the standing temples. This Severan layout is basically that which confronts the visitor to the site today. The granaries, fountain-house and range of shops have just been mentioned: the temples had already been standing for some short time, and they must have formed the most impressive portion of the town centre. Actual attributions cannot be made, but a wealth of religious sculpture and dedications has been recovered, showing Jupiter, Juno, and Minerva, Victoria, Imperial Discipline, Hercules, the Regimental Standards and Dea Roma amongst aspects of the official state religion worshipped either in the temples or the compounds. Of more exotic deities Jupiter Dolichenus is indicated by an altar and sculptured scenes, while The Unconquered Sun, the Great Mother, Tyrian Hercules

Altar to Jupiter Dolichenus and the Sky Gods of Brigantia (Corbridge)

and Astarte each have dedications. A third group comprises local and personal Celtic deities, some of whom, such as Mercury, Apollo Maponus and the Nymphs, were linked with their classical counterparts; while others were not. Altogether these cults make Corbridge quite beyond comparison on the northern frontier as a religious centre.

The compounds were originally separated by a north-south street, and each was surrounded by its own enclosure wall. In the western, double workshops take a large portion of the interior, but an earlier *schola*, or guild-room, was accommodated, and a small headquarters placed in the central position. The buildings of the east compound consisted of two junior officers' houses, another headquarters building, two *scholae*, and more workshops. At some later date the two compounds were united by a new northern wall, with central gateway, while smaller changes occurred within them. All of this has been laid out by D.O.E., and can be studied with the help of a site plan. The conspicuous "ditch" effect, across which some of the eastern compound walls have broken their backs, is the result of sinkage in a natural depression, on either side of the accumulated gravel road surfaces of successive forts, and does not represent the line of earlier fort defences, as once thought.

What is visible, however, is no more than the central area of a small, thriving country town which during the third century grew to perhaps 40 acres in size. Pre-First World War excavations and air-photography have produced the outline of streets and buildings which lie below the surrounding fields. Dere Street ran up the slope from the Tyne bridge to meet the Stanegate on the western side of the excavated area. The principal east-west street was lined with narrow strip-houses and shops on either side of the granaries, "forum" and compounds. To the east, Dere Street continued northwards, again running just outside the excavated area, and again for some distance it was lined with strip-houses. North of the "forum" lay more streets and houses, another two granary-storehouses, each considerably larger than the two already noted, what is probably a third storehouse, and a small set of baths. South, a large building, probably a *mansio*, lay towards the bridgehead. The most conspicuous find from this building is the famous Corbridge Lion, which was the fountain-head of a large, third-century water-basin.

This Severan layout represents a market town with military works-compounds and granary-storehouses lying at its centre. These latter are of the greatest interest for they are not the normal content of towns in the province, and must represent a collecting point for the *annona militaris*, the official corn levy which went to feed the army of the province, here represented by the Wall garrisons. The fertile northern banks of the Tyne have in recent years yielded increasing evidence of small native farmsteads, which no doubt were the producers of this grain.

The most spectacular small-finds, apart from the military material, are several pieces of Roman silverware, found in 1731-6 in the river banks west of Corbridge. One is the famous lanx, or decorated salver, now in Alnwick Castle, and another was a decorated bowl, now lost. Bruce noted two further vessels, but they were "speedily committed to the melting pot". In 1760 a fifth piece was found at Bywell, 4 miles lower down the river.

In addition, a gold betrothal ring, inscribed in Greek "Long Life to Aemilia", was found in a turnip field near the site, and is also at Alnwick. A second gold ring, found in the "forum" area in 1935, is also inscribed: "The love charm of Polemius". In 1908 and 1911 two hoards of gold coins were discovered. The first consists of 48 *solidi* of the late fourth century, which includes 13 of Magnus Maximus. The second was even larger, containing 160 *aurei* from Nero to Marcus Aurelius (A.D. 64-159/60). Both are now in the British Museum.

The later history of Corbridge is more obscure than it was once believed to be. Whether the military installations were run

The Corbridge Lion (*Corbridge*)

down late in the third century is uncertain, but certainly at some date the temples were totally demolished and their area given over to kilns, hearths and furnaces; in short, all kinds of industrial activity. The date of this is unclear, but it may well represent the result of an official suppression of pagan shrines and cults, following soon after the official acceptance of Christianity, and represented elsewhere by the spoliation of the Carrawburgh mithraeum. Later rebuilding and modifications are visible, and coinage shows that life continued at least into the period A.D. 388-402. The end of the site is also uncertain, although a sufficient number of Anglo-Saxon objects, including a pair of late fifth or early sixth-century brooches, has been recovered to suggest that a pagan Saxon cemetery existed somewhere within the central area of the Roman town. Later still, the Saxon tower of Corbridge Parish Church was built of stones from the Roman site, including an arch.

Of the inhabitants of the town we know little. Tombstones, mostly reused in the later levels of the site, record Julius Candidus and Barates, aged 68, a *vexillarius* and native of Palmyra, whose bare stone contrasts with that of Regina, his wife, commemorated on an elaborate memorial at South Shields. Three children's tombstones commemorate Ahteha, daughter of Nobilis, aged 5, Ertola, properly called Vellibia, aged 4 years and 60 days, and Julia Materna, aged 6, the very dear daughter of Julius Marcellinus. Lucius Valerius Iustus of the Sixth Legion is also recorded, as well as the trooper Flavinus, aged 25 years.

Defences, in the form of traces of a rampart and ditches, are known only on the north and north-eastern sides of the town, close to the modern Corchester Lane. At the point where Dere Street crosses these, two large stone foundations 8 feet square and 27 feet apart were found, perhaps indicating a gateway or arch. Ribbon development north is most likely, and a cemetary beyond is known.

East of the site the line of the Stanegate is known only for a few hundred yards, as it makes for modern Corbridge. In 1895 the tombstone set up by Julius Primus to his dear wife was found at Trinity Terrace, suggesting that a cemetery once lined the road there. The course of the road further east, however, is now not known, although pre-Hadrianic material from Benwell and Wallsend *may* indicate whither it was ultimately heading. Alternatively, the still undug fort at Washingwells, Wickham, may mark its course. A milestone dedicated to the Emperor Victorinus (A.D. 268-70) possibly came from the modern town side of the site.

The bridge bringing Dere Street across the Tyne has already been mentioned. The extensive remains of its southern abutment and 6 piers are still visible in the river bed, to the south-east of the site, and have been recorded. Another four piers and the northern abutment are considered to lie to the north, now covered by the Cor Burn and present bank of the river. The piers are of well-cut stonework, tied together in places with metal cramps. They have pointed cutwaters upstream only, and probably carried a timber upperwork taking a metalled roadway of about 30 feet in width across the river.

To the west, the line of the Stanegate is known for about a mile, then lost until beyond the North Tyne. After leaving the site the road runs across the field to the west, where it is known to have been lined by strip-houses. It then negotiated the Cor Burn by a series of right-angled bends, bringing it to the stream at its narrowest point. Remains of an abutment still survive, and pottery and coins show use to have continued into the latter part of the fourth century. In 1868 a mile stone dedicated probably to the Emperor Maximinus Dia (A.D. 364-78) was found on the western side of the site. Beyond the Cor Burn crossing the road ran south again, before turning west along the southern edge of Shorden Brae. Here, traces of occupation have been found which soon gave way to a cemetery of some size. Tomlinson records that when the course of the Cor Burn was straightened in the last century many bones, and some whole skeletons, appeared in the cliff face.

In 1958 the stone foundations of a large mausoleum (32 by 34 feet in size) were excavated on Shorden Brae. Although this was almost completely robbed of its stonework, traces of the original central burial were found. The mausoleum had been surrounded by a precinct wall of considerable size. Fragments of two stone lions, each devouring an animal, which had once crouched upon the south-eastern and south-western corners of this enclosure wall were also found, and are now at the site museum. A similar sculpture, known as the Corbridge Cuddy, for years stood in Corbridge market place.

Beyond the cemetery, on the west side of the Red House burn, a military bath-house was excavated in 1955-7. This had been a large and impressive building. An entrance portico (A) gave on to a spacious courtyard (B), on the southern side of which lay a cold room (C) with cold bath (c), a circular hot dry room (D) and a warm and a hot steamy room (E and F), all complete with furnace chambers (f) and a small latrine (G). The whole building had been constructed under Agricola, and demolished before the end of the first century. In 1974, excavations on the line of the Corbridge bypass, gave a reason for its existence: west again, on the river terrace, lay the remains of a large base or depot of contemporary date. Like the baths, it too had been systematically and carefully demolished, almost certainly on or shortly after the withdrawal from Scotland in *c*. A.D. 87, but unlike the stone baths, it had consisted totally of timber buildings. Although only the width of the bypass was available, excavations revealed a

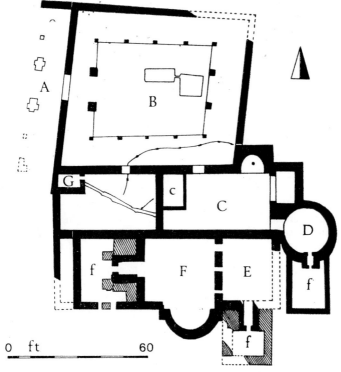

Plan of the Red House Baths, 1955-7

huge military enclosure 850 feet from east to west, containing a possible double legionary barrack, a workshop (*fabrica*) and a row of at least 13 open-ended buildings, which had been stores, worksheds or possibly stables. The extreme size of the site (it is unlikely to have been less than 10 acres and was probably over 20 in extent) and the unusual composition of its buildings indicates that far from representing a normal fort it must have been a depot or base, containing both workshops and a body of men large and important enough to have required an elaborate bath-house of considerable size. Such a site is at the moment unique on the northern frontier, and of the greatest interest and importance.

West of Red House the line of the Stanegate is unknown. It has been suggested that a fortlet should lie somewhere to the south of Wall village, but to date no trace of any such post has ever been found, and it may well never have existed.

Nearby, in Hexham Priory, St. Wilfrid's crypt (*c.* A.D. 675) is largely built with Roman stones from Corbridge. The Severan granary inscription mentioned above is reused in the roof of the north side-passage of the crypt, and the tombstone of Flavinus, standard bearer in the *Ala Petriana*, stands in the south transept. Other carved and inscribed stones are to be seen in the nave, along the north wall, and in other parts of the church.

FROM PORTGATE TO CHESTERS

Returning now to Portgate, the Wall and Vallum, about 80 yards apart, are very well preserved for the next three miles. The Wall ditch is in many places magnificent; the upcast that has been dug out of it is lying on the outer margin, rough and unlevelled, as if the workers were away in their dinner hour, attesting, in fact, unfinished work on the part of the digging gangs.

Turret 22*a* was found in 1930, nearly 200 yards beyond Portgate. It is the first structure in Standard A construction since 17*a*. Hereabouts the facing-stones of the Wall could once be seen in the road, giving a width at one place of 6 feet, but further on, before the summit, the full width of 9 feet 6 inches was again

Inscription to the Lightning of the Gods (Newcastle)

observed. From this vicinity, about a mile west of Halton-chesters, comes a remarkable stone discovered in 1850 and now in the Museum of Antiquities. It is inscribed FULGUR DIVO[RU]M, "The Lightning of the Gods", and had evidently been set up on the spot where a lightning bolt had struck. Turret 22*b* lay 540 yards further on, where a lane branches south. It is beyond this point that the Vallum becomes impressive and is seldom in more perfect state. In 1801 old William Hutton wrote with enthusiasm: "I climbed over a stone wall to examine the wonder; measured the whole in every direction;

surveyed them with surprise, with delight, was fascinated, and unable to proceed; forgot I was upon a wild common, a stranger, and the evening approaching . . . lost in astonishment, I was not able to move at all".

Milecastle 23 (Stanley), to be seen as a low mound on the south of the road, was examined in 1930. Its side walls are $9\frac{1}{2}$ feet thick and its internal width is 49 feet. There are traces of a ditch round it, as at milecastles 25, 29 and 51. In 1952, the Vallum was also excavated here. Its south mound runs through uninterrupted, but the north mound is broken by a gap giving access to the milecastle. The ditch had been re-cut, and, if a causeway existed, it was secondary. Turret 23*a* has been found by the roadside 543 yards beyond the milecastle, and turret 23*b*, 542 yards farther on again.

On the summit of the hill, the ditch of the Wall is 26 feet wide and 11 feet deep, cut in rock, while the Wall, 10 feet 5 inches wide, was formerly visible in the road. In places in this sector the upcast from the ditch can be seen, still in heaps as dumped by the excavators, no attempt having been made to level it into a counterscarp. Looking back east from the summit the Vallum is again very striking; the marginal mound is well developed, and the Military Way runs on the top of the north mound, a position which it occupies from just west of milecastle 23 to just east of 26, there being little room between Vallum and Wall.

In the north-east corner of the first arable field to the south of the road, milecastle 24 (Wall Fell) is a distinct platform and was found in 1930 to be 50 feet wide internally, with side walls 10 feet thick. Two fields farther on, at a dip in the road, is the site of turret 24*a* (Green Field); 24*b* comes opposite the ruined Tithe Barn. About a furlong short of the nineteenth milestone, the platform of milecastle 25 (Codlawhill) may be recognised to the south, opposite a gate in the north wall of the road. Its dimensions resemble those of milecastle 24, but it was protected by a ditch.

Turret 25*a* probably lay a little east of Hill Head, where to the right of the easternmost top-floor window of the main farm, a centurial stone bears the inscription, CHO VIII > CAECILI CLIIME—the century of Caecilius Clemens of the eighth cohort. About half a mile south of this point, at Fallowfield Fell, a Roman soldier, Flavius Carantinus inscribed his name upon the rock which he was quarrying (see p. 41). But this "written rock" has been cut out and removed to Chesters Museum, to protect it from defacement by thoughtless folk. The view from the fell is very extensive and fine.

At Hill Head the road swings to the south and leaves the line of the Wall, which runs through the fields some 50 yards north of it. The Vallum also crosses the road, which now runs upon its south berm. North of the Wall is St. Oswald's church which contains a Roman altar used as a cross-base; and by the roadside stands a wooden cross erected in order to mark

Centurial Stone at Hill Head

the traditional site of the battle of Heavenfield, where St. Oswald, King of Northumbria, defeated the British King Cadwallon in 634. Bede tells how "the spot is shown to this day, and held in much veneration, where Oswald, being about to engage, erected the standard of the holy cross, and on his knees prayed to God that he would assist his worshippers in their dire need. . . . Advancing towards the enemy at earliest dawn, they obtained victory, as their faith deserved. . . . The place is called in English *Heofenfeld*, or Heaven Field. . . . The same place is near the northern Wall with which the Romans formerly enclosed Britain from sea to sea, to restrain the attacks of the barbarians. . . . Hither, also, the brothers of the church of *Hagustald* (Hexham), which is not far away, made the habit of repairing yearly, on the day before that on which King Oswald was afterwards slain, to keep vigil for the salvation of his soul and, having sung many psalms, to offer for him in the morning the sacrifice of the holy oblation. And since that good custom has spread, they have lately built and consecrated a church there" (*Eccl. Hist.*, iii, 1-2).

Turret 25*b* is south-west of the church. It was excavated in 1959 and produced no pottery later than the second century. West of the roadside wooden cross the road swings southwards to cross the Vallum, which runs straight on behind the white cottage and through the little farm. Just east of this farm, Planetrees, the road swings north again to cross Vallum and Wall at the site of milecastle 26 (Planetrees), which was found in 1930 to have the same dimensions as the preceding three milecastles.

The house lies astride the ditch of the Vallum. A little farther on, to the north of the road, is the Black Pasture Quarry, which yields stone of the same nature as that used in the Wall in this vicinity. It is a first-class close-grained sandstone, and may be cut in blocks of any size.

Opposite the quarry and south of the road, a conspicuous piece of the Wall is preserved by D.O.E. When old William Hutton passed this way, on 22 July, 1801, he wrote: "Had I been some months sooner, I should have been favoured with a noble treat: but now that treat was miserably soured. At the twentieth milestone, I should have seen a piece of . . . Wall, seven feet and a half high, and two hundred and twenty-four yards long: a sight not to be found in the whole line. But the proprietor, *Henry Tulip*, Esq., is now taking it down, to erect a farm house with the materials. Ninety-five yards are already destroyed, and the stone fit for building removed. Then we come to thirteen yards which are standing and overgrown on the top with brambles." According to local tradition, it was owing to the old man's entreaties and tears that this fine piece of Wall was spared. The piece is exceptionally interesting, since it preserves a junction between the Broad Wall, on the east, and a sector only 6 feet thick, of the kind seen again at turret 26b. Many junctions of this kind must have existed to the east of the North Tyne, for we know of various places where the Wall is less than the broad gauge in width.

The road descends steeply, with a fine length of the Wall ditch on its south side. Turret 26a, opposite High Brunton House, was examined in 1959 and produced two levels of occupation, but no finds later than the second century in date. The road then swings to the north, and we pass Brunton House, west of which stands another excellent piece of Wall. This is reached by a stile on the Hexham-Chollerton road (A6079), about 200 yards south of the cross-roads at the foot of the hill. It is a fine stretch of Broad Wall, still 7 feet high, and exhibits 9 courses of facing-stones entire. The faces have been re-set in mortar, as found; but the core, now also mortared to preserve it, was originally set in tough puddled clay. In front of the Wall the ditch is very bold. Here also is turret 26b (Brunton), first excavated by Clayton in 1873. It measures internally 12 feet 9 inches by 11 feet 6 inches, and is recessed into the Wall about 4 feet. It has a door-way with threshold checked for monolithic stone jambs, as at turrets 29a and b. The Wall, which forms its north wall, stands 11 courses, to a height of $8\frac{1}{2}$ feet. The wing-walls of the turret are broad gauge, ready to take the Broad Wall, as that on the west does; but on the east the Wall is the Narrow Wall, 6 feet wide only, thus displaying a conspicuous example of the type of reduction already described.

The Military road crosses the North Tyne on Chollerford bridge, built in 1775. A medieval bridge, repaired in 1333, now lies some 300 yards downstream and wholly west of the river, on the island formed by the weir at Red Lion cottage. The abutments and piers of a second narrow bridge, seen at low water immediately downstream from the existing bridge, presumably belong to the later bridge, broken in 1733 and destroyed by floods in 1771.

From turret 26*b* the Wall runs straight to the river. Between the Hexham road and the disused railway a low platform indicates milecastle 27 (Low Brunton), excavated in 1952. It is a long-axis milecastle set in the Broad Wall, measuring 58 feet 9 inches by 48 feet internally; its type IV gateway matches those at milecastles 9 and probably 10. The milecastle is set in the Broad Wall and both its walls and the great Wall to the west were shown to have had a clay-bonded core.

Next is the most remarkable feature on the whole line of the Wall, the remains of the Roman bridge over the North Tyne, excavated in 1860 by John Clayton. This is reached by a path alongside the disused railway line from the east side of Chollerford Bridge. The ditches of both Wall and Vallum may be distinguished running down to the river. As it approaches the bridge abutment, the Wall is the Narrow Wall, standing on broad foundation. It is, however, only 6 feet 4 inches thick, but stands up to 8 feet 8 inches high. It terminates in a tower 22 feet square, standing upon the abutment. The main face of the abutment is 22 feet long, accommodating a roadway about 20 feet wide. Each face of the abutment is heavily splayed; the south side, originally as long as the north, has also been lengthened to check scour by the river. At the north end of the abutment, 5 courses of facing-stones stand 6 feet above the foundation course. Some are very large and come from Black Pasture Quarry, a mile to the east. All have a lewis-hole and grooves for iron tie-rods run in with lead. Their distinctive feathered tooling will be noted; and a *phallus*, for good luck, is carved on the northward water-face.

This fine bridge was not the first on the spot. Embedded in

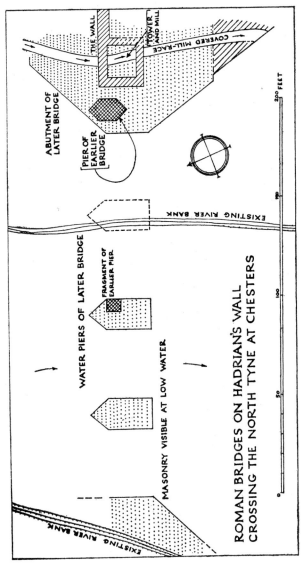

Diagram of the Roman Bridges at Chesters

the abutment is a mass of earlier masonry, forming a water pier. The main mass of a second pier of similar size is incorporated in the second larger and later pier in mid-stream, giving a water opening between the piers of 41-2 feet. The stones of both these earlier piers were tied by single dovetail cramps. This indicates an earlier and narrower bridge, designed, as at Willowford, to carry the Wall only. Its piers have starlings, or cutwaters, both up and down stream, like Hadrian's bridge at Newcastle, whereas the cutwaters of the second and wider bridge face upstream only.

Clayton, seeing that the second bridge was contemporary with the Wall, ascribed this earlier bridge to the period of Agricola. But at Willowford the bridge which also carried the Wall, or its walk, across the Irthing exhibits similar small and large phases (see p. 195), and its relation to the Wall is such as to show that the enlarged bridge must be a post-Hadrianic alteration, while the first bridge belongs to Hadrian.

The stone piers of the second bridge undoubtedly carried a timber superstructure. Several of its stones, now scattered about, have grooves for timbers, while not a single arch-stone (voussoir) has been found among the ruins. A highly unusual stone, however, is a large bollard 6½ feet long and 1½ feet in diameter; its square base is moulded to match the string course of the abutment, and it has evidently come from the abutment face, together with a fragmentary second example. Ingenious purposes for these stones have been suggested, but they are most probably a pair of large bollards, like uninscribed milestones, which stood at either side of the bridge ramp.

A channel, or race, 4 feet wide, runs across the abutment, passes through the tower and extends beyond the excavated area in both directions. Entering by a built opening, it may have served an undershot water-mill in the tower. Slabs, which formed a double covering for the channel, have been snapped across, apparently by the weight of fallen stonework, though some of them are one foot thick. They were found precisely as they now lie, in tumbled disorder partly caused by stone-robbing. Unhappily, no legible inscribed stone has survived to tell the history of the bridge, but it will be observed that the mill-race was not built until after the second bridge had itself been extended southwards.

The later bridge had three water piers, giving water openings of 35-6 feet. It is ascertained by excavation that one pier lies immediately under the present east bank of the river. Two others can be seen in the bed of the stream when the water is low and placid. They exhibit pointed cutwaters facing upstream, while lewis holes, by which the stones were lifted into position, and grooves for tie-rods and cramps can also be discerned.

The western abutment, of the same form and construction, is mostly submerged by encroachment of the river, but in favourable circumstances it can be seen from the west bank, where the large mass of masonry suggests that it, like the eastern, was furnished with a tower of defence.

On the North Tyne, about 1½ miles above Chollerford, stands Chollerton church. The columns of the south side of the nave are monoliths of Roman origin, probably derived from Chesters, as is the Roman altar once inscribed to Jupiter Optimus Maximus, and inverted for use in the church as a font.

CHESTERS (CILURNUM)

Perhaps no fort on the Wall so combines accessibility with interest as Chesters, now under D.O.E. guardianship. It lies 5½ miles from Haltonchesters, and guards the west side of the bridge across the North Tyne, just described.

Chesters is the CILURNUM of the *Notitia*, the name meaning "The Cauldron Pool", which is not inappropriate to the North Tyne at Chesters. It was garrisoned from the reign of Commodus onwards by the Second *Ala* of Asturians, 500 strong. Earlier in the second century it held the First Cohort of Dalmatians, but it had probably been initially built for cavalry. Its gateways, headquarters, part of its commanding-officer's house, and barracks, as well as a bath-house of special interest, are exposed to view; and it has a magnificent collection of Roman inscriptions, sculptures and other objects, forming a worthy monument to John Clayton who collected most of them. The Clayton Memorial Museum will not be here described, as a guide-book exists.

The fort measures 582 by 434 feet over the ramparts and contains an area of 5·75 acres. It is planned, as usual, in the form of a rectangle with rounded corners, and forms a bold platform with thick grassy turf now covering the masonry and the floor-levels. The defensive wall is 5 feet thick, with an earth bank inside it and a ditch outside. As at Benwell, Rudchester and Haltonchester, there are 6 gateways.

As in all the forts hitherto described, the Wall leaves about one-third of the fort projecting northwards. The Narrow Wall,

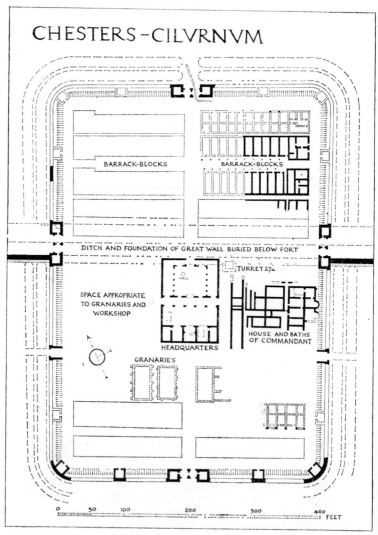

CHESTERS–CILVRNVM

BARRACK-BLOCKS

BARRACK-BLOCKS

DITCH AND FOUNDATION OF GREAT WALL BURIED BELOW FORT

TURRET 27a

SPACE APPROPRIATE
TO GRANARIES AND
WORKSHOP

WELL

HOUSE AND BATHS
OF COMMANDANT

HEADQUARTERS

GRANARIES

0   50   100   200   300   400   FEET

Chesters Fort: the heavy black line marks the visible remains. The granaries are known from excavation; the rest is a possible restoration standing upon the broad foundation, abuts on the fort at the south towers of its principal east and west gates. But the Wall ditch, already dug before the fort was laid out, runs right across the site presently occupied by the fort, and is buried below the main cross-street, as at Haltonchesters. In 1945, the broad foundation and turret 27*a* were found underneath the fort, the latter 136 feet west of the inner face of the east gateway. Finally, when the fort ditch was dug, it was brought so close to the foundation of the Broad Wall as to cause it slightly to collapse. The course of the Vallum here is not exactly known, but there are good reasons for thinking that it avoided the fort by the usual symmetrical diversion.

The visitor reaches the fort at the north gate (*porta praetoria*), which had two arched portals, separated by piers of masonry carrying arches at back and front; each portal is about 12 feet wide and was closed by double doors turning on iron pivots in socket-stones which are still to be seen behind the front jambs of the entrance. The west portal was still blocked when found, but it was then cleared down to its original sill-stone, which is still fresh and unworn, showing that the blocking took place at an early date. In the east portal, which was kept in use, are sills and the central stop-block of Wall Period II; the original ones lie buried beneath. There is also a later aqueduct channel, with cover-slabs of re-used stones, coming into the fort from the north-west. On either side are guardchambers with doors opening into the gate portals. Each guardchamber formed the lower storey of a tower.

The north rampart, clearly seen as a mound running east and west, leads on the right to the north-west angle; and so to the west main gate (*porta principalis sinistra*), again with twin portals and towers with guardchambers. The Narrow Wall, on broad foundation, is seen coming up to the south tower of the gateway. Both portals were evidently blocked very soon after being built since their sills are quite unworn; the north portal has a later paving of large stones; in the south, the original iron socket-cups of the pivots are still in place. Both here and at the corresponding east gate, the final stage in the blocking of the portals has been a walling-up of the inner entrance as well as the outer and the filling of the interior space with rubble. This massive platform would form an excellent base on which to plant the Roman spring-guns, which probably was done.

The guardchamber of the north tower has a feature of exceptional interest. Its north-east corner has been converted into a settling-tank, fed by a stone channel introduced through the front wall from outside the fort. The channel exemplifies a well-known type of military aqueduct. It enters at the highest point in the fort,

Dedication-slab of an Aqueduct-head, Chesters (Chesters Museum)

its source is probably a spring to the north of the fort. The bringing of water to the fort (*aqua adducta*) is recorded by two inscriptions of Ulpius Marcellus, governor A.D. *c.* 180-4, one here figured.

About 48 yards further south we come to the site of a single-portal gate (*porta quintana*), precisely similar to that on the opposite side of the fort, which has been left exposed. At the south-west angle there are scanty traces of a tower, followed, half-way between the angle and the south gate, by a fine interval-tower, with central doorway at the back. In front of the door the gutter of the street is seen and a column, probably from a barrack-block colonnade.

The south gate (*porta decumana*) has the usual twin portals and towers with guardchambers. The *spina* separating the two portals is in a more complete condition than any other at Chesters, and displays later blocking. The iron collar which held the pivot of one of the gates of the western portal was once to be seen in the pivot-hole. A similar collar was found in the other pivot-hole, and is now in the Museum. The covered stone channel outside the gate is a branch of the aqueduct already described, at the west gate, on its way to the bath-house.

In the east guardchamber much of a bronze tablet was found, dating to A.D. 146. This was the recipient's copy of a *diploma* or *tabula honestae missionis*, the official decree conferring Roman citizenship upon an auxiliary soldier at the time of his honourable discharge, after 25 years' army service, and legalising his marriage, past or future, with any one wife. Clayton presented the original tablet to the British Museum, but an exact replica is on view in Chesters Museum.

Beyond the south gate are seen an interval-tower and the south-east angle-tower. The walls of both stand about 12 courses high, enclosing an area about 13 feet by 10. Two infant-burials were found in the interval-tower. The external face of the rounded south-east angle stands well-preserved, 8 courses high.

Northwards, along the east rampart, lies the *porta quintana dextra*, a single portal 12 feet wide, which takes the place of an interval-tower and was no doubt surmounted by a tower itself. Most of the traffic from the bridge and beyond must have been carried to this gate along the Military Way, the mound of which is visible.

Next comes the main east gate (*porta principalis dextra*). The guardchambers stand up to 12 courses high. Each portal has been crowned by an arch, both

Inscription recording Legionary work under Antoninus Pius (Chesters Museum)

at back and front, and the impost-mould on the south rearward pier remains, with slots on its upper surface to hold the shuttering for the arch. The thresholds of each portal are quite unworn, suggesting they were soon blocked, like the west gates at Halton-chesters and Rudchester. A drain is seen in the flooring of the south portal. The Wall joins the south tower, a little south of the portal.

The headquarters (*principia*) lies in the centre of the fort. Its north half is a courtyard, bordered on three sides by porticoes. Bases of the piers which supported these remain, and the gutter-stones for their eaves-drips are in position. The court, which contains a fine well, has later been flagged, and on one paving-stone is carved a large *phallus*, a device much used in the Roman world to avert the evil eye.

South of the courtyard a large hall (*basilica*) extends across the building. Its monumental central doorway is now largely removed, and there are two lateral openings, probably once filled with grilles for light. Then comes a north aisle, entered from the porticoes and also by side-doors. The west side-door was used by small wheeled vehicles, perhaps hand-carts, for bulky objects. At the west end of the hall are the foundations of a raised dais or *tribunal*, from which the commanding officer administered justice. On its south side lie 5 rooms. The central 3 of these have wide open fronts, once spanned by arches, from which the fallen stones lie near. The central room, divided into ante-room and shrine, was the chapel (*aedes*) of the fort, in which the standards were kept; the rooms to each side were offices for regimental records, to the west, and pay, to the east.

Below the pay-room a large underground strong-room was later inserted, with steps leading down to it, one of which reused a fine building inscription of the First Cohort of Dalmatians. An oaken door, bound and studded with iron, was found at the entrance to the chamber, but fell to pieces shortly after being exposed. On the strong-room floor was found a number of plated *denarii*, chiefly of the reign of Severus. The roof is constructed with three parallel arched ribs, the intervals between them being bridged by large slabs.

Two remarkable stones, now in the Museum, probably once decorated the *principia*. The first is the top of a relief depicting a trooper holding a flag (*vexillum*) inscribed in Latin meaning "While the Emperors are safe, the Second *Ala* of Antoninus's Own Asturians is happy! The valour of the Emperors!" These loyal sentiments belong to A.D. 221-22, when Severus Alexander became the colleague of Elagabalus, who is the Antoninus mentioned, and later erased in disgrace after his death. The second stone is a great statue of Cybele, standing upon a heifer. Analogies suggest that this belongs to a group representing Alexander Severus as Jupiter Dolichenus and Julia Mamaea, the mother-Empress, as his consort. The hooves of another bovine animal, trampling a snake (standing next to Cybele in the Museum), could be the surviving part of the matching statue. Chesters fort has produced sculpture as fine as any from the Wall.

Two fragments of building inscriptions were reused in the headquarters and north-eastern barrack area. They belong to the reign of Antonius Pius and record modifications carried out by the Second or Sixth Legion about the time of the Antonine advance into Scotland. A third stone is a building inscription of about A.D. 205 from the *principia*, mentioning Severus and his sons, the governor Alfenus Senecio and the procurator Oclatinius Adventus. It closely matches a famous stone from Risingham, in Redesdale. While yet another stone belongs to the joint reign of Elagabalus and Alexander Severus, and commemorates the dedication of a building on the 30th of October,

A.D. 221. The name of the building is lost to us, but its provision doubtless helped to inspire the contemporary expressions of loyalty recorded above.

To the east of the *principia* are three blocks of buildings, excavated by Clayton in 1843. Immediately next to the *principia* is a long narrow range only 19 feet wide, of late date and uncertain purpose, overlying earlier structures which are visible here and there. East of this is a rectangular building, much altered by later work, including the wholesale insertion of hypocausts, some very rough in construction. Some of their furnaces appear to have occupied the passages of the original building, which must have been disused. This is most probably the commanding-officer's house, increasingly equipped with heating. The easternmost block is certainly the commanding-officers' private bath-house. It is admirably built, with a moulded base-course on the external walls, though excavation has shown that it is not the first building on the site: also, the hypocausts have been patched with columns borrowed from elsewhere. In a ruined part of its north wall was found the recumbent statue of Neptune now in the Museum, which must once have adorned a bath. A pair of cold baths lay in one of the chambers on the northern side of the group. When first exposed they were still lined with red, water-proof cement, or *opus signinum*. Immediately south of them is the dressing-room; to the east they give access to an intermediate warm room and so to a hot room with an apse. These ruined walls are the habitat of the rare rock-plant, *Erinus alpinus*, which, however, is known to have been planted here after the discovery of the bath-house.

North of these buildings is a street running east and west, with a central gutter, lined with numerous re-used shafts of columns. On either side of the street is a barrack-building, divided uniformly into rooms for 8 men apiece and fronted by a verandah. A group of larger rooms at the rampart end accommodated the two decurions or other officers. Each block lodged two *turmae* or 64 men, but some of the partition walls are of loose construction, as though the rooms had been subdivided at a later date, while the actual number of rooms appears to be 10, the number found in infantry, and not cavalry, barracks. The block to the south of this pair is usually called a stable, but it possesses characteristics of the "chalet" rooms to be seen in the fourth-century barracks at Housesteads, and elsewhere.

Among the refuse from these blocks, the shells of oysters,

mussels, cockles, and limpets were noted; the Romans relished this species of food, and, though Chesters is 30 miles from the sea, the garrison found means to procure it. The bones of red deer, roebuck, an extinct ox, wild boar, and sheep were also frequent. It is evident that the soldiery, when at their meals, threw the bones of their food, after they had picked them, amongst the rushes that covered the floor, and allowed them to remain there. But, since bones do not occur in the earliest level, it would appear that this unsavoury habit was not always allowed.

Julia Mamaea as Cybele
(Chesters Museum)

Between the pair of barracks just described and the north rampart lay another barrack-block, later rebuilt.

This appears to be matched by another barrack, just behind the east end of the south rampart, of which the colonnade is still visible, later alterations to it having been removed. Between both groups and the rampart lay an *intervallum* road, of river-gravel, which ran right round the fort inside the rampart.

Outside the fort, to the east, the mound of the Military Way can be seen leading to the bridge. Foundations of buildings are visible through the turf on both sides of it, and a portion of the Wall has been exposed between the east gate and the river. At the edge of the river, when the stream is clear, the foundations of the west abutment of the bridge are seen and, under exceptional conditions, the two piers lying in the river.

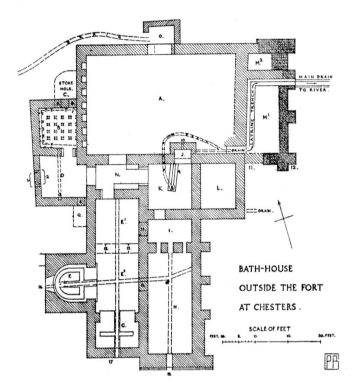

BATH-HOUSE

OUTSIDE THE FORT

AT CHESTERS .

SCALE OF FEET

A little below this abutment, and near the edge of the river, comes the bath-house of the fort. A small porch, O, a very late addition, leads into a large dressing room, A, about 45 feet long and 30 feet wide. This itself was an addition to the building, added probably in Wall Period II. It was paved with flagstones, on which the bases of central pillars supporting the roof were found. Its west wall contains 7 round-headed niches of a kind not unknown in other Roman baths, but of uncertain use. In front of this wall at an earlier stage of building there had been a long bench with stone uprights, a portion of one of which can still be seen. From the east side of the room opens a latrine, M, carried by a massive buttressed foundation on the steep river bank. It was flushed by the main outflow drain from the whole of the baths.

Passing out of the dressing room by a door in its south wall, we come into a vestibule, N, the floor of which and the steps that lead into the adjacent rooms, have been much worn by the tread of feet. Here the bather, turning east, entered the cold room (*frigidarium*), K. In the middle of this room stood a laver of cold water for douching; its base is still visible, and two drains from it, belonging to different periods, run away to the north wall. At the east end is the large cold bath, L, first reduced in size and then disused, late in the history of the building, and replaced by a much smaller cold bath, J, to the north.

The rooms lying to the south have all been modified, and some extensively, at various stages in their long life and a description of this part of the building is accordingly more complicated.

Another door led south from the vestibule into a room which originally gave extremely hot dry heat (*laconicum* or *sudatorium*), E1. This was heated by a furnace at Q, beyond its west wall, which induced heat into the hypocaust, or basement chamber, below the floor on which the bather walked. Today that floor is gone, but its level is indicated by the floor of the vestibule, and several door-sills at various points in the walls of the heated rooms. Later this room became part of the hot, steamy system of rooms I, H, and E2. At this time its place was taken first by room D, and later, when room D became an anteroom, by B. The furnace of B is still visible at C. It was for burning charcoal, to obtain a higher heat than in the steamy rooms. Here, as elsewhere in the building, will be noted the fine door jambs of stone, obviating wooden door-frames which would warp or rot in the dry or damp heat of the baths.

As an alternative to the hot dry room the bather went from the cold room into the first of the hot steamy rooms (*tepidarium*), I. Three apertures below floor-level in the south wall of this room admitted hot air into its hypocaust from that of the room beyond, but like the other rooms in this range the floor on which the bather walked has now gone. Later in the history of the building these hypocausts were dismantled and the chambers filled up with sand (now removed).

We next pass into the long room, H, which was a second warm room (*tepidarium*). Its east wall is strengthened on the outside by four buttresses. Its south wall has no buttresses, but is 4 feet 6 inches thick, and is built in stages. Originally the room ended at the third buttress, but later it was extended and a furnace provided in its south wall. In this room an alter was found dedicated "To the Goddess Fortune the Preserver, Venenus, a German willingly and deservedly set this up". The front exhibits a carved figure of the deity.

Altar to Fortune from Bath-house (Chesters Museum)

On clearing away the soil from outside the east and south walls of these rooms, 33 human skeletons were found, all of them in a remarkably perfect condition. The skeleton of two dogs and a horse were also discovered.

From the second warmroom the bather passed through another west door, now blocked up, into the hot room (*caldarium*), E2. This was the place where bathers sweated, washed in hot water, and were scraped with a strigil. The room contained two baths, one at G and the other at F. Originally, the hotter was at F, which had a furnace in its west wall, but later this was blocked and the bath had to rely on piped water, G replacing it as the main hot bath. The supports for the bath in F still remain, although the bath itself, like the room floor, has now gone. Some of the dark-red water-proof lime mortar (*opus signinum*) is still visible on the apse wall, and there is also a splayed window, 4 feet wide, outside which Roman window glass was found.

In excavating this chamber numerous small blocks of calcareous tufa were found, the use of which was explained by the late Parker Brewis. They are slightly wedge-shaped; a number of them put together would form an arch; a number of such arches laid parallel at close intervals would make a framework of ribs for a barrel-vault, and the intervals could be bridged by tiles laid on the upper and lower edges, as seen in the illustration. The whole would form a double ceiling, admirably light in construction and at the same time providing ducts for hot air

E

to heat the internal ceiling, and so prevent heavy condensation in the steamy room.

In the lowest course of masonry in the east wall of this chamber are two small stones lightly carved by a fanciful mason; one of them bears a *phallus* for good luck; on the other is a bird and the word NEILO above it.

From the hot room, in the original arrangement of the building, the bather returned to the first warm room to cool, then went through the vestibule into the cold bath to wash in cold water, thus closing the pores and avoiding a chill, and so back to his clothes. Later, room E1 was turned into another *tepidarium*, so that the bather could go from E2 by way of it back to the vestibule, or via a door (later blocked), into Room I. This circular progression round the rooms no doubt facilitated movement through the building. Later still, the party wall between E1 and E2 was removed and the two finally became a single room.

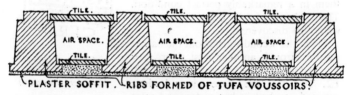

Section showing use of Tufa Voussoirs in an Insulated Barrel-Vaulted Ceiling

Near the bath-house, to the south and west of the fort, the remains of a very large extra-mural settlement have been observed from the air and on the ground. The cemetery lay further south still, where the river bends rapidly to the east and the sunken fence defining the park of Chesters joins its bank. A number of monumental slabs have been found at this spot, a place of great peace and natural beauty today.   One was erected to Aventinus, *curator* of the Second *Ala* of Asturians; another records Marcus Aurelius Victor, aged 50, who is shown mounted on his horse with raised arm. This is a variation of the well-known type of cavalry tombstone depicting a trooper riding down a barbarian, and best seen today on the Wall in Hexham Abbey (see p. 91). Lurio, a German, commemorated his sister Ursa, his wife Julia and his son Canio on a single stone, while Fabius Honoratus, tribune of the Cohort of Vangiones, and Aurelia Eglectiane set up a memorial to their most sweet daughter Fabia Honorata.

FROM CHESTERS TO CARRAWBURGH

For 500 yards west of the fort the Wall runs through the private grounds of Chesters house, where, at one point it is visible as four courses of facing-stones in position, covered in season with honeysuckle and other plants. On leaving the grounds of Chesters, it once more coincides with the Military road, and climbs the hill which leads to Walwick. On the hill its foundations used often to be seen in the road, before the modern surface was applied. The accompanying wood-cut was prepared when no new 'metal' had for long been placed on the road, and thunder-showers had removed all dust. In 1928, under similar conditions, the Wall was measured and found to be 7 feet 7 inches wide, the broad foundation extending another two feet two inches beyond it on the south.

The Wall in the road below Walwick, 1862

The Vallum is well seen in the field on the left. Where the road swings to the south, just west of a farm-track, the platform of milecastle 28 (Walwick) is to be seen, indicating a long-axis milecastle. Walwick Hall is next passed. The view from Walwick is exceedingly fine, commanding the vales of the North and South Tyne, with the Iron-Age hill-fort of Warden Hill between them, while another hill-fort appears east of the village of Wall and, to the south-east the distant view is closed by Hexham, with its priory church. The Military road now runs along the north mound of the Vallum, with the ditch of the Wall to the north, in excellent condition. Turret 28*a* is about 300 yards west of Walwick Hall; 28*b* at the usual distance beyond it.

Passing a cross-roads, we ascend sharply by Tower Tye, a cottage which once had a crenellated gable and was built about 1730 out of the stones of the Wall. On the summit the road swings into the Vallum ditch, but soon leaves it for the north mound. Beyond the summit, the remains of milecastle 29 (Tower Tye) are very distinctly marked to the north by the hollows made in robbing its walls. Here, as at milecastle 25, are also traces of a ditch. To the south of the Vallum a temporary camp, with traverses at its four gateways, lies in a plantation of firs and, further south still, is a native homestead site. A very fine piece of Wall, 6 feet high, is seen to the north, on Black Carts farm, running parallel with the road for a considerable distance. In this stretch turret 29*a* (Black Carts), was excavated in 1873 and again in 1971, before consolidation. It produced coins of Vespasian, Trajan, Hadrian and Constantine; more than are

Turret 29a, Black Carts, 1873

usually recovered. It measures internally 11 feet 4 inches by
11 feet 2 inches, has wing-walls to fit the Broad Wall and had
monolithic stone door jambs, like turrets 26*b* and 29*b*. The south
wall of the turret is almost completely robbed, only its lowest
course remaining, with a door-way three feet wide, but the Wall
in the recess is fourteen courses high. The wood-cut represents
it when first excavated. Opposite this point the gaps in the south
mound of the Vallum are very clear.

A little further west a road runs north to Sharpley and Simon-
burn through a break in the Wall known as the Hen Gap, beyond
which the Wall displays facing-stones of rather larger size than
normal.

Half-way between here and the summit of the hill is turret 29*b*
(Limestone Bank), excavated in 1912. Its occupation seems not
to have extended beyond the close of the second century, though
it had not been dismantled like some others whose occupation
had been equally short. It was approached by a branch path 11
feet wide, leading off at right angles from the Military Way.

The ditch of the Vallum is rock-cut all the way up the hill,
and exceedingly good, although somewhat overgrown with
hazels and other trees. All the way up the hill temporary crossings
are also seen at every 45 yards, many apparently half-finished;
also gaps in the south mound and, rarely, in the marginal mound.
The serious student will find the sector full of interest. The rock
removed from the ditch has mostly been broken up small and
packed into the mound, but four large masses lie on the south
berm as they were brought out of the ditch. The easternmost
block has holes for the chain-grips that were used to lift it.

At Limestone Corner, on the summit, several points demand
attention. The view to the north is wide and magnificent,
embracing the valley of the North Tyne, with Chipchase Castle on
its north bank, and the Simonside and Cheviot Hills in the
distance. Milecastle 30 (Limestone Corner) lies where the stone
dykes of the fields meet on the summit. Here, for the first time,
the Military Way can be plainly seen on the ground, coming up
to the south gateway of the milecastle and then swinging away
to run westwards. A hundred yards beyond the milecastle it
passes obliquely under the modern road, and then climbs onto
the north mound of the Vallum, along which it runs to Carrawburgh farmhouse. Excavation showed that the gaps in the north
mound had been filled to carry the Military Way.

The ditches of both Wall and Vallum should next be examined.

Each is cut through very hard quartz dolorite forming the hill, and the excavated masses of stone lie upon their brinks. The huge blocks that the Romans managed to dislodge and lift, or roll, are particularly well seen in the Wall ditch. On its north side lies an immense stone, now split into three by the frosts of winter, which, when first taken from the ditch, must have been one block weighing not less than 13 tons. In the ditch itself lies a comparable mass which has not yet been shifted; in its upper surface may be noticed a number of holes intended for the insertion of wedges. These wedge holes are all cut in the thin veins of quartz which intersect the dolerite, where the wedges, when driven in, would aid cleavage. Iron or wooden wedges were used, the former hammered, the latter expanded by having water poured upon them. Two such iron wedges found in the Wall structure at milecastle 26 have steel-faced tips and soft heads for hammering. The quarrying, by means of such wedges, and the lifting, by means of cranes, was heavy work, but by no means beyond what Roman engineers were accustomed to do.

It is noteworthy that while the Wall ditch is left unfinished, possibly at the end of a season's work, the Vallum ditch on the summit is fully dug, in spite of all the difficulties. For the Vallum, the ditch was an essential thing, while to the Wall it was an accessory.

South of the plantation and about 100 yards from the road, on the summit of the hill and a little to the east of the milecastle, is a temporary camp, about 55 yards square, with rampart, ditch, gateways and traverses all visible. From it there is a fine view of the valley of the South Tyne and Pennines, with Cross Fell in the far distance. Excavation in 1912 revealed inside the camp a number of paved areas representing the floors of tents or huts. The pottery dated an occupation, although not necessarily the first, to the third century.

Opposite the milecastle there is a causeway across the Vallum— a modern farm crossing—but thereafter Roman crossings, or slightings, are visible to the west, each opposite a break in the south mound. The north mound, on the other hand, is rarely breached and mostly displays its unmodified form, its gaps, in fact, having been filled to carry the Military Way. The view to both right and left is fine and the Vallum, particularly, is in very good condition. Next come the sites of turrets 30a and 30b, located in 1912; and then the farm of Carrawburgh. Here the marginal mound, which has been running along the south lip of the Vallum ditch, stops, and four consecutive causeways are seen in the ditch. The Military Way continues to run on the north mound. The farmhouse north of the road is called Teppermoor. Just west of a small quarry on the south comes the levelled remains of milecastle 31 (Carrawburgh), and shortly thereafterwards the fort of BROCOLITIA. The robbed west wall of the milecastle lies immediately beyond the car park.

CARRAWBURGH (BROCOLITIA)

The site of this fort, about 3½ miles from Chesters, is a bold platform, guarding both the Newbrough Burn and an easy approach from the north, along the western rim of North Tynedale. The fort measures some 460 feet from north to south and 360 feet from east to west over the ramparts, and contains an area of about 3·5 acres. Its ancient name was BROCOLITIA, meaning "Brockholes", and it was garrisoned by the First Cohort of Batavians in the third and fourth centuries. Its earlier garrisons are uncertain: it was built for a cohort 500 strong, possibly part-mounted, and a fragmentary inscription of the First Cohort of Aquitanians is usually attributed to the governor Sextus Iulius Severus (A.D. 130?-3) and taken to date the building of the fort. Otherwise attested are the First Cohorts of Cugernians, Frixiavones and Tungrians (only part of which could have been at Carrawburgh, as they were 1,000 strong), and also a detachment of the Second Cohort of Nervians. Some, however, may not have been in garrison as the Frixiavones and Cugernians are recorded on dedications to Coventina only.

Inscription of the First Cohort of Batavians from Carrawburgh (Chesters Museum)

The fort stands out boldly from the surrounding turf as a platform outlined by its ramparts and ditch: the defensive wall, if freed from rubbish, would be found to stand several feet high in places. The positions of the east, south, and west gateways are clearly visible, especially the south guardchamber of the latter, also an interval tower on the west rampart, a little south of the gate. A centurial stone, found in an upper course of its front wall and now in Chesters Museum, states that "the Thruponian century (built) 24 feet", doubtless the tower-front. In 1969 it was found that the south gateway had been completely blocked, probably at a late date.

Centurial Stone from Carrawburgh Fort (Chesters Museum)

The Narrow Wall apparently formed the north wall of the fort, joined by the side-walls at right-angles, as in the manner of the milecastles. This implies that the fort is either contemporary with or, more probably, additional to the Narrow Wall, resembling Great-chesters. The relation of the fort to the Vallum, however, is unique, for at Carrawburgh the Vallum ditch was proved in 1934 to have been filled up to make way for the fort instead of turning to the south to avoid it, as happens at other forts. Thus, the fort was not in existence when the Vallum was first dug, and so it must come late in the series of forts. This

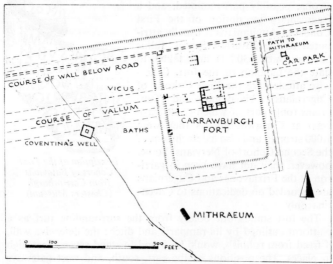

Plan of Carrawburgh Fort

wins some corroboration from the discovery here of the fragmentary inscription, probably of Sextus Iulius Severus, governor soon after A.D. 130, already noted.

Little excavation has been carried out inside the fort. The west wall of a granary is exposed south of the main cross-street, near the west gate, and monumental stones lie about, one bearing a fragmentary relief, another a large *phallus*. In 1967-9 excavation made contact with barrack-blocks, running east-west, in the north-western area of the fort; and uncovered much of the headquarters building. This consisted of the usual courtyard, cross-hall with western dais, and administrative offices. All had been badly robbed, but the *aedes* contained a sunken strongroom, probably added, and the two inner offices had received channelled hypocausts late in their life. Below these administrative rooms a length of ditch was found, 5 feet 5 inches wide and 2 feet 4 inches deep, running east-west, with a southern turn at its western end. Possibly this had been part of a temporary camp connected with the construction of the Wall, or a native settlement or shrine of pre-Wall date. Even earlier were plough-marks, in two directions, cut into the yellow subsoil: a witness that agriculture had been practised here in pre-Wall times. Below the courtyard and verandah the Vallum ditch was found, filled with material from the mounds. This filling had sunk in Roman times, necessitating the rebuilding of parts of the courtyard verandah: later, the courtyard had been flagged, a well added, and the verandah further altered. No evidence was found for any of these modifications either beginning or ending in destruction by enemy action.

East of the fort, an excavation in 1964, in advance of the construction of the carpark, showed that little survived in that area. Just east of the fort ditch two buildings were located, one of which was mostly robbed, the other, although also robbed, had been either a small temple or a substantial monument, presumably funerary.

By contrast, the western and southern slopes beyond the fort were once covered with the extra-mural buildings of the *vicus*, among them a bath-house excavated by Clayton in 1873. No attempt was then made to distinguish periods in its life, but some of the walling belonged to the fourth century, since coins of the Emperors Claudius II and Tacitus were found in its core. Its flooring, of stone slabs, embodied re-used tombstones now at Chesters, one exhibiting an auxiliary standard-bearer. The plan of the bath-house is a smaller version of the Chesters plan, suiting the smaller size of Carrawburgh fort. It shows, however, that even as late in the Wall-sequence as the building of Carrawburgh, the Hadrianic blueprint was still in use for bath-buildings. Tiles of the Sixth Legion were used for the hypocaust *pilae*.

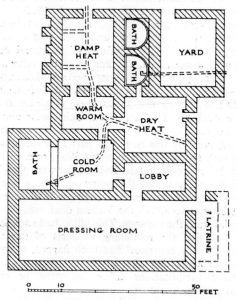

Bath-house at Carrawburgh, 1873

At the bottom of the west slope is the marshy source of a strong spring. In Horsley's day a rectangular basin was visible, cased in masonry. It was rediscovered in 1876, and can still be seen within a fence just west of the field-wall: it is usually full of water. When the structure was excavated by Clayton the top was choked with stones. Below came a mass of coins, followed by carved stones, altars, more coins, jars and incense-burners, pearls, brooches and other votive objects in an indiscriminate mass. The basin stood in the centre of a shrine, some 40 feet square internally, and there can be little doubt that in panic or fury its contents had been thrown into the sacred pool which already contained a mass of coins and votive offerings. The

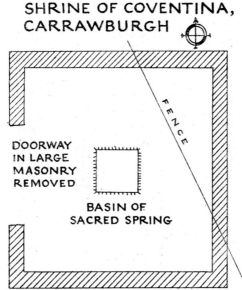

SHRINE OF COVENTINA,
CARRAWBURGH

FENCE

DOORWAY
IN LARGE
MASONRY
REMOVED

BASIN OF
SACRED SPRING

water-goddess was named Coventina and she is portrayed on some of the votive stones either singly or in triplicate to express her power. This latter is a well-known Celtic trait. The altars and other objects from the well are in Chesters Museum. An extraordinary number of coins was found. Clayton procured 13,487, four of gold, 184 of silver, and the rest of bronze, ranging from Mark Antony to Gratian, but many were carried away in a week-end raid upon the site by thoughtless folk. Amongst the coins were at least 327 examples of the brass denomination (*as*) of Antoninus Pius, in his fourth consulship, which commemorates the pacification of northern Britain after the disturbance of 155. BRITANNIA, disconsolate, sits upon a rock, her hair dishevelled, her head bowed, her banner lowered, her shield cast aside. This dejected figure differs totally from the triumphant Britannia of Hadrian or the proud first Britannia of Pius, who sit armed and alert on a crag, evoking Hadrian's watch between Tyne and Solway or the new frontier drawn by Pius between Forth and Clyde.

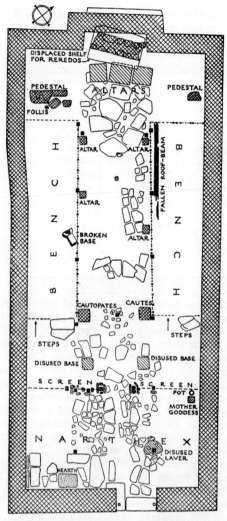

DISPLACED SHELF
FOR REREDOS

PEDESTAL   PEDESTAL
ALTARS
FOLLIS

B   ALTAR   ALTAR   B
E   E
N   ALTAR   N
C   BROKEN   C
H   BASE   ALTAR   H

FALLEN ROOF-BEAM

B   B
E   E
N   N
C   C
H   CAUTOPATES CAUTES   H

↑   ↑
STEPS   STEPS

DISUSED BASE   DISUSED BASE

S C R E E N   S C R E E N
POT
MOTHER
GODDESS

N A R T H E X
DISUSED LAVER
HEARTH

CARRAWBURGH MITHRAEUM
FOURTH CENTURY STATE

0   5   SCALE OF FEET   15   20

In 1949, a discovery no less remarkable than Coventina's Spring was made during the exceptionally dry summer. South-west of the fort, on the edge of boggy ground, a building was revealed in the shrinking peat, with three altars to Mithras still standing in position. Excavation showed it to have been a *Mithraeum* with a long and interesting history. The building now to be seen, consolidated by D.O.E., is the fourth-century shrine, the owner, Mr. W. J. Benson, having presented it to the nation. It is a typical *Mithraeum:* inside the door the worshippers first entered a small antechapel, in the south-west corner of which there was a large hearth, perhaps connected with the preparation of ritual meals, perhaps with tests by heat carried out during initiation ceremonies. In the north-east corner there is a statuette of a mother goddess, brought into the shrine after her own had been destroyed. Beyond the partition wall, the posts of which are represented by concrete uprights, lies the nave of the temple, flanked to left and right by low benches on which the worshippers knelt or reclined. Against each bench face there are two small altars, personal dedications to the god, while the two attendants Cautes and Cautopates stand at the ends of the benches. Cautes survives, except for his head, but of Cautopates only his feet were recovered in the excavation. Beyond the nave is the temple sanctuary with its three main altars, each dedicated by a tribune of the First Cohort of Batavians, Carrawburgh's garrison through the third and fourth centuries. The altar on the left shows Mithras as charioteer of the Sun, and was pierced so that a lamp placed in its rear recess would shine through the god's radiate crown. Behind and above the altars is a stone shelf on which the great Bull-Killing relief once stood, but this had been removed and smashed in antiquity and scarcely any trace of it remained. The earliest temple was shorter than the later buildings and the remnants of its rear wall were discovered in the later bench make-up, and are now visible. The altars and sculpture are now replaced with cast-stone replicas, and a full-scale reconstruction of the earliest *Mithraeum*, with commentary, is to be seen and heard in the Museum of Antiquities at Newcastle, where the original stones from the shrine are exhibited.

Immediately outside the door of the building was a small shrine to the Nymphs and *Genuis loci*, excavated in 1960, and further to the south-east a large hollow in the hillside indicates yet another important structure.

THE STANEGATE, NEWBROUGH AND GRINDON

MacLauchlan was shown the Roman road from Chesters to Walwick Grange, and himself had no difficulty in tracing it thereafter to the Stanegate. But the Stanegate itself, running west from the North Tyne crossing, was almost entirely obliterated. Skirting the north side of Warden Hill, it passes north of Fourstones to join the modern road where the lane runs to Frankham Farm (South View). Thereafter, it is mostly under the modern road through Newbrough, as far west as Barcombe. MacLauchlan records that all the way from Newbrough it was frequently found by roadworkers under the modern highway.

A mile and a quarter west of Fourstones lies NEWBROUGH. There, under the church of St. Peter's Stonecroft, a Roman fortlet was found in 1930. It is some 195 by 190 feet in size, that is about three-quarters of an acre in area. It was defended by a wall four feet wide, with a ditch 15 feet wide beyond. All the pottery recovered was of fourth-century date, and most belonged to Wall Period IV. A coin of Constantine I and traces of Roman buildings have been recovered in grave-digging, but little else is known. Newbrough lies a little over 7 miles from Corbridge and almost exactly 6 miles from Chesterholm: on its spacing a cohort-fort of some 3·5 acres could be expected initially to have lain here, as part of the Trajanic and early Hadrianic system.

The Stanegate then follows the modern road past Settling-stones and Grindon Hill, where a branch ran north-west to Housesteads. West of Grindon Hill, and south of the road on Grindon Common, there are two camps. The first is very small, the second is larger, some two acres in size. It has been argued that a small post should lie hereabouts, between Newbrough and Chesterholm, but no trace of any fortlet has ever been found and as the countryside is open moorland one may question whether there was, in fact, ever one.

FROM CARRAWBURGH TO HOUSESTEADS

West of Carrawburgh, turret 31*a* (The Strands) has not been located, but 31*b* was found in 1966 just to the east of Carraw farm and 1,080 yards from milecastle 31. Its doorway is to the east. The road here runs on the berm between Wall and ditch, past the farmhouse of Carraw, formerly a grange of the priors of Hexham. A quarter of a mile further on the platform of milecastle 32 (Carraw) is visible south of the road. It is of long axis type, but investigations in 1971 showed that it had been extensively robbed. The site of turret 32*a* lies at the normal distance beyond. Nearly half a mile to the south a small Roman camp, called Brown Dykes, occupies a hilltop with an extensive prospect. It is about 75 yards square with four gates and traverses. A smaller camp, 300 yards E.N.E. of it, is hardly visible.

The mounds and ditch of the Vallum and the ditch of the Wall are here very grand and very close to each other; the Vallum continues straight, while the Wall swings first slightly north, and then a little southwards, for the double purpose, apparently, of avoiding a bog on the north, and securing the crown of the hill. The road keeps to the south, parallel with the Vallum. In the field to the north, milecastle 33 (Shield-on-the-Wall) is evident. Its north wall and gate, of type II with larger backward projecting passage-walls than usual, are in good condition; while south of the stone wall, which divides two estates, slight remains of the milecastle's south gateway are to be seen, including its monolithic threshold. Here, too, the Wall ditch is remarkably bold.

Still further west, the cottage of Shield-on-the Wall lies to the south and beyond it a reservoir, supplying the Settlingstones barytes mine. Ahead is the ridge of the Whin Sill, an intrusive mass of quartz dolerite, along which the Wall runs in the central part of its length. Four successive crests are in sight, which belong to a single escarpment and seems to chase each other to the north. To the highest of these the Wall directs its course.

After the twenty-seventh milestone, 150 yards west of the site of turret 33*a*, the modern road takes to the south of both Wall and Vallum, at the bridge across the Coesike. The Wall and Vallum also part company; the Vallum running along the "tail" of the hill so that its ditch need not be cut in the hard whinstone; the Wall, on the other hand, makes for the heights, adhering most tenaciously to every projecting headland. The Military Way leaves the north mound of the Vallum and runs more or less parallel to the Wall. Passing the site of turret 33*b* we ascend the ridge and, quoting the words of Hutton, we now "quit the beautiful scenes of cultivation, and enter upon the rude of nature, and the wreck of antiquity". Turret 33*b* (Coesike) was excavated in 1968 and 1970, when it was found that its occupation had ceased before the end of the second century. The Wall had been rebuilt across the turret recess, and an inscription of the Sixth Legion was re-used in this work, in spite of the fact that the turret is usually assigned to the Twentieth Legion. On the ascent to Sewingshields farmhouse the Wall has been robbed out to furnish building stones for the house and field walls. The ditch is most pronounced where it begins to mount the hill, but on reaching milecastle 34, marked by a clump of trees, it ends abruptly, the height on the cliffs rendering it unnecessary.

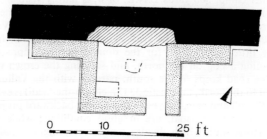

Coesike Turret, 33b: Narrow Wall black, demolished turret stippled built-up re-cess shaded

Milecastle 34 (Grindon) is of type II. South of it, and the modern road, lies a small Roman temporary camp with traces of three entrances, each with a traverse in front. Two other, and smaller camps are not visible. At the next field-wall beyond milecastle 34 is the site of turret 34*a*, found in 1913 and further investigated in 1971. It is notable for its unusually short wing-walls, and like other turrets in this sector it too went out of use in Period II. North of the Wall two sites of interest lay opposite the milecastle and north-east of Sewingshields farmhouse, respectively. The first was an ancient inhabited site on an island in Fozey Moss; the second was Sewingshields Castle, called by Sir Walter Scott, in *Harold the Dauntless* (canto 6), the Castle of Seven Proud Shields.

When Dr. Lingard was there, its walls were 5 feet high. Later, the vaults were removed and the whole area ploughed. Scott described this state of affairs romantically

> .   .   .   . "No towers are seen
> On the wild heath, but those that Fancy builds,
> And, save a fosse that tracks the moor with green,
> Is nought remains to tell of what may there have been."

But a more striking tale was preserved by the Rev. John Hodgson and Miss Carlyle.

"Immemorial tradition has asserted that King Arthur, his queen Guenever, court of lords and ladies, and his hounds, were enchanted in some cave of the crags, or in a hall below the Castle of Sewing-shields, and would continue entranced there till some one should first blow a bugle-horn that laid on a table near the entrance into the hall, and then, with 'the sword of the stone', cut a garter also placed there beside it. But none had ever heard where the entrance to this enchanted hall was, till the farmer at Sewingshields, about fifty years since, was sitting knitting on the ruins of the castle, and his clew fell, and ran downwards through a rush of briars and nettles, as he supposed, into a deep subterranean passage. Full in the faith, that the entrance into King Arthur's hall was now discovered, he cleared the briary portal of its weeds and rubbish, and entering a vaulted passage, followed, in his darkling way, the thread of his clew. The floor was infested with toads and lizards: and the dark wings of bats, disturbed by his unhallowed intrusion, flitted fearfully around him. At length his sinking faith was strengthened by a dim distant light, which, as he advanced, grew gradually brighter, till all at once, he entered a vast and vaulted hall, in the centre of which a fire without fuel, from a broad crevice in the floor, blazed with a high and lambent flame, that showed all the carved walls, and fretted roof, and the monarch, and his queen and court, reposing around in a theatre of thrones and costly couches. On the floor, beyond the fire, lay the faithful and deep-toned pack of thirty couple of hounds; and on a table before it, the spell-dissolving horn, sword, and garter. The shepherd reverently but firmly grasped the sword, and as he drew it leisurely from its rusty scabbard, the eyes of the monarch and his courtiers began to open, and they rose till they sat upright. He cut the garter; and, as the sword was being slowly sheathed, the spell assumed its antient power, and they all gradually sunk to rest; but not before the monarch had lifted up his eyes and hands, and exclaimed,

> 'O woe betide that evil day,
> On which this witless wight was born,
> Who drew the sword—the garter cut,
> But never blew the bugle-horn!'

. . . . Terror brought on loss of memory, and he was unable to give any correct account of his adventure, or the place where it occurred."

Yet another local tradition of King Arthur attaches to the high points called the King's and Queen's Crag, half a mile north-west of Sewingshields, beyond the Wall:

"King Arthur, seated on the farthest rock, was talking with his queen, who, meanwhile, was engaged in arranging her 'back hair'. Some expression of the queen's having offended his majesty, he seized a rock which lay near him, and with an exertion of strength for which the Picts were proverbial, threw it at her, a distance of about a quarter of a mile! The queen, with great dexterity, caught it upon her comb, and thus warded off the blow; the stone fell about midway between them, where it lies to this very day, with the marks of the comb upon it, to attest the truth of the story. The stone probably weighs about twenty tons!"

Between Queen's Crag and the Wall there are many traces of Roman quarrying, including wedge holes in the rock, while on the north face of Queen's Crag itself, in 1960, an inscription was found. It records the names of two centurions, Saturninus and Rufinus, and the *optio* Henoenus.

Centurial Stone, at Sewingshields

The farmhouse of Sewingshields is entirely built out of Roman stones, turret 34*b* lying under its buildings. A centurial stone is preserved there, it may be read "The Century of Gellius Philippus".

From Sewingshields to Carvoran the Military Way is almost everywhere visible. It is always to the south of the Wall, but it does not necessarily keep parallel with it, as it selects the easiest gradients with skill. It is, however, generally visible to the discerning eye.

After a walk westwards through a small plantation, the columnar formation of the dolerite rock soon attracts attention: it cleaves easily and tends to break off, and every thunderstorm throws down some of the cliff. Next follows Cat's Gate, a narrow chasm in the rocks by which, says local tradition, the Scots crept under the Wall. Milecastle 35 (Sewingshields), much robbed for repairs to the farmhouse, lies some 540 yards west of it, and had gates of type II. It had been considerably restored in Period II. A hundred yards before the summit of the hill comes the site of turret 35*a*, Sewingshields Crag, located in 1913 and excavated in 1958. Its occupation ended in the second century; later the turret was demolished, and the Narrow Wall built up across its recess. From the summit one can see Broomlee Lough (to the west) and the smaller Grindon Lough (to the south of the Military road).

Excavation has shown that for many miles along the crags, west from milecastle 35, the Wall is normally the original Hadrianic Narrow Wall, on either narrow or broad foundation. Some rebuilding does occur, however, especially across the recesses of demolished turrets, and at milecastle gateways, which appear to have been thoroughly rebuilt in Period II, as mere posterns, and without their towers. All of this indicates the extent of the modifications of the Hadrianic system, carried out after A.D. 180.

Just beyond the summit a Saxon boundary earthwork, known as the Black Dyke, may be seen running towards the Wall from the north across the moors. From the north the Dyke seems to have run up to the Wall at King's Hill, a little beyond milecastle 36, and followed the Wall to this summit. It consists of a ditch, with its upcast disposed in a mound on the east, so that the work faces west. It runs from the North Tyne at Tarset, across the heads of the westward valleys, to the South Tyne at Moralee.

Turret 35*b*, tested in 1947, had gone out of use in Roman times. West of it comes Busy Gap, where the Wall ditch reappears, as at all such breaks in the escarpment. The triangular enclosure in the gap is post-Roman. On the west side of the gap is a wicket gate through which a drove road passes to the north. This part of the Border long suffered from the incessant wars and raids between England and Scotland, and Busy Gap was a pass much frequented by raiders. A "Busy Gap rogue" was in medieval Newcastle a well-known term of abuse. When Camden and Cotton visited the Wall in 1599, they did not dare venture into these parts. From Carvoran the former wrote (as Philemon Holland translated): "the Wall goeth forward more aslope by Iverton, Forsten, and Chester-in-the-Wall, near to Busy Gap—a place infamous for thieving and robbing, where stood some castles (chesters they call them) as I heard, but I could not with safety take the full survey of it, for the rank robbers thereabouts".

Milecastle 36 (King's Hill) is soon reached, standing on a slope of one in five. It is a long-axis milecastle, the north gate of which was first rebuilt as a postern and then finally blocked. Next follow in rapid succession two narrow and rather steep gaps without names, and Kennel Crags, on whose summit stood turret 36*a*. To the west are the Knag Burn and the famous fort of Housesteads, Camden's Chester-in-the-Wall.

In the bottom of the valley is a gateway, discovered in 1856, which is one of the very rare gates through the Wall, elsewhere than at a milecastle or a fort. It was possibly used for civil as opposed to military traffic. There was another at Portgate but nothing is known in detail of its plan. Here, by contrast, the plan is of special interest. It is a single passage flanked by guard-chambers, and pivot-holes at back and front show that there were two sets of doors, so that parties could be admitted for examination and the payment of tolls, and allowed through the second door in either direction only when the process was complete. It thus affords a glimpse of Roman frontier control rarely given by archaeology. When originally found, in 1856, the structure yielded coins of Claudius II and Constantius I, and re-excavation in 1936 showed that it had been inserted in the Wall in the fourth century. Similar gateways are known on the African frontier near Gemellae, where they occur at Roman-mile intervals instead of milecastles, with a single turret halfway between every two gateways.

The Knag Burn passes under the Wall in a culvert, as it must have done in Roman times. Between the burn and the fort are traces of extra-mural buildings, and the Military Way may be seen winding up to the east gate.

Many visitors will not have walked along the Wall from the Coesike but will have motored along the Military road. Six hundred yards west of the bridge they pass the small camp already described. Further on, beyond the schoolhouse, again on the south, are outcrops of coal from which the Romans probably took the coal used in the fort of Housesteads; there is also an outcrop of limestone which has been much quarried by them.

The farmhouse of Moss Kennels is next reached on the south of the road, and then the house called Beggar Bog. Just beyond the car-park and the gate leading to Housesteads there is a round tumulus, probably of the Bronze Age, to the south of the road, and another still further south in the valley.

HOUSESTEADS (VERCOVICIUM?)

Housesteads is, to most present-day visitors to the Wall no less than it was to William Hutton, "the grandest Station in the whole line". Its ancient name is abbreviated in an inscription as VER, which establishes VERCOVICIUM for the BORCOVICIUM of the *Notitia*, the initial constants being interchangeable in later Latin. That name would mean "Hilly Place", or the like, but the *Ravenna List* gives Velurcion, and Collingwood suggested Verlucione as a possibility. Its garrison, for whom the fort was probably built under Hadrian, was the First Cohort of Tungrians, 1,000 strong, reinforced in the third century by the *cuneus Frisiorum*, or formation of Frisian cavalry, and the *numerus Hnaudifridi*, or Notfried's unit of irregulars. In the second century, presumably during the Antonine occupation of Scotland, a legionary holding-force is known.

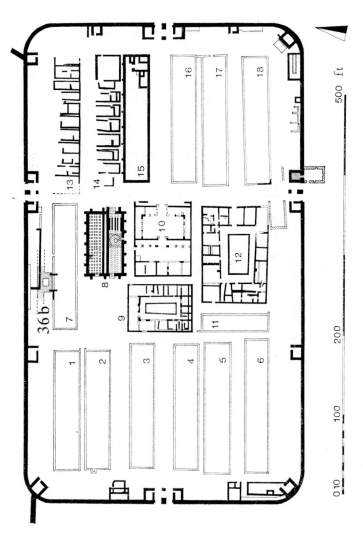

Plan of the Fort of Housesteads

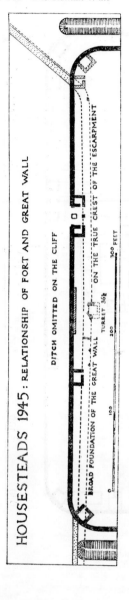

HOUSESTEADS 1945 : RELATIONSHIP OF FORT AND GREAT WALL

DITCH OMITTED ON THE CLIFF

ON THE TRUE CREST OF THE ESCARPMENT

TURRET 36½

BROAD FOUNDATION OF THE GREAT WALL

0   100   200   300 FEET

The fort lies 4¾ miles from Carraw-burgh and covers just over 5 acres. Its plan is the usual rectangle with rounded corners, 610 by 367 feet in size. Its long axis runs from east to west, as at no fort so far described: this is because the fort is planted at the very edge of the cliff, on a narrow shelf which itself slopes sharply southwards. A better site further west was sacrificed in order to overlook the Knag Burn gap, carrying an ancient traffic route from the north.

The site, including the Knag Burn gateway and milecastle 37, was bought by the late Professor G. M. Trevelyan in 1930 and presented to the National Trust, which also owns the Wall as far as Peel Crag. The fort is in the guardianship of D.O.E. and visitors are asked, while visiting it, to keep to the acknowledged paths, and not wander about the farm-land.

The Narrow Wall joins the fort at its rounded northern angles. It is evident that the fort was then already erected, because its north-east angle-tower was actually moved (see p. 145) to suit the final arrangement. But, before any fort was built at all, the Broad Wall and turret 36*b* had been laid out on the crest, and their demolished remains were overlaid by the rampart and *intervallum* road of the fort. The fort was thus added after the broad foundation had been laid, but before the Narrow Wall had been built. As at Rudchester, the Vallum passes so far south as to require no deviation from its straight course. Its ditch, levelled and obliterated by buildings of the Roman extra-mural settlement, was found 85 yards south of the fort in

1934, and was crossed opposite the south gate by a causeway of living rock.

Considerable excavation has been carried out, and this is still the most completely exposed fort on the Wall. The defences and some of the interior were investigated by Hodgson and Clayton, and the rest of the interior by R. C. Bosanquet for the Society of Antiquaries of Newcastle in 1898. More recently buildings have been excavated for D.O.E. by various directors.

The plan of the fort is best appreciated by entering the south gate and walking uphill to the centre. There the *via praetoria* leads eastwards from the headquarters building (10, *principia*) to the main gate or *porta praetoria*, while the *via principalis* runs across the fort to the north gate, *porta principalis sinistra*, and the south gate, *porta principalis dextra*. The space east of this road was filled with four long narrow barrack-buildings (13-18), and a pair of other buildings (15-16) which face each other across the east-west street. The northern of these had a fine flagged floor and a small bath unit inserted into its eastern end. On the north side of the *principia* lie the granaries (8, *horrea*); on the south, the commanding-officer's house (12, *praetorium*). Behind this central row of buildings came a hospital (9, *valetudenarium*) and near them miscellaneous buildings of uncertain purpose (7, 11): then 5 more barracks (1-3; 5 and 6) and a workshop (4). Finally come the west rampart and west gate, *porta decumana*.

A more particular survey may begin by examining the *principia* (see plan). The visible building, which had a front portico, projecting into the street, was first built in the Second Period and remains of a Hadrianic *principia* have been found below it. Large masonry at the entrance, from which probably came reliefs of Mars and of Victory now at Chesters, has been robbed away, leaving only a threshold with pivot-hole. The entrance leads into a courtyard bordered on three sides by an open colonnade, later closed by walling. A doorway beyond leads into a hall with eastward aisle and north side-door. In its north-west corner is the packing of a dais (*tribunal*), from which an ornamental front and the top have been removed. Beyond this lie the usual 5 rooms. The middle one is the shrine of the standards, and beds are cut in the stones flanking its threshold, to receive low stone screens, as seen at Chesterholm. The south wall of the shrine and the pay room to the south are much ruined.

In the record-room to the north, heated by a hypocaust, were

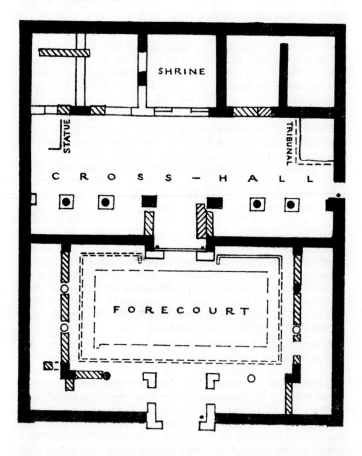

SHRINE

STATUE

TRIBUNAL

C R O S S — H A L L

F O R E C O U R T

0   10   70
FEET

Plan of Severan Headquarters, Housesteads. Later additions are shaded

found over 800 iron arrow-heads with fragments of wooden shafts: the place had thus finally become an armoury. The pay-room, to the south, was modified and a new wall at its back cut off space for a lavatory. The paymaster, who was the regimental standard-bearer, was now living in his office.

Between the south gate and the *principia* are the remains of the commanding-officer's house (12). This began as an L-shaped pair of wings to the north and west, and was later extended to become a normal courtyard house. The room at the north-east corner was a kitchen, with large oven, while that in the centre of the north range was turned at an early date into a bath-suite with heated room and cold bath. In the last Period the hypocaust went out of use and was filled with fourth-century pottery and coins (the latest of A.D. 346-78). The central room of the west range began as a latrine, in the drain of which second-century pottery was found, together with a solid gold signet-ring with an engraved intaglio showing a theatrical mask. In Period II the latrine was filled and replaced by a urinal, to the north.

The south end of the west range contained a group of heated living rooms, entered directly from the courtyard. When the south range was built its two western rooms were added to these private apartments. The two eastern rooms, on the other hand, were flagged and had certainly been stables, at lower ground level, possibly with servants' quarters above, at courtyard level. The principal entrance remained throughout in the centre of the east range, giving on to the central courtyard; which, as we now see it, has a modified central area built-up with re-used stonework, including a broken door or window head.

A smaller building (9), immediately behind the *principia*, was a hospital. This was a courtyard building, consisting of small rooms alternating with narrow passageways, arranged round a central courtyard. In its first state the courtyard contained a verandah; later this was removed and the whole central area flagged. Alterations also occurred in the south range, where some of the rooms had as many as three floor levels of beaten earth and pebbles.

North of the headquarters building lie two granaries side by side (8). These are buttressed buildings, whose floors, now removed, covered a ventilated basement in which rows of piers, still visible, carried the joists of a wooden floor. Joist-holes are seen opposite each row of piers in the south wall of the north granary. The object of the ventilation was to keep the floor cool and dry for corn-storage. Doors at the west end opened onto platforms up to which carts could be brought for unloading grain. Like the visible *principia*, the existing buildings are secondary and the south buttresses of the north granary have been founded upon bases and caps from a dismantled portico, suggesting that the original granary had been a single, undivided building with a central colonnade, which was later turned into two separate buildings. In the southern of these a post-medieval kiln for drying grain has been inserted.

Beyond the granaries comes the rampart, which, as usual in Hadrian's time, consisted of a stone wall backed by an earth bank. The earth bank has, however, mostly been removed in later Roman times, to make way for buildings. West of the gateway the base of a staircase ramp is visible, beyond which may be seen foundations of an interval-tower, with adjacent rain-water cistern. Here also are seen the foundations of turret 36*b*, demolished when the fort was built, but occupied before demolition, as its hearths show.

Statue of Victory from Housesteads
(Newcastle)

The north gate is very fine, the large blocks of its foundation exhibiting very close joints: an embanked roadway, which led out from it, was removed to display them. The gate has twin portals, divided by piers, the innermost standing to a consider-able height. In the east portal excavation in 1930 showed that pivots for the doors had not yet been fitted when blocking-masonry was inserted. The west portal had a later threshold, now removed, about three feet higher than the original one, and one of its pivot-blocks lies at the back of the gate. The flanking guardchambers are in good condition, and, in rebuilding the west one, part of an altar to Jupiter Optimus Maximus was used as a walling stone, and is now in Chesters Museum.

Outside this chamber is a large water-tank. Its stone sides, themselves of re-used material, were run in with lead in vertical slots at the joints and cramped with iron at the top. Their tops are worn by sharpening swords or by washing clothes, as in tanks found in more than one Roman fort. Many tanks at Housesteads are related to the towers, collecting water from their flat roofs; for here water is not plentiful below ground and rain-water became particularly valuable.

At the north-east angle the Narrow Wall abuts on the fort at the north end of the curving angle. At some date, the tower, originally placed in a normal position in the midle of the curve, was pulled down and re-erected at the junction as now visible. The foundations of the original tower have been discovered but are not displayed, though the patching executed when its walls were pulled away from the fort-wall can still be seen.

Further south, behind the east rampart, an interval-tower lies midway between the angle and the gate. The high level of its floor shows that the existing structure is a rebuilding and, just north of it there is another large water-tank, at an earlier and lower level.

At the east gate (*porta praetoria*) the foundation-work carrying the external wall of the south tower is worth noting. The south portal has been blocked, but not before its threshold and pivot-blocks were renewed in Period II, as seen on the north side: the blocking therefore presumably belongs to the fourth century. When blocked, the portal became a guardchamber, while the older guardchamber to the south became a coal-store, in which nearly a cart-load of coal was found in 1833, no doubt won from local out-crops (see p. 138). Two successive holes in which iron cups for the door-pivots were fixed, remain on the north side, and one on the south. The stone stop-block for the doors is also seen, and Roman wheel-ruts, 8 inches deep, appear in the checked threshold. Like the ruts at Pompeii, they approximate closely to the British railway gauge, and the local legend is that George Stephenson took his gauge from this gateway. His standard, however, had been reached by averaging the wheel-gauge of a hundred carts, some years before these gates were uncovered.

On the north side of the *via praetoria*, leading west from this gate, is a long building (15) of massive construction, with buttresses and a wide southern doorway, large enough for carts. Excavation in 1961 showed that it had apparently begun as a normal barrack-block, which was rebuilt after a fire during the second century. The visible building is the third-century replacement, which continued in use into the early fourth century, and later. It is a buttressed store-building, constructed of exceptionally long stones with feather-tooling. The bath-block at its eastern end looks like an even later insertion. In it can be seen a bath, and voussoirs from an insulated double ceiling, as at Chesters. To the north lay barrack 14, excavated in 1959-60 and in part displayed. The Hadrianic building was a normal barrack-block with verandah, projecting centurion's quarters and 10 barrack-rooms, all under a single roof. Little remained of its Period II successor, but the Constantian rebuilding was entirely different. Instead of a single building, 7 individual barrack units, each with its own side walls and evesdrips, were found, flanked to the west by a workshop and to the east by the officer's accommodation.

Threshold of North Portal, East Gate, Housesteads: Looking West. The Right-hand or North Rut is now broken

Later modifications were widespread, although the form remained the same. The coins go down to Gratian's issue of A.D. 367-375.

The corresponding barrack to the north (13) is under excavation. It, too, began as a normal block, with a centurion's suite at its eastern end. In the fourth century, however, it was rebuilt as a row of individual one or two roomed units (chalets), the eastern 6 of which were each independently built, while the western four or five had party walls. The eastern chalet contained a bread-oven in its southern room, and was entered from the east. The others were all entered from the north, except number two, which had doors in both its north and south walls. Although the chalets had a common south wall their north ends were individually built, some having a flagged area beyond, others not. The length of the chalets, too, varied considerably.

This change to chalets was apparently accompanied by the removal of sections of the fort rampart backing-mound and its replacement by extra buildings. These alterations are comparatively rare, being known for certain only at Greatchesters and High Rochester on the northern frontier, and Caernarvon in Wales. Chesters, too, and Risingham, may possibly have received chalets late in their lives.

South of the east gate, a staircase ramp is attached to the inner side of the fort-wall, and then come several other additions of late date, including an interval tower. At the south-east corner, on the outer face of the wall, large blocks are seen at the tower position, as they are at the north, west and east gates, among other places, suggesting that where necessary the towers and gateways of the fort were built upon reinforced stone rafts, to prevent slip on the steep hillside. At the angle, and for some distance along the east and south walls, much of the outer face has been heavily rebuilt. Its excavator, in 1911-12, found that this came late in the structural sequence, so that it can more easily be attributed to repairs after general neglect in the late third century, than any barbarian damage in A.D. 180.

The original entrance to the angle-tower was replaced by another to the south west, after it had become masked by a very fine water-tank, which completely blocked it. This tank was well constructed and its stone sides are still joined with lead flashings and iron cramps. At least two more such tanks lay close by on the north, as shown on photographs in the Museum.

The over-flow from the tanks was used to flush the men's latrine, a rectangular building with a long axial passage, on each side of which seats were arranged over two deep sewers. A stone channel in front of them carried running water for washing sponges, the Roman equivalent of toilet-paper, and at one end there is a stone basin for washing hands. The outfall-sewer disappears under the rampart, to discharge at a point as yet unknown, further down the hillside. As now seen the building is entered from the west, but originally its doorway was in the eastern wall, which explains why the sewer runs round the north, east and south sides.

More barracks lay to the north and an interval-tower is seen on the south. Then comes the south gate, a massive structure with two portals, the pivot-holes for the doors of which are visible. The gate has guardchambers on either side, and when excavated by Hodgson the east portal was found to have been walled up, blocking which is probably to be dated to the third century. In the thirteenth century, a Border farmer built a vaulted undercroft with central pier outside the east guard-chamber, and in the guardchamber itself is a later corn-drying kiln. The lower part of the eastern external steps to the upper living-room of this habitation is less easy to see.

Stone lintels with arched heads were used to crown the windows or doorways of the gate-towers, and several lie here ornamented with circular or cruciform designs (the latter without Christian significance). The best are in Chesters Museum. Inside the fort and near the south gate were found in 1853, a gold ear-drop, a gold signet-ring with paste *intaglio* of Mercury, and a *sestertius* of Commodus dated to A.D. 181, all now in Chesters Museum.

The south rampart is in good preservation and stands 10 courses high. At the south-west angle of the fort the tower front is built with larger stones than normal, as already has been noted in other towers. Just north of the angle-tower a long staircase-ramp extends to the next interval-tower, which has again been re-constructed from a low level and contains an oven.

The west rampart is still 11 courses high and has a bonding-course of stone slabs, while the west gate stands higher than any of the others. Its north impost remains to full height, ready for the cap and springer, similar to those to be seen at the main east gate of Birdoswald. At the back of the outer central pier, bolt-holes for the bar of the doors and slots for its manipulation

Mars, probably from the principia *at Housesteads (Chesters)*

are visible; they go with corresponding holes behind the imposts. The existing threshold and stop-block in the south portal belong to the Period II reconstruction, after which this portal was blocked, presumably under Constantius, in the early fourth century. The north portal, on the other hand, was blocked with rougher masonry, probably in the reconstruction of A.D. 369. Bruce's wood-cut here retained, shows the different character of the work, a point not realized at the time of excavation, when the blocking was removed. The guardchambers were also later converted into heated rooms, as at the east gate of Birdoswald.

Against the inner face of the west rampart, both north and south of the gate, are several additional buildings of a type already noted near the east gate, but no interval-tower now appears to the north. The area between the west rampart and *via quintana* was occupied by 5 barracks (1-3, 5 and 6) and, on the south side of the westward road, a workshop and smithy (4).

The West Gate, Housesteads, from the West, showing Blocking Walls in both Portals, now Removed

Like the north-east angle, the north-west angle of the fort antedates the Narrow Wall, which makes contact with the front of a normal angle-tower. Excavation has shown, however, that the west ditch cut into the broad foundation while leaving space for the Narrow Wall to pass between its end and the cliff.

Immediately west of the fort, and on the Military Way, a series of conspicuous and regular enclosures is visible as mounds and ridges in the ground. The area has never been subjected to systematic excavation and its true nature remains unknown, but the plots could represent individual holdings, lining the Roman road.

South of the fort lies the Museum, which houses a small but interesting collection of objects, models and photographs. Of special interest is a relief of three deities in hooded cloaks, a well-carved figure of Mercury and a bold panel of Hercules and the Nemean lion, all from the *vicus*. Amongst the inscriptions are fragments of a dedication to Severus and Caracalla from the fort headquarters building. Most of the earlier discoveries, however, are in either Chesters Museum or the Museum of Antiquities, Newcastle.

South and east of the fort there are widespread visible remains of Roman extra-mural buildings, indicating a *vicus*, or civil

settlement, of no small size. Earlier antiquaries were astonished both at the extent of the buildings and at the number of inscribed and sculptured stones which they saw on the slopes and in the valley. Excavation and air-photography have confirmed the number and variety of these buildings. Just outside the south gate of the fort are very massive foundations and a group of shops or taverns is erected upon terraces, blocking the approach to the east portal of the gate. On inspection these show good sills to take shuttered

Relief of Mithras, pierced for illumination from behind, from Housesteads (Newcastle)

fronts. Excavation has shown that the settlement dates, in its most highly-developed form, to the third and fourth centuries, and an inscription indicates that, like all such settlements, it had local self-government. The place was not, however, without sensation: the excavators of the 1930s found that one building had been a gamblers' rendezvous, another a coiners' den while below the early fourth-century floor in the rear room of another, probably a tavern, two skeletons were found. One was a short robust man of middle age, with the point of a sword still between his ribs, while the other was slighter and probably a woman.

The bath-house of the fort once stood on a rocky shelf on the east bank of the Knag Burn, opposite the middle of the fort. It was heated by hypocausts and soot was found still in the flues. Though it was ransacked many years ago, to supply stones for neighbouring field-walls, fragments of walling hint at remains still worth examination. Nearer the Wall is a fenced spring, cased in Roman masonry, which seems to have supplied the baths with water. Opposite this, and west of the burn, a Roman lime-kiln has been found.

On the hillside, east, and especially, south of the fort, small platforms and large terraces are clearly visible, particularly when the sun is low. The smaller of these are usually house-platforms, the Romanized counterparts of the native dwellings visible on so many Northumbrian sites. The larger terraces mark the remains of cultivation fields, some possibly pre-Roman, others Roman in date, the rest mediaeval and later. Together, platforms and terraces have obscured a good stretch of the Vallum. By and large, on the hillside the ancient terraces run east and west, and the more recent field-strips north and south. Elsewhere, the distinction is not always so clear.

South of the *vicus*, in the marshy valley, rises the ridge called Chapel Hill. Beyond its west end, close to where a spring still flows, is the site of a half-underground temple, dedicated to Mithras and first discovered in 1822. Excavations of 1898 revealed a long narrow nave, flanked by trenches for reclining worshippers. Beyond this was the sanctuary, which yielded fragments of the great Bull-Killing scene, a very notable relief of Mithras rising from the rock, surrounded by the signs of the Zodiac, so designed and placed that it would be illuminated from behind, statues of the attendant deities Cautes and Cautopates, and several altars. Two of these were dedicated to *Mithras, Lord of the Age*. One, bearing the names of Gallus and Volusianus, consuls for A.D. 252, probably marks a refurbishing of the temple some time after its foundation earlier in the century. Most of the stones from this temple are in Newcastle, the others in Chesters. A small altar to Jupiter, Cocidius and the Guardian Deity of the Locality, reused in the *Mithraeum*, and originally erected by a detachment of the Second Legion acting as garrison, recalls the early Antonine occupiers of the fort.

The large and imposing stones in Chesters Museum dedicated to Mars Thincsus were found on the north side of Chapel Hill. This German deity was attended by pairs of Alaisiagae, female spirits or Valkyries, whose names are given as Beda and Fimmilena, Baudihillia and Friagabis. The shrine also yielded a remarkable arched door-head, on which are carved the god and male attendants, represented as Mars with Victories. Their worshippers belong to two units of irregulars, the *cuneus Frisiorum* and the *numerus Hnaudifridi*, which formed part of the third-century garrison. Excavation in 1961 at the site of discovery yielded foundations of a round third-century shrine, 13 feet in internal diameter. Below lay traces of the second-century civil settlement, no doubt kept south of the Vallum and its crossing.

Altar to Mithras (Newcastle) and Impost from the Shrine of Mars Thincsus (Chesters Museum), from Housesteads

Another group from Chapel Hill is a series of altars dedicated to Jupiter, Best and Greatest and the Spirit of the Deified Emperors, by the Tungrians, under their commander. Such inscriptions are usually part of the official state cult, as practised by the army. Also in Chesters is a fragment of an elaborate Diocletianic building-inscription, one of a very small number from Wall-forts. Finally, an inscription now in the Museum of Antiquities, Newcastle, was set up by the Cohort according to the interpretation of the Oracle of Apollo at Claros, and is paralleled by similar inscriptions at Volubilis and Cuicul in Africa, Corinium in Dalmatia, Sliven in Thrace and Nora in Sardinia.

Tombstone of Anicius Ingenuus, Medical Officer, from Housesteads (Newcastle)

The sculptures which Housesteads has produced are among the best in the frontier-forts. Those of Mithras and Mars Thincsus have already been noted. But the seated mother-goddesses, found in the *vicus* and now in Newcastle, equal any found in the north of England. Even more striking are the reliefs of Victory and of Mars, forming a pair, which came from the front of the *principia* and are now in Chesters Museum, while another Victory from the *principia* is in Newcastle. In Housesteads Museum are to be seen the hooded deities, Mercury, and Hercules and the Nemean Lion, already mentioned.

The cemeteries lay beyond the extra-mural settlement, one to the west of the fort, south of the Military Way, and one on either side of Chapel Hill. In the low ground to the east human remains have been found in draining, while tombstones have been discovered to the south. One records Anicius Ingenuus, a medical officer, and shows a crouching hare carved above the inscription.

Like Chesters, Housesteads was connected with the Stanegate, and MacLauchlan surveyed a road running south-east from the fort to the Stanegate at Grindon, which Bruce had no difficulty in tracing from near Moss Kennels farmhouse to Grindon Shields. Horsley thought that a second road went south-west to the Stanegate near Chesterholm.

THE STANEGATE AT BARCOMBE

Two and three-quarter miles west of the crossroads on Grindon Common, at Crindledykes, 5 complete and two fragmentary milestones were found in 1885. They record the Emperors Severus Alexander (A.D. 223), Probus (A.D. 276-82), Maximinus Caesar (A.D. 305-9), Constantinus Caesar (A.D. 306-7), and Constantinus Augustus (A.D. 307-337). They are now in Chesters Museum. The stone dedicated to Severus Alexander records the distance XIIII miles, showing that the road was measured from Corbridge 14 miles to the east.

The Stanegate then runs below Barcombe, from the summit of which, if the day is clear and the bull not about, there is an excellent view of the Wall, Vallum and Stanegate. Roman quarries will be noted. East of the "Langstane", a small bronze arm-purse was found in a quarry reopened in 1835, carefully deposited beneath stone-chippings. It contained 63 coins, apparently wrapped in leather. Three are of gold, the rest of silver. The *aurei* belong to Claudius, Nero and Vespasian; of the *denarii* 9 are republican, the rest imperial, extending from Nero, with 17 of Trajan and 4 of Hadrian. The high proportion and excellent preservation of this last group indicates that the coins were laid aside and lost early in Hadrian's reign, when the quarry was being worked for building the Wall.

North of this quarry and north-east of the Langstane, on a shoulder which commands a view of the Wall from Sewingshields to the Nine Nicks of Thirlwall, is a British fortification, with a rampart tolerably complete, and, in its north-west corner, a Roman signal-station, linking Chesterholm with points east and west. This is a sub-rectangular or circular enclosure measuring 65 feet from north to south, with a turf-built rampart still standing 2½ feet high, and outer ditch with possible causeway. No trace of any timber structure has been found but Flavian pottery occurred in a secondary feature.

From Barcombe the Stanegate descends into the valley to cross the Bradley Burn, and make for Chesterholm.

CHESTERHOLM (VINDOLANDA) AND THE STANEGATE

Where the Stanegate crosses the Bradley Burn, on its western side, there is a large natural hummock with an uninscribed Roman milestone standing in its original position beside the road. Just east of the stream is the entrance-way to Chesterholm house, now a museum: the main entrance-way and carpark for the site, however, lie to the west, and are approached from that direction.

Beyond the Bradley Burn the road crosses Brackie's Burn and, after a steep climb, runs past the northern edge of VINDOLANDA, modern CHESTERHOLM, once known as Chesters-Iverton or Chesters-on-Caudley.

The Roman name Vindolanda ("White Close") is indicated by an inscription from the *vicus*, while the *Notitia* treats the fort as one of the Wall system and gives the Fourth Cohort of Gauls as its garrison. The same cohort was in occupation during the third century. Earlier garrisons are uncertain but possibly a Cohort of Nervians was stationed here at some time.

The fort, covering 3.5 acres, occupies a prominent platform, sheltered by hills to the north and east, and naturally strong on every side but the west. Its function was to guard the north-south gap in which it stands. The walls, north gate, west gate and headquarters, excavated by Professor Eric Birley and presented by him to the nation, are now in the custody or D.O.E. The central building is a fine example of a fourth-century headquarters, in which the *tribunal* and stone screens of the cross-hall deserve attention: and in the chapel of the standards the unusual pit-like sunken *caisse*, for the chests of the regimental funds, should also be noted. Below this building, which faces north, the discriminating eye can pick out foundations of a third-century headquarters, facing south, which had been constructed with small stone infilling between larger piers, like many Roman buildings in Africa.

The north and west gates, as visible, are both of fourth-century date, with single passageways and slightly projecting guardchambers. The south gate is of the same date but is a pedestrian passageway only, without guardchambers, as apparently was the east gate. The north-west angle tower is earlier, but has been reduced by the later, fourth-century wall.

Among the dedications are two altars to the Genius of the *Praetorium* by prefects of the Fourth Cohort of Gauls. The

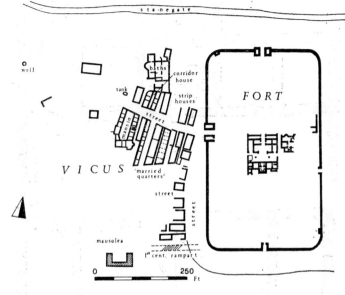

Plan of Chesterholm Fort and vicus

praetorium was the commanding-officer's house and the altars were unearthed in its ruins. Another fragment, however, from a Hadrianic building inscription, now in Newcastle, is so similar to those of the Second Legion from the Wall milecastles that it must be considered an import.

Excavation has proved that the first fort here lay to the west of the visible one. Like other forts on the Stanegate it was a Flavian foundation, perhaps dating to the late 80s, and it came in due course to form one of the series of garrison-forts for the first phase of Hadrian's Wall. When the forts were removed from the Stanegate to the Wall, it was not retained in commission. Just how a fragment of an inscription mentioning the governor Calpurnius Agricola relates is uncertain, but in Period II, if not earlier, a new fort was built on the present site, to the east, facing south. A declaration of loyalty to Caracala in A.D. 213 by the Fourth Cohort of Gauls is now in the Museum of Antiquities, Newcastle. The existing fort, however, is a complete reconstruction

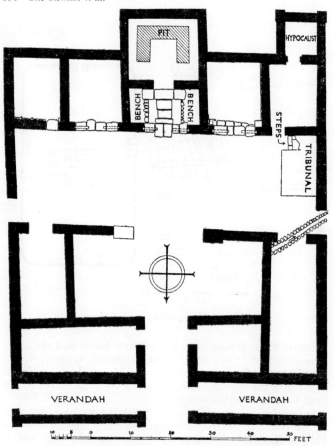

Chesterholm: Early Fourth-century Headquarters

by Constantius I, and faces north. There were extensive repairs in
A.D. 369, while coins recovered suggest that occupation continued
until late in the century. Life may have continued later still, in fact
well beyond the abandonment of the fort, for the inscribed tombstone of Brigomaglos, found near the site, has the language and
lettering of a sub-Roman Christian monument of the fifth century.

West of the fort lies a considerable *vicus* or civil settlement, parts of which have been uncovered and consolidated in recent years. Its history differs slightly from that of the fort, however, for it appears to have been built, as a single operation, sometime after 140, that is, well after the abandonment of the earlier fort. It consisted principally of the buildings described below: the bath-house, corridor building and several strip-houses, to the north

Fragment of an Inscription attesting Devotion to Caracalla (Newcastle)

of the east-west street, and the "married-quarters" block, *mansio* and accompanying buildings to the south. The workmanship was of good quality, with well-laid small ashlar throughout, and the whole gave the appearance of having been of one creation. At some date these buildings were surrounded by a broad clay rampart. The unusual nature of this settlement has led its excavator to wonder if it was constructed for some special purpose, connected, perhaps, with the mining of lead, iron and coal in the vicinity.

This settlement was subsequently demolished, to be rebuilt, in part at least, as the *vicus* of the third-century fort, to the east. The second period workmanship, however, was of noticeably inferior quality, with large stone blocks providing the seating for timber upperwork. Individual buildings too, had undergone much reconstruction, and many traces of metal-working were visible. Associated with the latest occupation material in a building of this second period was a hoard of 111 radiate coins, which, terminating with issues of the Emperors Postumus and Victorinus, must have been buried by A.D. 270. Later, a small amount of rebuilding occurred, which is associated with pottery types common after A.D. 369.

The settlement visible today is partly that of the second century, and partly that of the third. It consists of buildings lining the main east-west road, and a north-south side-street running on the line of the earlier fort ditch. Immediately outside the west gate of the fort strip-houses are to be seen to the north and south. These are the normal *vicus* buildings of any age, similar to those described at Housesteads; further west more exceptional buildings occur. On the north side of the road there is a group of larger dwellings once joined by a rear wall. The most westerly of these began as a corridor house with three rooms opening off each side of a central passageway. Later, it was split into two separate ranges when the corridor was turned into an access-alley leading to the bath-house behind.

The baths were constructed as part of the earlier settlement. Later modifications, and stone robbing, have affected the original building plan, but in essence it seems to have consisted of two ranges not unreminiscent of the Hadrianic block-type baths, although different in plan. In the south-eastern corner lay the cold room and bath, with a warm room to the west, and the hottest room and its baths occupying the north-western portion of the building. The north-eastern corner contained the hot dry room, entered directly from the cold room.

Later modifications gave additional rooms to this complex, including an introductory changing room which now forms the most easterly room of all. To the north is a latrine and to the south rooms of uncertain purpose.

Next, on the south side of the main road, are two long narrow buildings rather different from the normal strip-house, which have been interpreted as married quarters. The more easterly consists of two ranges, one subdivided into rooms not unlike a normal barrack-block. These, it has been argued, may have been quarters for the soldiers and their families after the abolition of restrictions on marriage, although their date is probably too early. The other range contains no internal divisions now and may have been a communal hall. Last, on the southern side, is the *mansio* or official rest house. This is a courtyard building: private rooms, a latrine and a kitchen comprise the east and west ranges and a small bath-house forms the southern side. Again, the visible building was constructed in the mid-second century, but it had a long life and there were major alterations, including the rebuilding of the entire east wing in large masonry. Traces of other buildings can be seen to the west, including a store and water tanks, and to the south two mausolea have been uncovered.

The *vicus* lies over the early fort, portions of which have been found to the south, including timber internal buildings and the turf rampart. It is from this area that many of the recent small

Altar showing Forest Glade, Chesterholm (Chesters)

finds have come, including leather shoes and wooden writing tablets, some of which may now be seen in the site museum. Also to the south are examples of a stone wall with turret, and turf wall with mile-castle gateway, giving a valuable three-dimensional example of how the original features may possibly have appeared.

A small museum has recently been opened, which contains many of the more important new finds from the site. These include leather shoes and cloth, metal tools and implements, pottery and animal bones. Also on view are some of the wooden writing tablets from the late first-century levels, stamped tiles of the sixth Legion and inscribed and sculptured stones. Many small altars and other religious dedications have come from the *vicus*, but perhaps the most interesting single inscription is an altar, now in Chesters Museum, which records the *vicani Vindolandenses*, showing that the *vicus* here too was a self-governing community. A further altar, now in Newcastle, was found in Beltingham churchyard, 2 miles to the south-east. It comes either from Chesterholm or a local shrine, and is of great interest in that it is dedicated to the goddess Sattada by the *curia* or council of the Textoverdi, apparently a local tribal unit or sub-division, not otherwise attested.

Apart from the mausolea beside the stone and turf reconstructions, two cemeteries are known, one to the west of the site and the other to the north of the Stanegate. From the northern cemetery comes the tombstone of Ingenuus, who lived 24 years 4 months and 7 days, now in the site museum.

Altar from Chesterholm, erected by the vicani Vindolandenses *(Chesters Museum)*

Beyond the site entrance and car park the Stanegate continues westwards, with the base of the next milestone standing on the north side of the road about 1700 yards (rather more than a true Roman mile) west of the Chesterholm stone. Its shaft, broken up to make a pair of gateposts, bore the inscription, in large coarse letters, BONO REIPUBLICAE NATO, "To him who was born for the good of the State", paying a compliment to the reigning Emperor.

A little beyond this milestone base the road to the Once Brewed (see p. 171) crosses the Stanegate, which continues beyond it as the farm road to Seatsides, where the farmhouse lies in the centre of a marching camp, the northern portion of which still survives. Two further camps, no longer visible, lay to the north, and another pair, much smaller, once lay to the east. This series serves to mark the beginning of a group of 19 camps which stretches as far as the western end of Haltwhistle Common, giving us a picture of what the whole length of the Wall was probably once like, littered with the traces of temporary and marching camps, associated with the construction of the Wall and the movement of units, or, in the case of the smaller examples, practice works where troops were trained in the construction of earthen defences.

Beyond Seatsides the road continues, running along the northern edge of the ridge, past the point where another milestone was found, and onwards to the north of Hill Top farm. In this stretch it is complicated by later alignments, but its general direction is clear. By Hill Top it swings north-west and crosses the Military road obliquely at the lane leading to Shield-on-the-Wall. Across the Military road it aims for the Mare and Foal, but curves south and runs parallel with the modern road towards Haltwhistle Burn fortlet. To the south, at Milestone House, part of another marching camp survives, including one side over 600 yards in length.

Altar set up by the Curia Texotverdorum, *Beltingham (Newcastle)*

FROM HOUSESTEADS TO GREATCHESTERS

In walking westwards, those who wish to avoid fatigue will best take the Roman Military Way, which was once lined with Roman buildings west of the fort. It is easily found, because all the field-gates are placed upon it; and no-one should need to be reminded to close the gates after him in this land of flocks and herds.

The Military Way was in use as a public road not very long ago. The family of Wright were hereditary carriers between Newcastle and Carlisle for more than 100 years, and so continued till driven off the road by the railway. The representative of the family at the time the first edition of this book was prepared was the tenant of Housesteads farm. He stated that the tradition in the family was, that the traffic from east to west was originally conducted on pack-horses, and that the carriers, in the central part of their journey between Newcastle and Carlisle, were accustomed to resort to the Roman way. In certain parts of their journey they had to camp out all night, and one of their camping places was opposite the Twice Brewed, a carriers' inn of which old Hutton gave a picturesque description (see p. 171).

Those who choose to walk along the Wall leave the fort by the west gate and make north-west for a small plantation. The Wall here has been cleared of tumbled stones on either side, and it is interesting to compare the masonry thus exposed, but not renovated, with that of the Wall west of milecastle 37, which was extensively repaired when freed from fallen material in the nineteenth century; or, again, with the Wall as consolidated by D.O.E., which is firm and good when time has removed its first new look. For many visitors this walk will be the most memorable item in their tour: for here in particular can be re-created by every imaginative soul the conditions of the watch and ward which the Romans kept.

The walk along the whin-sill is exceedingly beautiful, and the traveller will notice that the Wall differs slightly in width in different places, as is shown by the offsets and insets of a few inches on the south face. This is reputedly due to different gangs working simultaneously on different parts of the line, the centurion in charge of each exercising, within narrow limits, his own judgement as to the width of the Wall. The north face of the Wall, however, is everywhere flush.

At 450 yards from Housesteads comes milecastle 37 (Housesteads), excavated in 1853, 1907 and 1933. It measures internally 57 feet 7 inches from east to west, and 49 feet 7 inches from north to south, with side-walls 9 feet thick. The north wall was

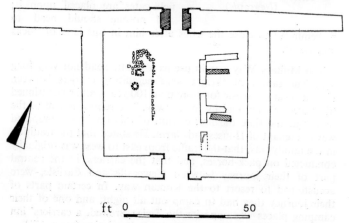

Plan of Milecastle 37 (Housesteads), later walls shaded

laid out to broad gauge at the north gate, and thence tapered to narrow gauge at either side, a treatment not found anywhere else. The gateways are of type I, like short-axis milecastles 38 and 42, and the occurrence of Second Legion building inscriptions in each of these three cases allows a firm attribution of short-axis milecastles with type I gateways to that Legion.

The south corners are rounded externally and squared on the inside. In building this milecastle's wall, two courses of thin sandstone slabs were used for bonding, as at Housesteads, much as tiles are used in many Roman structures. If a third represented the base of the rampart-walk it would give a wall 15 feet high, with crenellations adding a further 5 feet. This fits well the north gate, 10 feet wide, of most substantial masonry, where the springers of the arch are in position, and several arch-stones lie upon the ground, inviting restoration. Each stone has a lewis-hole in it, so placed that the stone would hang on the crane at the angle which it was to occupy in the arch. The jambs, from the floor to the top of the impost, are a little under 6 feet high, the arch giving 5 feet more of head-room. That the gate was built first, before the adjacent walling, is shown by the raking joints seen on both sides in the south face. Later, the gateway was narrowed to 3 feet 9 inches, and the floor of this later postern, 3 feet 6 inches above the sill of the original, covered a set of secondary pivot-blocks. The south gateway, now in poor state, had also been reduced to a postern.

These alterations explain the layers revealed by excavation. At foundation level, within the north gate, mason's chippings and a mason's chisel were discovered, and these belong to the initial construction. Upon the chippings, near the walls, a first floor of flags had been laid. To the west of the axial road a wooden stores-shed was built and on the east side a stone barrack of two rooms, the south unoccupied and used for arms, the north serving as living-quarters and associated with Hadrianic pottery. Next, above a levelled mass of stones and rubbish, came a second floor belonging to the visible building, once butting against the main walls. A devastation is thus suggested, and is usually taken to be that carried out by the Caledonian tribes, which ended Wall Period I. About the same time the jambs of the north gate were levered out of perpendicular and so remain, with the masonry of the Period II postern-gate built up against them. As such would require masons' tools, and time to achieve, it is best seen as part of the Roman demolition of the gate-tower at a time when many turrets were also being dismantled, rather than destruction by the Caledonians, who, in any case, would be more interested in pillage and sack than the destruction of inanimate stonework.

Left-hand bottom corner of Hadrianic dedication slab, Milecastle 37 (Housesteads), in Chesters Museum

Structural evidence for fourth-century occupations had been removed, but pottery later than A.D. 369 was recognised in 1933. The most valuable relic, however, found in 1853, was a fragment of the inscription commemorating the original building of this milecastle by the Second Legion under Hadrian's legate, Aulus Platorius Nepos. When complete, it was the same as those from milecastles 38 and 42. The stone was re-used in flooring of a later period and is much worn. At the foot of the cliff was found an altar dedicated to the Cumberland war-god, Cocidius; and another, to Jupiter, was found south of the milecastle.

In the gap between Housesteads Crags and Cuddy's Crag the Wall ditch is again supplied. From the top of Cuddy's Crag there is a well-known view back to Housesteads and Sewingshields. Then come Rapishaw Gap and Hotbank Crags. Immediately on gaining the ridge the site of turret 37*a* is found (Rapishaw Gap). This turret, like all others in this craggy sector, was demolished in Period II, the Wall being rebuilt and carried across its site. In the valley to the south the Vallum is seen to be overlooked at close range by high ground on each side. Hesketh Hodgson, an excavator of the nineties, noted how this siting disposed of the theory that the Vallum was a defensive earthwork against the south, remarking that "bar gunpowder, a party of schoolboys could stone the best troops in the world out of the Vallum".

The view from the summit is extensive and fine. To the north, all four loughs, Broomlee, Greenlee, Crag, and Grindon, are in sight. The ridge between the first two was extensively quarried by the Romans and a small temporary camp, at West Hotbank, occupies its west end. Beyond the waste, to the north-east, lie the Simonside Hills and beyond them Cheviot. The heather-clad hill immediately to the south is Barcombe (see p. 155), another quarry-area from which the Romans won stone. West of Barcombe the gorge leading to the South Tyne is seen and the platform of the fort at Chesterholm, which guarded it, is conspicuous. South of the Tyne, Langley castle lies near the angle of a large plantation; beyond it are the chimneys of the disused smelt-mills. The valley of the river Allen is seen joining the South Tyne; and a little above their confluence are the ruins of Staward pele, on the east side of the Allen. In the distance, to the southwest, lie the Pennine summits of Cross Fell and Cold Fell, with Lakeland Skiddaw and Saddlebank emerging from far behind the latter.

At the west end of the crag, beyond the site of turret 37*b*, Crag Lough comes into full view, adding much to the beauty of this wild and interesting region. Water-hens build among the reeds at its west end, and wild duck and swans are to be seen on its surface. In Milking Gap milecastle 38 (Hotbank) is evident, in the field opposite Hotbank farm. This milecastle,

Hadrianic dedication-slab from Milecastle 38 (Hotbank): fragments at Durham and Newcastle conjoined

excavated in 1935, is of short-axis type, measuring internally 50 feet from north to south by 62 feet from east to west. Its gates, of type I with renewed pivot-blocks, were reduced to posterns in Wall Period II, when a tombstone was used as a pivot-block. Pottery of the late fourth century was found. The broken inscribed slab shown in the figure also came from this milecastle. Its left-hand half, now in the Chapter Library at Durham, has no provenance, but the right-hand half, now at Newcastle, was built up in the farmhouse of Bradley, only a quarter of a mile to the south-east. It records building by the Second Legion, under Aulus Platorius Nepos, governor of Britain A.D. 122-6. But a second and more perfect example, still retaining traces of red paint in its letters, also came from Hotbank; for in 1757 a local correspondent wrote to Stukeley that it "was found at a *statio per Vallum*, nigh the east end of Craig-loch". This can only mean milecastle 38, and removes a longstanding ambiguity. It also shows that the north and south gates of milecastles each had a similar inscription. The comparable stones from milecastles 37 and 42 will not be forgotten.

At the bottom of the gap the Wall turns sharply to ascend the west crag, and is accompanied by the ditch across the gap itself. Hereabouts, Hutton noted a length of 60 yards of Wall still standing 8 feet high. South of this point and just west of the farm track to the Military road, before it crosses the Vallum, some rough foundations of whinstone outline a British settlement, excavated in 1937. The date of its occupation has been given as Antonine, but it is probably, in reality, Trajanic, on the evidence of the pottery found. The Vallum twists sharply southwards, so as to avoid a marsh, as can best be seen from the heights.

West of Milking Gap, the majestic cliffs, their magnificent columnar formation towering above the lake, afford as romantic a setting as any on the line of the Wall. A number of goats, in a half-wild state, used to frequent the crags, adding to their romantic aspect, but they have since been destroyed. Turret 38*a* is halfway up the rising ridge west of the gap; 38*b* on the summit of Highshield Crag, above the west end of Crag Lough.

Hadrianic dedication-slab from Milecastle 38 (Hotbank) now at Newcastle

On the east edge of the next gap the Wall has been conserved by D.O.E., showing how, on the steep descent, the coursing is kept horizontal and is stepped downhill. The method of building the core is also well seen. After a course of rubble has been placed slantwise a layer of mortar has been laid and then another course of stones. This hard white mortar is of the Period II reconstruction and astonishingly tenacious. The Wall now again ascends steeply, turning sharply north on to a high hummock. In 1928 this was named *Mons Fabricius* in honour of the great German *limes* scholar, Professor Ernst Fabricius, who visited Hadrian's Wall in that year. From the hummock the Wall drops into the gap of Castle Nick, so named from milecastle 39, which lies 1,529 yards from milecastle 38 and 1,806 from 40, considerably more than a Roman mile.

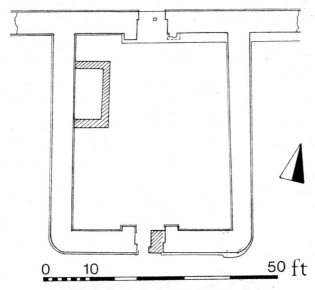

0   10   50 ft

Castle Nick Milecastle, 39. Later walls shaded

Castle Nick milecastle was first investigated by Clayton in 1854, and again by Simpson in 1908-11. It measures internally 49-51½ feet from east to west and almost 62 feet from north to south, which long-axis proportions, together with its type II gateways (both features also displayed at milecastle 40), show that we have here a different legion at work from milecastles 37 and 38. The side walls, 7 feet thick, are in excellent preservation, with 6 or 7 courses of stone standing. The gateways, of type II, are built predominantly of small stones, and display considerable rebuilding in Period II, when they were not only narrowed to posterns, but lost their inward projecting passage walls. The north shows an unusual feature: the gateway is built on broad foundation which, however, becomes narrow foundation immediately to the west of the western passage wall, and so continues up the slope to the west. Vestiges of a small lean-to barrack remain against the west wall.

The Military Way may also be studied to advantage, as it negotiates the climb out of the gap to the east and west.

After another small eminence, another break in the ridge occurs, called Cat Stairs. Here it is possible and convenient to view the crags from the north by going down the stairs, and walking along the flats to the north of the Wall as far as the next gap, where the basaltic columns of Peel Crag rise in pillared majesty.

On Peel Crag the Wall is again in fine condition, Narrow Wall on narrow foundation. This stretch of Wall, however, owes its very survival to the labours of F. G. Simpson, who excavated and restored it in 1909-11. During that work a total of 169 chamfered stones, apparently coping stones from the upper part of the Wall, were found on its north side. Such coping stones form one of the few pieces of evidence in support of a rampart walk.

Turret 39*a*, Peel Crag, was excavated in 1911, and found to have narrow side walls and an eastern door. It had been demolished in Period II, when its recess was built up, unusually, with extremely large ashlar blocks. This blocking, however, was not carried right to the Wall top. At some date before it occurred, the bodies of a young man and an older woman had

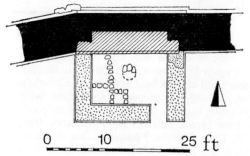

Peel Crag Turret, 39a: Narrow wall black, demolished turret stippled, built-up recess shaded.

been buried below the floor in the north-west corner of the turret, an apparent breach of Roman religious law, as stated in the XII Tables. Today, only slight traces of the turret's side walls are visible below the turf, and the blocking wall has been built up to full height.

The cutting and embanking of the Military Way, as it approaches the gap from the east, are well worth study.

In Peel Gap the ditch begins again, and runs as far as Winshields milecastle. Both it and the Wall here, splendidly conserved, form a bold re-entrant, making both the climb and the defence easier. It is likely that the low ground north of the Wall was a swamp in Roman days. The modern road passing through the gap leads to Kielder, and so into Scotland; but it soon degenerates into a mere track. The Wall itself, from turret 39a to milecastle 40, is unexpectedly narrow, varying from 6¾ to 5½ feet in different stretches. In some places this appears to be original Narrow Wall, but in others it is a rebuilding of the Narrow Wall, which has been called the Severan Narrow Wall, and linked to other rebuildings at Throckley, Matfen Piers, Portgate and elsewhere. In truth, however, we know too little of these variations to be dogmatic about their date or significance.

To the south, on the Military road, is the Once Brewed Youth Hostel. The modern Twice Brewed Inn lines a little west of the Youth Hostel. Before the construction of the Newcastle and Carlisle railway, however, the present farm of East Twice Brewed was the inn, much frequented by carriers who plied between the two cities. Up to 20 men and 50 horses used to put up there for the night. Hutton had great difficulty in getting a bed, without sharing it with one or more carters; and, at supper, concluded that they had no barricades in their throats, and that eating was the chief end of man.

Just west of Milking Gap the Vallum takes a sharp swing south to avoid a large area of bog, which it skirts for the next mile and a quarter. From High Shield, the Military road has been running along its south berm. At the Twice Brewed they part and the Vallum swerves northward to begin slowly to converge upon the Wall.

On the west side of Peel Crag formerly stood the farmhouse of Steel Rigg, and on the west side of the modern road lies the site of turret 39b (Steelrigg), excavated in 1911. Here, the Wall foundation is broad, and the turret was built with broad wing walls, which later took the narrow curtain, but in Period II it was disused, dismantled and built up, as were many others. In this case the Wall itself was almost totally rebuilt, with its width reduced by nearly 18 inches, as already said.

The Wall now quits the dolerite crags and runs along a ridge of sandstone. It is at first in bad condition, but the ditch, with upcast-mound to the north, is well preserved. The crags shortly commence again, and the ditch ceases, in unfinished state. Before reaching the top of Winshields, and where the ditch ends, is milecastle 40 (Winshields), excavated in 1908. Its dimensions are similar to those of Castle Nick, measuring 60 feet from north to south and 48¾ from east to west. The milecastle lies on a slope of 1 to 6, and has gateways of type II. The northern is unique, in that there is a 15° turn at its east jamb. Both gates were extensively rebuilt in Period II, when they lost their backward projecting jambs, and were narrowed to posterns. Later, the south was farther narrowed. In the south-eastern angle an oven was found, together with the south wall of an inserted lean-to building.

The distances between milecastles 39, 40 and 41 are exceptionally long, measuring 1,806 and 1,850 yards respectively. Winshields stands 1,230 feet above sea level and is the highest point on the Wall. The prospect is very fine in every direction: on a clear day the Solway is easily seen, with Burnswark in Dumfriesshire and Criffell in Kirkcudbrightshire forming a noble background.

The Wall, in good preservation, is here under the guardianship of D.O.E., who have grouted the core afresh and reset the facing-stones. About 220 yards west of the summit of Winshields and 80 yards south of the Wall, in a sheltered spot called Green Slack, MacLauchlan observed British hut-circles. Turret 40a, 624 yards beyond the milecastle, has narrow walls, and its door to the east. Next comes the deep valley of Lodham Slack, where the Wall, standing upon the broad foundation, has its ditch again. Here MacLauchlan observed a native earthwork to the south. Turret 40b, with narrow walls, is on the summit of the next ridge, and a gentle descent leads to milecastle 41 (Melkridge), a short-axis milecastle with narrow side-walls and type I gates.

The next gap, a bold one, is named Bogle Hole, and then comes Caw Gap. The way in which the Romans defended a re-entrant is well shown here. The Wall bends south on each side of the gap, so as to enfilade any attack. The ditch is discontinued on the west side as soon as the crag attains height, but when the ground drops again for a few yards, opposite turret

41a, it reappears. A road passes through Caw Gap, and to the north lies the solitary house of Burn Deviot, once a resort of smugglers and sheep-stealers. Lights are believed to flicker at night about the windows, the spirits of those murdered in the house.

West of Caw Gap, the Wall is largely uprooted for some distance. In 1967 turret 41a was found to have been dismantled and the Wall rebuilt across its recess. The foundations of the broad wing-walls of the turret can still be seen, somewhat larger to the east than the west, but the wing-walls themselves were removed when the Wall was rebuilt across the turret. To the south two large stones, overlooking the Military road, are called "The Mare and Foal" and one more is marked on Armstrong's *Map of Northumberland:* the three are probably remains of a Bronze-Age circle.

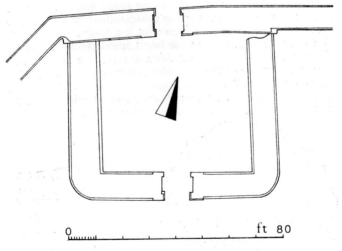

0   ft 80

Plan of Milecastle 42 (Cawfields)

Proceeding onwards there is a point where the Wall is reduced in thickness by one foot at a single inset. The cliffs are again high and in columnar formation. After Bloody Gap and a second gap called Thorny Doors, comes turret 41b, which was found by Simpson in 1912, 558 yards from milecastle 42, but could not be relocated in 1967, in advance of consolidation. The Wall hereabouts is once more in excellent state.

Here, fallen from the cliff, a building-stone like a centurial stone was found, commemorating work by the Durotriges of Dorset through one of their tribal sub-divisions. It is matched by a duplicate from the same area and compares with similar tribal building-stones from Thirlwall and Howgill. West of here there are again slight offsets and insets in the south face of the Wall, varying its thickness by several inches, as already noted west of Housesteads.

On the east side of the next gap, named Hole Gap, is milecastle 42 (Cawfields), excavated by Clayton in 1848. It lies 1,641 yards west of milecastle 41, and measures internally 63 feet from east to west and 49 from north to south. Its walls stand 7 or 8 courses high and are 8 feet thick. Both gates are of type I, in massive masonry, and the south gate displays a bar-hole for the doors. Excavation in 1936 showed that the north gate and wall were built to the broad gauge, before the rest of the milecastle. Clayton's excavations produced two inscribed stones. The more important is a fragmentary inscription of Hadrian, matching those found at milecastles 37 and 38. The other is a tombstone, cut down to serve as a hearth-stone, and what remains of the inscription has been translated as "To the divine shades: Dagvalda, a soldier of (such and such a unit of) Pannonians lived . . . years; Pusinna erected this tablet". As this Cohort of Pannonians is not attested in garrison at the

Re-used Tombstone, and fragment of Hadrianic dedication-slab, Milecastle 42 (Cawfields), in Chesters Museum

nearest fort, Greatchesters, it may indicate the source of the milecastle forces.

South of the milecastle, on the Roman Military Way, three milestones have been found; one of Severus Alexander (A.D. 222-23), the second of Numerian (A.D. 283-4), while the third, uninscribed, still lies on the spot. North of the Vallum and close to a vanished spring, an altar to Apollo was found. All the inscriptions are now in Chesters Museum. In Hole Gap there is a short length of ditch, but from the adjacent summit to Haltwhistle Burn the Wall has been destroyed by Cawfields Quarry, now happily bought out by the nation. Here and at Carvoran the visitor may form a clear idea of what can happen to the most august Roman monument in Britain, in the noblest part of its course, at the remorseless hand of industry.

In this sector the Vallum, descending from Shield-on-the-Wall farm to Haltwhistle Burn, is in a perfection hardly equalled in any other part of its course. Excavation in 1939 revealed that, in the low wet ground between the track to the milecastle and the road to the quarry, the sides of the ditch had been revetted in turf-work, capped with clay and founded upon flagging. Uphill to the east, the ditch has later been cleaned out and the marginal mound is present, while the crossings are absent. The gaps for the crossings, however, are clear in the north mound throughout this sector, with three long intervals at the east end; but in the south mound only three complete gaps have been dug, immediately west of Shield-on-the-Wall. Then comes a series of gaps only marked out by a couple of V-shaped notches in the crest of the mound; next a length where not even that has been done; and then, half-way down the hill, the completed gaps begin again. Here, as at Wallend Common (p. 191) and High House (p. 217), the crossing-system was never completely finished. The causeway opposite milecastle 42 has been found, on excavation, to be secondary, like the others.

The planning of the Military Way is also interesting. Opposite milecastle 42 it crosses the north mound of the Vallum, travels for 250 yards along the north berm and then recrosses the mound. The position of the Vallum in relation to the steep hill left no room for the road; but if the road had been contemplated when the Vallum was laid out, nothing would have been easier than to place the Vallum a little more to the south. The road is thus demonstrably later in the frontier-scheme than either Wall or Vallum.

On the Haltwhistle Burn, the Cawfields quarry-spoil has now buried the site of a Roman water-mill, found just below the point where the burn is crossed by the Military Way, and excavated in 1907-8. An artificial channel had been cut across a bend of the stream, and a weir constructed to direct water into it. Something like 20 feet of this channel had been widened and deepened, and partly, at least, lined with timber. Here, on the bank above, a rectangular stone building lay, measuring 22 feet 9 inches by 15 feet 8 inches in size. It was so placed that its north-west wall formed one side of the widened channel. Fallen stone-work, several large millstones and pottery were all recovered during the excavation, enabling the excavator, F. G. Simpson, to interpret the building as a water-powered mill with undershot wheel, dating to the third century. The whole had been surrounded on three sides by a rampart and ditch, and was almost certainly connected with Greatchesters fort. The large millstones are now in Chesters Museum.

West of Burnhead farmhouse the Wall ditch is bold, but the Wall is mostly destroyed. Turret 42*a* (Caw Burn) has been destroyed by quarrying; 42*b* lies opposite the large temporary camp beyond the Wall, close to the point where the Wall bends westward towards Greatchesters.

HALTWHISTLE BURN FORTLET AND THE STANEGATE TO CARVORAN

Where the Stanegate approaches Haltwhistle Burn, 3½ miles from Chesterholm, a small post stands, 65 feet above the stream, on a very bold bluff. The natural defences are good, to which deep ditches of irregular plan have been added.

The fortlet was excavated in 1908, when it was found to be some 208 by 167 feet, giving an area or about three-quarters of an acre. It was defended by ramparts of earth with a stone facing, set not in mortar but in clay, and had gates in its east, south and west walls, the latter a postern giving on to the burn. At some stage the east gate had been blocked completely by a closing wall. Inside the fort the remains of several buildings were found, the surviving walls of clay-bonded stone, which originally most probably served to carry timber upperwork. These buildings appear to have been a barrack for a *centuria* (II) with separate centurion's quarters (III), and possibly another centurion's or officer's quarters (I) just inside the east gate: the two last buildings are about the same size and shape, although

III was better built. In the southern portion of the fort a roughly constructed building (IV), about 40 by 30 feet in size, had secondary buttresses, and an added, partly walled area (V), on its western side. It is possible that this was a combined storehouse-granary and armoury, with perhaps an enclosed yard-area to its west. Roads lead in from the three gates to a central paved area, where the smallest building of all (VI) stood. This, like building III, was of better masonry than the others, and had been provided with an internal fireplace, all suggesting that it had been the administrative building, or office, of the fort.

On the strength of these buildings it appears that the garrison had been a vexillation, detached from its parent unit, for although a storehouse seems to be present, there is no proper commanding-officer's house nor headquarters building. In this case the term fortlet is more appropriately applied to the post than fort.

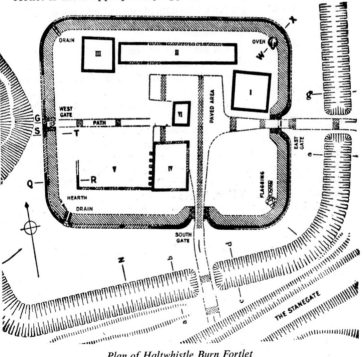

Plan of Haltwhistle Burn Fortlet

The finds alone are not conclusive in dating the lifespan of the post, but taken with other evidence they suggest a foundation during the reign of Trajan, but later than the destruction of c. A.D. 105. The fortlet had clearly been occupied for some time, for the east gate had been walled up and other signs of long-term wear were noted by the excavators. Abandonment had been accompanied by careful and thorough demolition, and the robbed west rampart was sealed by the refuse of a quarry, which lay immediately on the dismantled wall. Clayton was shown the letters LEG. VI. V. on a rock-face of this quarry in 1844; a record of the Sixth Legion cutting stone, presumably for the Wall. The life of the fortlet clearly ended with demolition, no doubt when the garrisons were moved to the line of the Wall itself about the year A.D. 125.

The Stanegate swings round the fortlet to the south, descends the burn on a well-graded embankment, then climbs the opposite bank in a deep cutting, to run west as a line visible across the fields.

Near the fortlet is the majority of the remarkable group of temporary camps already noted. Some are still visible on the ground, others need to be traced with the aid of the Ordnance Survey *Map of Hadrian's Wall*. Two lie north and north-east of the fortlet, another, very small, is just south of the Vallum, while a large and a small camp lie north of the Wall itself. Five hundred yards west along the Stanegate, at its junction with the branch road to Greatchesters, a large camp occurs, with a smaller later addition in its north-eastern corner; and west again three more camps of varying sizes can be seen, while two others are known from air-photographs. Finally, a large camp lies on the highest point of Fell End. These cannot all be of the same date; and it has been suggested that some housed men to build the Wall, while others were constructed and modified for training or exercise.

After crossing the Haltwhistle Burn the Stanegate again takes the line of the ridge across Haltwhistle Common, continuing all the way on the north side of the modern road. Another marching camp is passed at Sunny Rigg and a little further west yet another, and considerably larger example, lies on Fell End. Here again the road is confused by later lines, and traces of quarrying and mining are visible all around. Near this camp a milestone of Aurelian (A.D. 273-275) was found in 1932, very like that of Probus (A.D. 276-282) from Crindle Dykes (see p. 155). On Fell

End the road turns slightly north to run directly to Carvoran fort, from where this last length of its course can be seen as a particularly clear line as it descends the hillside. Just to the east of the fort the road was lined by a cemetery on its northern side. The distance from Haltwhistle Burn to Carvoran is just under 3¼ miles.

GREATCHESTERS (AESICA)

Greatchesters fort, like Carrawburgh, lies wholly south of the Wall. It is nearly 6 miles from Housesteads, measures 419 by 355 feet over its ramparts and covers just over 3 acres. Its function is to guard the Caw Gap. Like Housesteads, it faces east; the Military Way enters by the *porta praetoria* and leaves by the *porta decumana*, and a branch of the Stanegate, on the site of the farm-road, comes in by the *porta principalis dextra*. The ancient name of the fort was AESICA (of uncertain meaning, but perhaps the name of the Haltwhistle Burn), and its third-century garrison, according to inscriptions, was the Second Cohort of Asturians, with a detachment of *Raeti Gaesati*. The Sixth Cohort of Nervians, and the Sixth Cohort of Raetians, successively, formed the second-century garrison, while the *Notitia* mentions a First Cohort of Asturians, if this is not a slip for Second.

In Gordon's day some walls of this fort were standing 12 or 13 feet high. Today only the rampart and ditch system are clearly defined, there being no less than four ditches on the west side, which is the weakest.

Excavations in 1894 determined many features. The ramparts were partly cleared and, as at several other Wall forts, were found to have had lean-to buildings set against their inner face at a late date. The west tower of the south gate yielded a famous hoard of jewellery, comprising an enamelled brooch shaped as a hare, a gilded bronze brooch

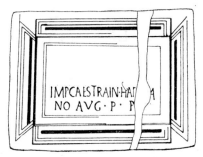

Hadrianic Inscription from Greatchesters East Gate (Chesters)

which has been described as a masterpiece of Celtic art, a silver collar with pendant, a gold ring and a bronze ring with Gnostic gem. Replicas are on view in Newcastle.

The west gate is of very special interest because it is now the only gate on the Wall which still exhibits, intact, the various blocking walls by which it was first reduced to one portal and then finally closed altogether: at other forts we know that such additions existed, but they were cleared away by the excavators,

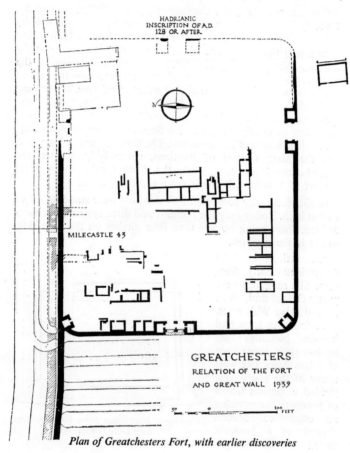

HADRIANIC
INSCRIPTION OF A.D.
128 OR AFTER.

MILECASTLE 43

GREATCHESTERS
RELATION OF THE FORT
AND GREAT WALL 1939

50   0   100
                      FEET

Plan of Greatchesters Fort, with earlier discoveries

usually without record. A large building inscription of Hadrian mentioning the title of *Pater Patriae* conferred in 128, was found outside the east gate and is in Chesters Museum. Unfortunately, however, it records neither the governor nor the unit concerned; but it does serve to show that the fort was not completed until after the year A.D. 128.

The most interesting part of the defences is the north-west angle, excavated in 1894 and 1925. The angle itself was rounded, but the angle-tower is planned with a projection and bonded with the Narrow Wall, which is thus clearly contemporary with the fort as it stands. In spite of this, however, the Narrow Wall overrides the butt-ends of the four west fort ditches, which terminate behind the broad foundation. In addition, the angle-

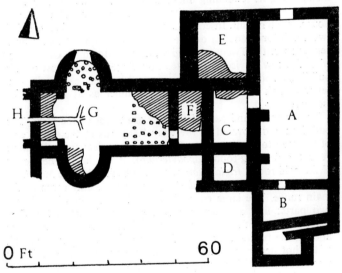

Plan of Greatchesters Baths

tower had been very substantially rebuilt some time after A.D. 342, as a coin of Constans (Trier mint 342/8) found in the mortar proves. A number of stone ballista balls were found beside the tower when first excavated.

The reason why the Narrow Wall here was not built upon the broad foundation was discovered in 1939. Aesica occupies the site of milecastle 43, which had already been built on the broad foundation when the change to narrow gauge took place and the resolve to build a fort was made. The north gate of the milecastle could not be embodied in the defences of the fort, which were accordingly built just behind it, the milecastle being then demolished at leisure.

Our knowledge of the internal buildings is fragmentary. The *principia* was partly uncovered in 1894, disclosing the cross-hall and administrative offices. Its vaulted underground strong-room, now ruinous, was described by Lingard in 1807. It lay below the shrine of the standards, whence came an altar to Discipline also noted by Lingard. To the north of the headquarters a granary produced a fine inscription, now at Newcastle, commemorating its rebuilding under Severus Alexander in A.D. 225. To the south excavation disclosed the commanding-officer's house, much rebuilt. Inscribed stones re-used in its walls included two tombstones and an ornate altar to Jupiter Dolichenus by a centurion of the Twentieth Legion, Lucius Maximius Gaetulicus, who also saw service at Newstead on Tweed. South-west of this building 6 rooms of a barrack may still be seen, each built as a separate unit in the fourth-century manner as at Housesteads (see pp. 146-7).

To the south and east of the fort are traces of the *vicus*. The bath-house, discovered in 1897, lay 100 yards to the south, east of the road to the Stanegate. Its features are clear from the plan: A is the dressing-room (*apodyterium*), B the latrine beside it; C the cold room, *frigidarium*, with cold bath D; E the *laconicum* of dry heat, F a small *tepidarium*, or warm steamy room of the main range. The large room G beyond should be divided into two parts: first a square *tepidarium*, then the *caldarium* (hot steamy room) with apses for lavers and hot bath next to the boiler and H, the furnace, the flue of which is visible in the west wall of the hot steamy room. The final abandonment of the *caldarium* was associated with a hoard of late third-century coins.

The Vallum passes south of the fort and was crossed by an original revetted causeway, of which the east side was found in 1951. Further south are traces of barrows, where the cemetery of the fort seems to have been; but the "remarkable" barrows noted near the Wall by Brand would seem to have been prehistoric burials. Cultivation-terraces on the hillside west of the fort resembling those at Housesteads are associated with medieval or later homesteads. Little is known of the civilian population, but several tombstones survive. One is to Lucius Novellius Lanuccus, aged 70, set up by his daughter, a second to Aelius Mercurialis, by his sister Vacia, and a third to Nigrina set up by Aurelius Casitto, a centurion of the Sixth Legion. There are also two to young girls: one to Pervica, the other set up by Aurelia S . . . illa "to her very dear sister" Aurelia Caula who lived 15 years, 4 months.

A remarkable feature of this fort is the aqueduct which feeds it from the north. Lingard noted that the "water for the station

was brought by a winding aqueduct still visible from the head of Haltwhistle burn. It winds 5 miles". This is a channel or leet, three or four feet deep and proportionately wide, running along the north margin of the basin of the Caw Burn. In order to cross its northern tributaries, an extremely winding course is taken, but the line is so well planned that only once has a bridge or embankment been necessary. This structure is now gone, but its site is named Benks Bridge. The aqueduct is in fact 6 miles long, though the direct line is little more than 2¼. By this means the water of the Caw Burn was so brought to within about 350 yards of the fort. The aqueduct is then lost but owing to a fall in the ground, the water could only have been brought over this part of its course by an embankment or an inverted siphon. The course is indicated on the Ordnance *Map of Hadrian's Wall*.

Tombstone of Pervica from Greatchesters (Newcastle)

G

FROM GREATCHESTERS TO CARVORAN

Near Greatchesters the Vallum is of great interest. A quarter of a mile west of the causeway serving the fort it runs almost straight, into a large field directly south of Cockmount Hill farmhouse. Here 10 successive crossings are visible in their complete state, with causeways in the ditch and gaps in both mounds, though a modern track has somewhat obscured those in the south mound, while a modern drain in the ditch has slightly disturbed the causeways. Excavation in 1939 showed that the causeways were made when the ditch had been open sufficiently long for the upper half of its very steep sides to have washed down into the bottom. Vegetable matter then grew, to be succeeded by the causeways. These preserved, behind their mass of filling, the steep profile of the original ditch, modified only by the weathering that had occurred before the causeways were constructed. Elsewhere the Vallum ditch has been re-cut, as in the next field, where upcast from later clearing can be seen piled in heaps on the lip. The Vallum then runs along the north slope of Blake Law, avoiding the marsh at its foot. The ditch is cut into the slope for 250 yards and for the western 100 yards the slope is stepped to form the south berm and the south mound is unusually broad. Then the Vallum swings north, across

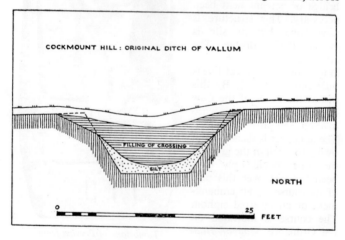

COCKMOUNT HILL : ORIGINAL DITCH OF VALLUM

FILLING OF CROSSING

SILT

NORTH

0   25   FEET

The Vallum Ditch, in Original Form

the marsh and runs along its north margin. In the Allolee grounds cultivation has reduced it to poor condition.

The Narrow Wall, leaving Greatchesters, runs behind the broad foundation up to turret 43*a*, which had already been built upon the latter. Broad foundation and Narrow Wall then run parallel again as far as Cockmount Hill Wood. Here both are exposed to view, but before leaving the wood they gradually converge, so that the Narrow Wall runs on the broad foundation once again. The reason for this long divergence may have been due to insistence by the engineers of the Narrow Wall upon a deeper foundation, though they were normally content to use the shallow, broad foundation. From Aesica to Allolee the Military Way is very clear, and an uninscribed milestone from it forms the west post of the gate at the west end of Cockmount Hill Wood, on the Wall-line.

The Wall now climbs gradually. Turret 43*b* is 100 yards beyond the edge of the wood. The ditch hereabouts is very irregular, now dug fully and now to half width only, or often not at all. Here and there the north face of the Wall is seen for short lengths.

East of Allolee farmhouse, the site of the long-axis milecastle 44 (Allolee) is very distinct. Beyond it, the rebuilt north face of the Wall stands up to 9 courses high for about 200 yards, while the south face is not exposed at all. Opposite Allolee farmhouse only the core is to be seen. Of two centurial stones recorded in the south wall of the farmhouse, one is lost and the other now very indistinct. Beyond milecastle 44 the crags are broken by frequent gaps, known as the "Nine Nicks of Thirlwall". The Wall climbs and descends them unflinchingly, seizing the crest of the rugged cliff wherever possible.

In the first two nicks the ditch reappears and the Wall makes a re-entrant; turret 44*a* occurs at a turn on the crest between them. Beyond the second nick comes Mucklebank Crag, 860 feet high. There, in a bold angle of the Wall, turret 44*b* was excavated in 1892. Because it lies in an angle, its north and west sides are both recessed into the Wall. In it were found three occupation-levels, a coin of Valens (A.D. 364-378) and a centurial stone. The stones from an arched window are now attached to the turret wall. These most likely come from a first-floor window in the north wall of the turret, as depicted on the Rudge Cup and the Amiens Skillet.

Walltown Nick is a wide one. The Wall enfilades it on either side and runs across it in a stright line, accompanied by the ditch. Close behind the Wall, in the middle of the gap, is a spring now enclosed in a shaft, called "The King's Well" or "King Arthur's Well". Hutchinson records a tradition that here Paulinus baptised King Egbert; and himself suggested the King probably to have been Edwin; but neither notion is true. Camden learnt of a more picturesque tradition, connected with chives, which still grow abundantly in the crevices of the crags near Walltown House. "That the Roman souldiers of the marches did plant heere every where in old time for their use, certaine medicinable hearbs, for to cure wounds: whence is it that some Emperick practitioners of Chirurgery in Scotland, flock hither every yeere in the beginning of summer, to gather such simples and wound herbes; the vertue whereof they highly commend as found by long experience, and to be of singular efficacy". In fact this plant (*Lilium schoenoprasum*), though rare, frequents rocky pastures in widely distributed parts of Britain, and the suggestion that the Romans introduced it, although not impossible, is not proven.

Walltown is also the site of the tower inherited by John Ridley, brother of the Protestant martyr. The present Walltown farm-house is modern, but a fragment of the tower remained in Wallis's time and MacLauchlan saw its foundations, north-west of the present house. These have now vanished, as has the old village of Walltown, which lay on the south slope nearby. East of Walltown farm a small hill carried a British entrenchment.

After climbing the steep west side of Walltown Nick, the Wall, of which much core is visible, runs along the crags to milecastle 45 (Walltown). This is a long-axis milecastle, and large stones robbed from its gateway can be seen lying behind troughs to the east of Walltown farm. A fine piece of the Wall runs to the edge of the Greenhead Quarry, 150 yards away. This extension of the quarry has removed the Wall for a quarter of a mile. Beyond it turret 45a and some 400 yards of Wall are under D.O.E. guardianship, and rank among the finest stretches of the Wall, especially in the fifth nick, beyond the turret. This turret is especially remarkable, for it was built as a freestanding tower before the Wall was brought up to its east and west sides, which has prompted speculation that it might have ante-dated the Wall system. However, its foundations, examined in 1959, produced early Hadrianic potsherds, showing that it was constructed as part of the Wall, all be it an early part. It is situated on a prominent point, 100 yards short of the normal measured position, with Pike Hill, Carvoran and Haltwhistle Burn all visible from it (weather permitting), suggesting that it may also have served as a forward observation or signalling tower during the construction and in the early days of the Wall.

The huge western bite of the Greenhead Quarry has then removed the rest of the Nine Nicks and the Wall with them, including turret 45*b*; one of the most savage and deplorable incursions of industry upon the Wall.

West of the Carvoran quarry-buildings the Wall and Vallum start again, the Wall running in the second field north of the fort. The Vallum swings north to make a wide and regular detour around the fort on the north, similar to its normal detours to the south of other forts, except that this detour excluded Carvoran. Such a detour suggests that Carvoran was a Stanegate fort in origin given up on the building of the Wall. A fragment of the ditch and northern mound of the Vallum are clearly visible at the east end of the detour, two fields north of the fort; thereafter they run under the field wall and away to the south-west, where they are less pronounced. The line of the Wall here is visible, but it has been well robbed of its facing stones.

CARVORAN (MAGNA)

Carvoran is the MAGNA of the *Notitia*, which records its garrison as the Second Cohort of Dalmatians, also attested by a

tombstone. The name possibly means "The Rocks". In Hadrian's day it was held by the First Cohort of Hamian archers, a special Syrian unit, 500 strong, whose native weapon was the bow. Their commander, Flavius Secundus, set up an altar for the health of Aelius Caesar, in A.D. 136-138. The same unit was again in garrison under Calpurnius Agricola in A.D. 162, when it set up altars

Building Inscription of Flavius Secundus, Carvoran (Newcastle)

mentioning the prefect Licinius Clemens; these are now at Newcastle and at Chesters. A further unit, the First Cohort of

Batavians, recorded on building stones, may have been constructing the Vallum rather than garrisoning the fort.

The site lies at the junction of the Stanegate and the Maiden Way, which ran south via Whitley Castle, Cross Fell and Kirkby Thore. Its purpose was primarily to guard the road-junction and the important gap of the Tipalt valley, and for this reason it may have been a pre-Hadrianic creation, although no structure of such a date has as yet been found. On the other hand a connection of the fort and Stanegate is borne out by the deliberate exclusion of the site from the military zone of the Wall by the

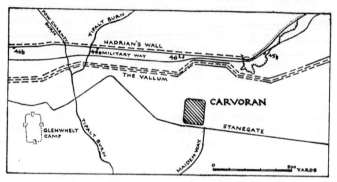

The Wall, Vallum, Fort and Stanegate, at Carvoran

Vallum, which specifically and regularly deviates to the north of it. A secondary crossing in this deviation carried a roadway from the fort's north gate.

The fort measured some 440 by 360 feet over the ramparts, giving a size of about 3.5 acres; similar to Chesterholm and Castlesteads. Centurial stones show that it was walled in stone by the Hamians themselves, under Flavius Secundus, late in Hadrian's reign. The north gate was located in 1972 and its west portal shown to contain secondary blocking. The north-west angle-tower is visible, but little is known of internal buildings. In 1599 Camden found the ruins very evident, but agriculture had begun to destroy them by 1776 and the process was completed in 1837. The only building then observed was the bath-house with plastered walls, situated, as at Risingham and Bewcastle, just within the south wall and near the south-west

FORTVNAE·AVG·
·PRO· SALVTE·I·AEII
·CAESARIS·EX·VISV
·T·FLA·SECVND VS·
PRAEF·COH·I·HAM
IORVM·SAGIIIAR
·V· S· L·M·

angle of the fort. Its dressing-room contained the altar for the health of Aelius Caesar already noted.

Knowledge of Carvoran thus depends largely upon relics. The most important building-stones are fragments of a monumental inscription mentioning Hadrian, not more specifically to be dated, and the inscriptions from the fort-wall, recording its construction when the Hamians were in garrison, not long before A.D 135-8.

The deities who came with the Syrian archers are represented

Altar for the Safety of Aelius Caesar, Carvoran (Newcastle)

by dedications to the goddesses Syria and Hammia. There is also a very remarkable metrical dedication to the Virgin of the Zodiac, with reference to Julia Domna, by a prefect honoured with tribune's rank, and a small altar set up to Jupiter of Heliopolis, that is, the great Ituraean god Jupiter-Hadad, whose worship was centred at Baalbek in the Lebanon. More unusual are the dedications to Fortune, by a centurion who had served in all three British legions, and to the Nymphs, by Vettia Mansueta and her daughter Claudia Turianilla. A small altar to Epona, the ostlers' goddess, smacks of the fort stabling (and the Dalmatians were a part-mounted cohort). A well within the fort yielded fine stag's antlers,

IMMINET·LEONI·VIRGO· CAELES
TI·SITV   SPICIFERA·IVSTI·IN
VENTRIX· VRBIVM· CONDITRIX·
EX·QVI S·MVNERIBVS· NOSSE·CON
TICIT·DEOS ERGOEADEM·MATEROIVM
PAX·VIRIVS·CERES DEA SYRIA
LANCE·VITAM·ETIVRA PENSITANS
IN·CAELO·VISVM·STRIA SIDVS EDI
DIT LIBYAE COLENDVM·INDE
CVNCTI·DIDICIMVS
ITA·INTELLEXIT·NVMINE·INDVCTVS
TVO   MARCVS·CA E CILIVS·DO
NATIANVS·MILITANS ~ TRIBVNVS
IN·PRAEFECTO·DONO·PRINCIPIS

Metrical Hymn from Carvoran (Newcastle)

eloquent of hunting prospects, also a perfect iron javelin-head, with a double barb on a long stem, socketed for a wooden shaft. The weapon is of the kind used in the later Roman period by German tribes, and reminds us that a *Numerus Magn* . . . is recorded at the fort, at some date unknown. Many of these inscriptions and objects are now in the Museum of Antiquities at Newcastle.

The extra-mural settlement is represented by many dedications to the god Vitiris, whose altars are confined to the Wall and its neighbourhood and centre upon Carvoran, as if the cult had its seat in this vicinity. He is equated with the Roman Hercules and also with the Celtic god Mogon; and, by confusion of *Vitiris* with the Latin *veteres*, sometimes he gets a ghost plural as *di veteres*. This deity seems to have been German, but an undoubted north-British deity, Belatucadrus, is named on another altar.

The cemetery has produced tombstones, notably that of Gaius Valerius Tullus, from Vienne, a soldier in the Twentieth Legion and one of the few legionaries in garrison on the Wall who is known to have been buried there. In the eighteenth century a mound east of the fort, now vanished, yielded a stone coffin-case containing organic remains and two gold rings. Other tombstones include that of a standard bearer of the Dalmatians, and four erected to the memory of women: Aurelia Aia, daughter of Titus, from Salonae; Lifana and two others each also called Aurelia, one set up by a bereaved mother, the other by a sister.

One discovery is rare indeed. In 1915, just north of the north-east angle of the fort, what looked like an old bucket was seen sticking out of the ground. This proved to be a Roman *modius*, or dry-measure, in bronze. Of excellent workmanship and in perfect condition, it is of truncated conical shape, like an inverted bucket, about a foot high and wide, weighs nearly 26 pounds and holds 20 pints. It bears an inscription in elegant lettering, certifying its weight and capacity and once naming the Emperor Domitian, under whom it was made; his name, however, has been erased following the condemnation of his memory by the Senate. The measure is stated to hold $17\frac{1}{2}$ *sextarii*, now 16·8 pints, but will hold almost 20. It has been suggested that this was a device to defraud provincials under obligation to deliver a certain amount of wheat; but Roman certified measures are normally quite accurate, and a gauge set lower than the brim may be missing, since there are rivet-holes for vanished accessories. This most unusual object is one of the notable exhibits in Chesters Museum.

FROM CARVORAN TO BIRDOSWALD

The site of milecastle 46 (Carvoran) lies just west of the northward deviation of the Vallum, mentioned above. Both here and as far as Thirlwall Castle, the Wall ditch is particularly striking; while the lines of the Vallum, running parallel with the Wall, are also clear almost as far as the river Tipalt. A Roman inscribed stone is inserted, upside down, in an out-house at Holmhead and reads CIVITAS DVMNONI(*orum*), in a latish style of lettering. The Dumnonii were the British tribe occupying Devonshire, Cornwall, and part of Somersetshire. This stone would seem to record work on the Wall by their levies; similar stones record work in other sectors by the Catuvellauni of Hertfordshire and the Durotriges of Dorset. They constitute a highly instructive exception to the practice that the Wall was, in the main, built by military labour. On this occasion at least the tribal levy, or *corvée* was called into service, but for repairs rather than original building.

The Wall and Vallum reappear on the slope west of the road and railway. West of the road the broad foundation stood three courses high and the ditch was about 33 feet wide and 6 feet deep. Between Wallend and Chapel House, the ditch of the Wall is unusually large. Its north side, or

Building-stone of a British tribal corvée, *Holmhead*

counter-scarp, is 15 or even 20 feet high. Towards the west end of Wallend Common the Vallum is particularly notable. Gaps for the crossings have been dug in both mounds, but the material has never been used to make the causeways, and lies untidily outside the gaps in small heaps as it was dumped from baskets by the diggers. The crossing system has evidently never been completed, as at Shield-on-the-Wall and High House.

Three hundred yards east of Chapel House comes milecastle 47 (Chapelhouse), excavated in 1935, and measuring internally 69 feet from north to south and some 60 feet from east to west. Its gateways are said to be of type II, but they could, in fact, have been of type III. As at milecastle 48 (Poltross Burn), a large

Part of a Hadrianic dedication-slab from Milecastle 47 (Chapel House), at Newcastle

barracks lay on each side of the roadway. Part of the original dedication-tablet, erected by the Twentieth Legion, was once built up in a stable at Chapel House. This is the only fragment of a Twentieth Legion dedication so far found and it differs in style from the Second Legion's tablets. Turret 47a (Foultown) stood at the normal interval westwards. At the hamlet of Gap, on the watershed between Tyne and Irthing, the Vallum, here very distinct, takes higher ground than the Wall. In the lowest course but one of the gable end of an out-house, a centurial stone is seen, upside down: it reads, translated, "The century of Claudius Augustanus, of the third cohort". Just beyond the hamlet is the site of turret 47b.

The ditch of the Wall between Gap and the railway at Gilsland is unusually wide, measuring 50 feet in several places, and in 1971 the glacis was found to be some four feet high and at least

Sculptured fragment from Rose Hill, Gilsland, at Rockcliffe, Cumberland

30 feet wide, when it was removed behind the Station Hotel, Gilsland.

On a knoll called Rose Hill, later removed in making Gilsland railway station, Lingard observed "a platform on the top 12 yards in diameter, with a ditch round it. Here was a figure of flying Victory". His description of the hill strongly suggests a medieval motte: and builders of such castles elsewhere took packing-stones for their wooden structures from Roman sites. The stone, much weathered but of particular interest, is now at Rockcliffe, north of Carlisle. It shows a flying Victory, backed by a representation of a domed shrine comparable with Arthur's O'on, near Falkirk. It may have been one of a pair of matching supporters for a monumental inscription, all on separate stones.

Immediately west of the railway station the wooded gorge of Poltross Burn divides Northumberland and Cumbria. The Vallum, here under the guardianship of D.O.E., approaches the stream by deep cuttings on each bank, the steep sides of its ditch being revetted with masonry. The Military Way, swerving southwards to ease the gradient, crosses the burn between the Vallum and the Wall, avoiding milecastle 48. On the west bank of the burn, the Military Way breaches the north mound of the Vallum and runs along the north berm, where it remains for at least 600 yards.

Milecastle 48 (Poltross Burn) is also under guardianship (plan, p. 22). It measures internally 70 feet from north to south by 60 feet 9 inches from east to west. All its walls were built to the broad gauge, the Narrow Wall on broad foundation joining its wing-walls about 12 feet away from the milecastle on either side. The north gate, $9\frac{1}{2}$ feet wide and of type III, had secondary pivot-blocks and was reduced in the Period II reconstruction to a four-foot postern. Enough remained of a flight of steps leading to the rampart-walk at the north-east corner to show, by calculation, that the rampart-walk lay 12 feet above ground level, which, allowing for the steep hillside, suggests 15 Roman feet as the external height of the Wall without its parapet.

A series of superimposed ovens had been constructed in the north-west angle of the rampart, and a pair of barracks face each other across the axial road. These originally consisted of four rooms each, 13 by $12\frac{1}{2}$ feet in size, which could have accommodated a garrison of 64 men, the largest number possible in a single milecastle. Later, the barracks were altered to three rooms each. No inscription was discovered, but the finds recovered in

1909 proved an occupation from early in the reign of Hadrian until the fourth century. In particular, the coins enabled the excavators to propose that the first period ended with the great invasion of A.D. 180, and the second not long after 270; dates which were soon applied to the whole Wall, and remained accepted until 1929.

At this milecastle type B construction (as west of milecastle 17) is again seen in the Wall foundation. It comprises three courses of stonework above the flag foundation, followed by an offset marking the commencement of the superstructure. This construction continues to Willowford Bridge.

The Wall crosses the railway immediately beyond milecastle 48, and can be seen standing several courses high in the garden to the east of Gilsland school, once the old vicarage, and now belonging to Romanway Guest House. This is a good place to study the broad foundation in relation to the Narrow Wall. The flag footing-course of the Broad Wall, visible at the bottom of the garden, carries one course of Wall-stones; a little way up the slope a second course is seen, and then a third. But no appreciable time can have elapsed between laying these lower courses of the Broad Wall and building the Narrow Wall upon them, for the mortar core of the two is homogeneous and continuous. Here was found a centurial stone, inscribed COH I> OPSILI, "The first cohort, century of Opsilius": there are also two Roman altars, once built into the sanctuary steps of the Norman church at Over Denton; one uninscribed, the other dedicated by a tribune to Jupiter, Best and Greatest and worn by use as a threshold or by sharpening implements or weapons.

Across the Brampton road Wall and Vallum converge until the north mound of the Vallum comes within some 15 feet of the Wall. A fine stretch of the Wall is here seen, as Narrow Wall on broad foundation. In it were found four centurial stones, two reading COH VI>LOVSI SVAVIS, two of >COCCEI REGVLI, both known in other sectors, the former thrice. On Willowford Hill, to the south, there is a well-preserved temporary camp with two gates protected by traverses, in contiguous sides. It is 1¼ acres in size.

From the Romanway Guest House as far as Willowford the Wall is now preserved and displayed by D.O.E. Just east of the point where river, Wall and Vallum are closest comes turret 48*a*, with well-preserved wing-walls of the broad gauge. Two hundred yards farther on, the farm-track crosses the Wall and occupies the ditch, here enhanced by the cart-track which occupies it. The remains of turret 48*b* stand high and bold just before reaching the farm-yard.

The Wall then descends to flat ground bordering the river, and reaches the bridge by which it crossed the Irthing. On the east, the first feature is a large tower, founded upon massive re-used masonry and built against the back of the Narrow Wall, here resting upon four courses of broad foundation. The west wall of this tower coincides with the east end of the wing-wall of an original turret, built as part of a length of Broad Wall, which marked the original termination of the Wall in the river Irthing. Only the north-east corner of the recess of this turret, however, now remains, all else having been removed in a drastic Roman reconstruction, which included extending the Broad Wall west, perhaps as the river moved its course. The turret guarded the abutment of the original bridge, now seen as a splayed foundation slightly further west.

The reconstructed Wall rides across this earliest abutment and terminates over a pair of narrow culverts of large masonry, which possibly served a mill. The front of this Wall was once faced in large blocks, now mostly replaced by a patched face; and these bonded with a massive stone apron, revetting the end of the berm as it approached the river. The north front of the apron is cut to match the slope of the ditch, and there are traces of paving in the adjacent river-channel. Next, the early splayed

EAST END OF ROMAN BRIDGE, WILLOWFORD

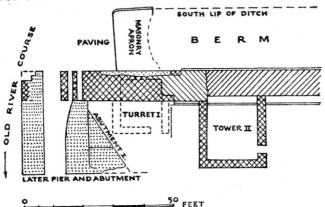

abutment was enlarged, by blocking the east culvert, while a correspondingly large pier was added in the stream, forming a new culvert, with paved bottom, which may have served as the race for an under-shot water-mill wheel. Both enlargement and water-mill are matched at the North Tyne, where a bridge sufficiently wide to carry the Military Way replaced the narrow first bridge and a mill-race is associated with the later work. Likewise, both here and at Chesters, the original stonework was bonded with dovetail cramps here visible in the outer stone pier of the original pair of narrow culverts.

The main water-piers of the bridge are represented only by the large pier already described, which incorporates work of the first period at its north end. It also embodied re-used masonry, including a voussoir. Two levels of occupation were found in the later tower, but the excavators observed that the very earliest Hadrianic pottery was absent, thus confirming what is visible structurally; that is, this tower is an addition to the Narrow Wall, replacing the earlier tower.

Excavations in 1940 showed that the river once flowed immediately west of the abutment in a rocky gorge, which contained foundations of two further water-piers, now 10 feet below the surface of the holm. The turbulent Irthing has evidently changed its course since Roman times, so that it now lies entirely west of the Roman bridge. This means that the western cliff

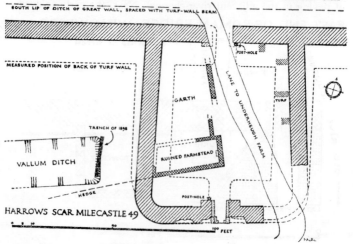

SOUTH LIP OF DITCH OF GREAT WALL, SPACED WITH TURF-WALL BERM

MEASURED POSITION OF BACK OF TURF WALL

GARTH

LANE TO UNDERHEUGH FARM

POST-HOLE

TURF

TRENCH OF 1898

VALLUM DITCH

RUINED FARMSTEAD

HEDGE

POST-HOLE

HARROWS SCAR MILECASTLE 49

100 FEET

may then have been considerably less steep and thus easier for the Wall to climb.

On the cliff summit, named Harrow's Scar, the Wall stands 7 courses high. Here is milecastle 49 (Harrow's Scar), found in 1898 to measure internally 75 feet long from north to south by 65 feet wide from east to west. In 1953 further excavation revealed part of the Turf-Wall milecastle below it, and showed that the Vallum ditch, ending just short of its southwest corner, did not descend the cliff. The south gate of the stone milecastle was of type III, reduced in Period II to a foot-way.

At the Irthing the Broad Wall came to an end and its counterpart, the Turf Wall, began. When the latter was replaced in stone, the new Stone Wall was the Narrow Wall, and this, between Harrow's Scar and a point west of Birdoswald, is conserved by D.O.E. and forms a fine sight. At about 50 yards west of the milecastle the Wall makes a northward turn of about eight degrees: had it not done so, it would have aimed for the main east gate of Birdoswald fort. This is the course actually taken by the Turf Wall, whose ditch has been traced at this point running below the foundations of the Stone Wall. Thus, when the fort was built it projected beyond the Turf Wall, just as the forts at Chesters, Halton, Rudchester and Benwell project beyond the Stone Wall. Accordingly, the north portal and guardchamber of the main east and west gates of the fort bestride the ditch, upon a special foundation of large stones. The ditch was again traced, running under the fort, and then across the field to the west of the fort. It appears on the surface in the adjoining field, whence it is visible until the Stone Wall crosses its line at Wallbowers.

The Vallum at first runs parallel to the Turf Wall; on approaching the fort it makes a symmetrical diversion, as at several other forts, so as to skirt its south side. It has, however, no north mound. In order to avoid impinging too closely upon milecastles and the fort in this sector, where the escarpment of the Irthing leaves little room, the upcast from the Vallum ditch has been disposed in a south mound of twice the normal size. Opposite the south gate of the fort the Vallum ditch was crossed by a causeway of undisturbed subsoil revetted vertically in stone, with foundations for a central gateway, as at Benwell.

The section of Stone Wall between Harrow Scar and Birdoswald differs from earlier stretches both in its width, and in another particular: the drainage channels through it, built to carry off surface water, are placed very much more closely together than in the earlier lengths of Wall. Here they occur at regular intervals of 20 feet, or occasionally even more closely. In the consolidated stonework a number of centurial and other interesting stones are still in their original positions. This is the only stretch of the Wall where such may now be seen. Most of the stones are in the topmost remaining course, or the string course, but the phallic symbols are at half this height. The position of each is marked by a small metal strip set between the lowest courses of the Wall. Sixty-nine yards from the west wall of the milecastle there is an almost illegible stone recording "The Century of Marcus Rufus"; at 74 yards a clearer stone of "The Century of Carus Scipio"; at 211 yards a phallic symbol; at 268 yards "The Century of Julius Primus, Cohort VIII"; 10 yards further "The Century of Secundinus Verullus built 30 paces"; at 301 yards there is a stone with a very worn ansate tablet and < P P, "The Century of the Primus Pilus" (senior centurion of the legion); at 382 yards "The century of Tertus"; at 409½ yards another phallus and about 435 yards the end of the Wall. Some 10 further inscribed stones had fallen from this length of Wall.

The area south of this length of Wall contained the fort parade ground. From Birdoswald a most impressive group of official parade-ground dedications is known, including one to the Standards and the Deity of the Emperor, and over 20 to Jupiter Best and Greatest, all officially dedicated by the First Cohort of Dacians, Hadrian's Own. Some were found re-used in Birdoswald Farm, others in buildings further afield, but 5 were found either a short distance east of the fort, or at Underheugh Farm to the south, including one discovered in the face of the cliff above the farm, suggesting that it might have been buried as the parade-ground altars at Maryport were. Another 5 of these altars came from Willowford Farm, to the east of the bridge abutment.

BIRDOSWALD (BANNA?)

Birdoswald fort is nearly 3¼ miles from Carvoran. Its position is striking. In addition to the bold scarp on the south, at the foot of which the Irthing winds, a valley to the north takes the overflow of Midgeholm Moss into the Irthing. The west side now appears weak, but was in Roman times a fairly deep bog, drained below the fort into the gully which emerges in the cliff west of Underheugh. The prime function of the fort, however, was to guard the Irthing bridge and to watch the route from the north across the shoulder of Gillalees Beacon.

The previously accepted name of the fort was CAMBOGLANNA, but there is good reason for suspecting an error in the *Notitia*, and that Birdoswald's name was BANNA (a Tongue or Horn), as given on the Rudge Cup and Amiens Skillet. The Hunters of Banna are recorded on an altar from the site. Camboglanna would then attach to Castlesteads. The garrison in the fourth century was the First Cohort of Dacians, Hadrian's Own, 1,000 strong, who were also in garrison in the third century. Early in that century the First Cohort of Thracians, part-mounted, are also recorded on a building inscription. A stamped tile from the vicinity of Hare Hill, 3½ miles to the west, is usually read as "The First Cohort of Tungrians", and on its strength it has been suggested that this unit, too, may have been at Birdoswald. The Second Tungrians at Castlesteads, however, seem at least as likely an origin for the tile.

The fort measures 580 by 400 feet, and has an area of 5.3 acres, showing that it was originally built for a milliary cohort, probably the same Dacians attested here later. In that case Dacian tribesmen taken into the regiment when it was first raised would still have been serving when it took up its position on the Irthing.

The north gate lies under the modern road, where the foundations of one of its jambs used to be seen in the metalling. The curved north-west angle of the fort, 12 courses high, forms the east side of the drive entrance to Birdoswald farm and the Wall abutted upon it with little attempt at bonding. The Wall had, in fact, been rebuilt in the late fourth century over a ditch, as if the fort had been cut off from the Wall for independent defence during a crisis, as Kipling fancied in *Puck of Pook's Hill*. The well preserved angle-tower was used as a cook-house, its ovens often rebuilt during the second century. The fort-wall then continues southwards and exhibits an interval-tower standing high except at the west, where the face has been robbed. The shrubbery in the farmhouse garden covers

Altar from Birdoswald, by the First Cohort of Dacians (Tullie House)

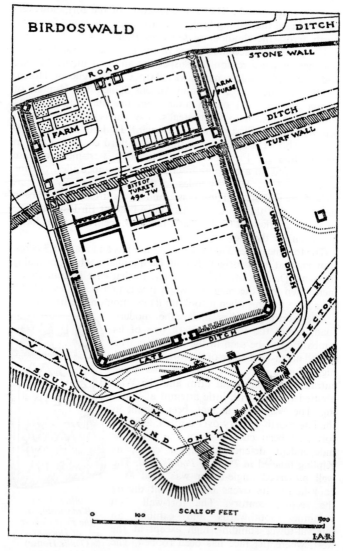

BIRDOSWALD

Birdoswald Fort, with Turf Wall, Vallum, and Stone Wall

the main west gate. The west postern has wheel-ruts in its threshold and pivot-holes for a two-leaved door. It was blocked during the Roman period, probably in Period II, when internal buildings spread across the street which it served.

At the south-west angle the rampart, though not high, bears marks of very thorough reconstruction; two successive periods are probably Roman work, but a third is to be associated with a long-vanished farm-building.

The south gate, cleared in 1851, is the usual twin entranceway. The east portal was blocked soon after erection and converted into a guard-room. Late in the Roman period, the west portal was also closed. The blocking walls were removed in 1851. The east guardchamber contained two late-Roman ovens; the west has since become choked by its own ruins. Its east wall is reconstructed, following complete demolition, in large and irregular masonry in the style of the late fourth century. West of the guardchamber there is a corn-drying kiln of post-Roman date.

Both gates on the east side of the fort have been excavated, but no trace of the blocked postern is now to be seen. In the late fourth century the fort wall was entirely rebuilt here, on the crest of the bank, after having already been reconstructed in large masonry in the third century. The rampart backing, between the south-east angle and the postern, was cut back to form a flat revetted shelf used for cooking-ovens in the early fourth century, while the rampart-walk had a vertical back.

The main east gate, in excellent preservation, was excavated in 1852, when many traces of the alterations which it had undergone were removed. Its north portal and tower are founded in the Turf-Wall ditch. More recent re-excavation, before consolidation, showed that the central pier of the gateway had been strengthened and a second-period roadway and new pivot-stones had been provided. Also in Period II, a platform for large ovens had been built of tiles inside the tower. Later, the whole tower had collapsed, probably at the time when buildings in the central range of the fort were in ruin, to be rebuilt early in the fourth century. The north portal was now blocked, becoming a guard-room of which the back wall still stands, the front one having been removed in 1852. The Romans also blocked the west door of the original guardchamber and opened a new door in its south wall, giving access from the new guard-room built in the portal. At this time the south guardchamber may have received a hypocaust.

Fallen masonry found in 1852 outside the south tower included a re-used inscription, which may be translated: "Under Modius Julius, Imperial propraetorian legate, the First Aelian Cohort of Dacians, commanded by Marcus Claudius Menander, tribune". Modius Julius was governor in A.D 219, and the stone was doubtless matched by another bearing the name and titles of Elagabalus, under whom the work was done. Left of the inscription is the palm-branch of victory, to the right the curved native sword of the Dacians. Several round-headed lintels for doors or windows come from near this and other gateways,

The right-hand member of a pair of building-stones from the East Gate, Birdoswald (Newcastle)

as at Housesteads; one was placed over the door of the north guardchamber in 1852, but incorrectly. North of the gate a fine stretch of fort-wall and an interval-tower are to be seen. Between tower and gate a bronze arm-purse, like that from Barcombe (p. 155) was found in 1949. It contained 28 *denarii* current under Hadrian and had been accidentally buried when the rampart-backing was piled against the fort-wall, behind which the purse had been momentarily laid aside.

The whole interior was once marked with the line of streets and the ruins of buildings. Towards the rear of the fort traces of the normal type of barracks have been found, and a coin-hoard of 30 *denarii*, again those current under Hadrian, was concealed in the primary floor of one of them. Later, the buildings were drastically reconstructed and extended across the *via quintana*. Near the east postern a building of three rooms, 9 or 10 feet square, was excavated, one of the rooms was heated by a hypocaust, and to judge from similar buildings in other forts, was the baths of the commanding-officer's house. It yielded a fine seated statue of Fortune, identifiable by the tip of her rudder. The stone is now at Tullie House Museum, Carlisle.

West of this, in the centre of the fort, stood the headquarters building. Trial trenches in 1930 showed that, because the

Statue of the Goddess Fortuna from Birdoswald Baths (Tullie House)

ground here dipped into a natural gully, the back wall of the building stands some 15 courses high, while the voussoirs of its arched front lie just as they had fallen. The front wall, on the other hand, is only two courses high.

West of the headquarters one or more granaries lay parallel with the main cross-street of the fort. In 1859, in making the garden in front of the farmhouse, the south wall of one of them was adapted as a retaining-wall. It is 3 feet 6 inches thick and 92 feet long. It was not uncovered to its very bottom, but has been shown to stand at least 8 feet in height. It has 9 external buttresses, between each of which is a vertical slot or ventilator. The buttresses supported the thrust of the heavy roof, and the air-vents ventilated the space beneath the damp-proof floor and kept it cool. Three sleeper walls, to support the flagged floor, were found to the north and many roofing slabs lay among the fallen rubbish.

The *praetentura*, or area to the north of the central buildings, contained barrack-blocks lying, as at Chesters, across the fort. Those immediately north of the *via principalis* overlie the filled-in ditch of the Turf Wall and one of them, excavated in 1928-9, produced inscriptions important for the history of the fort, described below. The life of this barrack had been a long and complicated one, with many changes of plan and shape. In the *retentura*, or rearward part of the fort, trenching has shown that in Period II buildings were laid across the *via quintana*, to house the extra troops then added to the garrison.

The relation of the Stone Wall, Turf Wall and Vallum to the fort is complicated and has given rise to much curious planning. The Stone Wall is brought up to the fort's north angles. The Turf Wall, running straight from milecastle 49, abutted upon its principal gates, like the Stone Wall at Chesters. But both the Turf Wall and its ditch were constructed before the fort was begun, for, in 1945 and 1894 respectively, they were found to pass below it. The site of turret 49*a* TW was also found in 1945, although nothing was left except the gap in the Turf Wall and a scatter of mason's chippings left from the removal of the tower, all sealed below the *via principalis* of the fort.

The Vallum is diverted round the south side of the fort, only just slipping between it and the Irthing escarpment, at the cost of omitting the north mound. Opposite the south gate of the fort the Vallum was interrupted by a causeway of undisturbed subsoil, revetted vertically on each side with stone and closed by an undefended gate, as at Benwell. In fact the first arrangement of the fort, in relation to Turf Wall and Vallum is normal.

Three points, however, differentiate Birdoswald from other sites. First, the Vallum cuts through a pair of ditches which appear to have been an earlier native promontory-fort, itself occupied by a small Roman rectangular post associated with early second-century pottery. Secondly, the Vallum was obliterated at the fort very soon after its creation, and wooden buildings were erected across it. These were apparently cut through by the fort ditches. Such a sequence, if correct, would be unusual by comparison with other Wall forts, and it may not be correctly understood: on the other hand the situation at Birdoswald may have been more complex than elsewhere. Thirdly, the Stone Wall was run up to the northern angles of the fort, possibly to gain room for a parade ground and other buildings to the east (see p. 198); for west of the fort the ground was boggy and undeveloped in Roman times, although a tombstone found there in 1961 may indicate that it contained the fort cemetery.

This tombstone was to G. Cossutius Saturninus, a soldier of the Sixth Legion, from Hippo Regius, modern Annaba. Others commemorate Aurelius Concordius, who lived 1 year and 5 days, the son of Aurelius Julianus, the tribune recorded on the Severan granary inscription (see below), also Decibalus and Blaesus, aged 10, set up by their brother. Decebalus was the name borne by a famous Dacian king.

The history of the fort was illuminated by two large inscriptions, found in 1929 and now at Tullie House Museum, Carlisle. One records the restoration of a granary (*horreum*) by the First Dacian Cohort and the First Cohort of Thracians, under the command of Aurelius Julianus, in A.D. 205-8; the second states, in translation, that the Cohort "restored the commanding-officer's house (*praetorium*), which had been covered with earth and had fallen into ruin, the headquarters building (*principia*), and the bath-house (*balneum*)", under the Emperors Diocletian and Maximian. It dates to the period A.D. 297-305. These inscriptions were for long taken as giving definite dates for the commencement of the Second and Third Periods of occupation long recognized at Wall sites, and the terminology of the second stone was

Diocletianic Record of Rebuilding after Decay, Birdoswald (Tullie House)

interpreted as a euphemism for hostile destruction. In recent years, however, such views have been doubted, and it is better to see the first inscription as indicating general third-century rebuilding and modernization, as does the gateway inscription of A.D. 219, and as do numerous inscriptions from the frontier forts (see p. 7). The second inscription is a literal admission of the decay and collapse after the fort garrison had been withdrawn by Carausius, or a little earlier, and far from euphemism it is a blunt statement of truth, illuminating the contemporary humus layers archaeologically attested in the abandoned, or clearly reduced forts of South Shields, Rudchester and Halton-chesters, to the east.

Four objects of interest, visible from Birdoswald, may also be mentioned. In the valley, not half a mile due south, is Over Denton church. Its chancel-arch, of the eleventh or twelfth century in date, and 6 feet in span, is built of Roman arch-stones, whose original tooling was unfortunately removed by recutting in 1881. A quarter of a mile south-west of the church, is the signal-tower of Mains Rigg (see p. 208). The third object, seen to the north-west from the road north of the fort is a ruined wall of Triermain Castle, celebrated by Scott in *The Bridal of Triermain* and by Coleridge in *Christabel*.

The fourth object lies near the summit of Gillalees Beacon, on the horizon a little west of north, and is seen as a small cairn-like mound in good weather, named Robin Hood's Butt. Its excavator, Haverfield, was cautious about its Roman nature, but comparison with Mains Rigg has led to it now generally being accepted as a Roman signal-tower, flanking the Roman road to Bewcastle. Signals from it could be seen at Birdoswald or on the Wall, but not by an enemy to the north, so that a surprise intercepting move could be prepared in terrain well adapted to ambush (see p. 320).

THE STANEGATE, THROP AND NETHER DENTON

From Carvoran fort the Stanegate turns north-west to nego-tiate the steep slope of the Tipalt Valley. Towards the bottom of its descent it swings back again southwards, at a point where MacLauchlan found a very perfect portion of its surviving. Across the Tipalt it crosses the present Gilsland road and the railway and again makes a dog-leg, as it climbs the slope, passing north of Glenwhelt Leazes Camp. This measures some 495 by 264 feet over its ramparts, giving an area of about 3 acres. It is of a rare type, as MacLauchlan observed, having an external straight traverse combined with an internal *clavicula*, or curved terminal of the rampart, at each of its four gateways. About ¾ of a mile west there is a second camp, with the same type of gateways, at Chapel Rigg. These two alone of all the camps found on the Wall have this peculiarity. The third camp, with conventional traverses, lies at Crooks, approximately a similar distance further west. It measures about 390 by 270 feet, giving an area of some 2·25 acres. These three are all temporary camps, similar in construction and purpose to those already noted beside Haltwhistle Burn.

North of Lawn Top (Loanhead), the Stanegate swings southwards again and crosses the Poltross Burn 350 yards upstream
from the Wall. Two hundred yards west of this crossing, on the
crest of the ridge north-east of Throp farm and just under 2¼
miles from Carvoran, stood the small Roman post of THROP.
It was excavated in 1910 and found to resemble in size and date
the fortlet at Haltwhistle Burn. About 200 feet square, it covers
c. 0·9 of an acre, and was defended by a rampart of turf laid on
a stone foundation 16 feet wide. Its two gateways, situated
in the north-eastern and south-east sides, were of timber, and

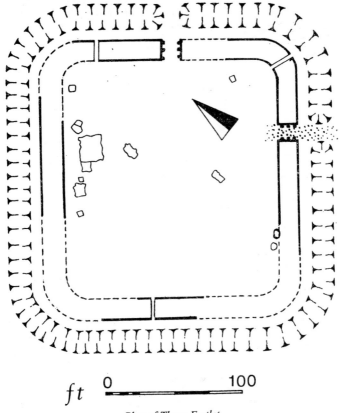

ft 0 ———————————— 100

Plan of Throp Fortlet

so doubtless had been the internal buildings. Of these, only patches of rough flagging and a series of hearths close behind the north-western rampart had survived the heavy ploughing. An oven was found at the back of the south-eastern rampart.

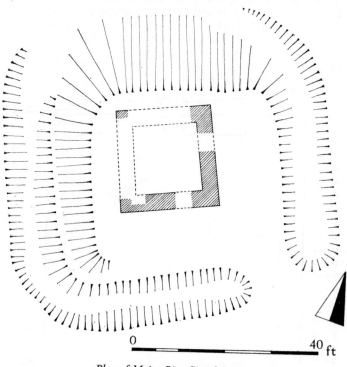

Plan of Mains Rigg Signal Station

Little stratification remained, but the pottery recovered suggested the same early occupation as at Haltwhistle Burn, terminating with the building of the Wall; but in this case followed by a second brief period of use in the fourth century.

From Throp the Stanegate runs directly to Nether Denton, almost 2½ miles away, taking the shortest and most direct route. After passing the northern edge of Throp farm it falls in below the modern Gilsland-Low Row road just east of Upper Denton, and after crossing the railway line, continues to Nether Denton. Just south of the railway crossing, and overlooking it from the hillside of MAINS RIGG, above three young oak trees, a Roman watch- or signal-tower was identified in 1928 and partly re-excavated in 1971. It consisted of a stone-built tower 21 feet square, surrounded by a ditch, also square in plan, about 10 feet wide, with an undug causeway of about 10 feet at the south-eastern corner. The tower walls were 3 feet wide with offsets, and clearly showed that there had been no ground-floor door to the building. Instead, it had been entered by means of a removable ladder to a door in the first floor, as some of the upper-German watch-towers were. The post links the forts of Throp and Nether Denton, which are invisible from each other, and also communicates with the bluff on which Birdoswald fort stands.

NETHER DENTON is the next of the posts on the Stanegate line. It lies on a narrowish ridge-top now occupied by the church and rectory of the same name, overlooking a steep descent to the Irthing on the north. In 1868, when the rectory was being built, *fibulae* and other metal objects, 89 coins ranging from Republican times to Trajan, and Flavian-Trajanic pottery in abundance, including stamped amphora handles, were found, together with structural remains including clay and cobble foundations and stone flagging, and "traces of fire-places" with much blackening. All of this lay on firm gravel so that it is perhaps unlikely that the structures represent the hypocaust system of an external bath house, as has been suggested.

In 1933 excavation produced "thickly occupied ground", with many tiles, down the hillside from the church. Twenty yards north of the east-west service track, morticed timbers were found 6 feet down, resting on what appeared to be ditch filling, together with pre-Hadrianic pottery. A short distance nearer the church a massive laid-turf rampart was found, 30 feet thick at its base and still standing 5 feet high. Some 60 yards of this were traced, running west and swinging slightly northwards as it neared the shoulder of the hill, where a corner might be expected. Two coins of Domitian (one dated A.D. 87) were found at Church Hill House, and during the excavation samian and coarse ware of pre-Hadrianic date were recovered.

From this, and the contours of the hill-top, it has been argued that a cohort fort of about 3 acres existed here, mostly under the church, farm and rectory: although, when one considers the site on the ground the area is actually less than 3 acres. Recent air-photography, however, has shown that the discoveries of 1933 lie within a considerably larger fort, the ditches of which run to the west of the church, from the Irthing bank to the field south of the east-west farm track, then turn and run east towards the junction of the farm track and the main road. The size of this fort must have been considerable, something near 6 acres, but its details, and date, have not yet been ascertained. As two distinct building periods, one of timber and one of stone, have been suggested for the site, and occupation appears to run from the reign of Domitian through that of Trajan, the

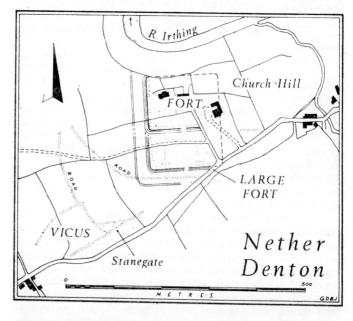

simplest solution would be for a large Flavian fort to have been replaced by a smaller Trajanic post, abandoned, like others on the Stanegate, with the decision to move the garrisons on to the line of the Wall.

South of the Gilsland road (the Stanegate) in 1911 and again in 1933, walling, areas of occupation and second-century samian were found. Two cremations were also recorded from this area, and some of the pottery recovered has been dated to the second half of the second century, suggesting that civil occupation continued after the presumed abandonment of the fort. Air-photography has also recorded a considerable area of what appears to be *vicus* on the north side of the Stanegate, south-west of the fort.

Beyond Nether Denton the Stanegate line is uncertain, but some 700 yards west, a cemetery is known at High Nook farm. In 1861, 1909, and 1965 cinerary urns were found there, with a date range from Flavian-Trajanic times to the 170s. This bears out the probable continuation of burials at Nether Denton, and suggests that the Roman road may have run towards the Irthing before turning south-west to make for Castle Hill Boothby.

FROM BIRDOSWALD TO CASTLESTEADS

The Wall, westward from Birdoswald, is the Narrow Wall, on a foundation less deep than that between Wallsend and Newcastle. Its remains are on the south side of the road, and have been preserved by D.O.E. to beyond turret 49*b*. This was excavated in 1911, when two floors subsequent to Period IB were found, and a few fragments of late pottery, showing that the turret had not gone out of use at an early date. Unfortunately, the rear and side walls were greatly reduced in height in 1837.

The Wall ditch is often very well preserved hereabouts, and is visible over long stretches at least as far as Banks.

A little more than half a mile from the fort, on the crest of the hill, is the site of milecastle 50 (High House), also excavated in 1911 and found to measure internally 76 feet from north to south and 60 from east to west. It resembles milecastles 48 and 49 in plan and details, although its internal area is considerably greater, and its walls are narrow (7 feet 7 inches) since it was built with the Narrow Wall. The north gate is of type III, and the original internal buildings appear to have been of timber, although little trace of them remained. In Period II two large stone buildings had replaced them, similar to those at Poltross Burn, although considerably more ruinous when found. This milecastle has produced fragments of three legionary building inscriptions. Two indicate the Sixth Legion, the other refers to a vexillation of the Second, but is probably later in date.

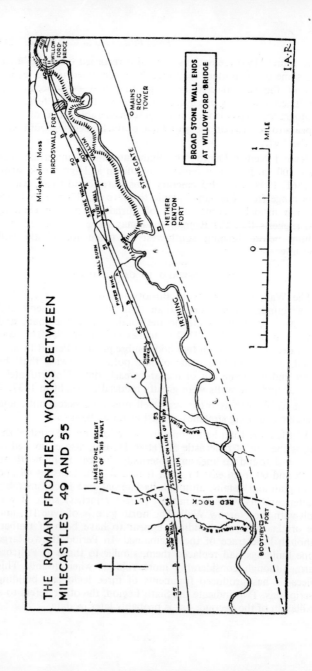

THE ROMAN FRONTIER WORKS BETWEEN
MILECASTLES 49 AND 55

BROAD STONE WALL ENDS
AT WILLOWFORD BRIDGE

The next two turrets were also excavated in 1911. The first, 50*a* (High House), was found to have been dismantled in Period II when the Wall was built across its recess. It provided two inscriptions of the Sixth Legion. These, together with a cohort stone built into the stable at High House, and three other, unprovenanced, stones now preserved at Lanercost, all of the Sixth Legion, suggest that it was that Legion which was responsible for the rapid rebuilding of the first 5 miles of the Turf Wall (but see p. 46).

The second, turret 50*b* (Appletree), by contrast, had remained in use after the end of the second century. At both turrets 50*a* and 50*b*, as well as at 49*b*, fragments of window glass were found.

The Turf Wall, running south of the line of the Stone Wall from milecastle 49 to milecastle 51, is first visible in the second field west of Birdoswald, behind turret 49*b*. Mound and ditch are here faint and have been washed out on the steep slope, but soon become bold and so continue to milecastle 51. When the Turf Wall was discovered, in 1895 (its ditch had been noted previously, though not understood), the view was advanced that Hadrian had constructed a Turf Wall from sea to sea, but that only this short piece remained, the rest having been dismantled when Severus built the Stone Wall on the same line. It was argued that any Hadrianic remains associated with milecastles and turrets elsewhere could not disprove this, since they might have belonged to the supposed Turf Wall just as well as to the Stone Wall.

Fragment of Hadrianic building-inscription in oak, from Turf-Wall milecastle 50 TW (Tullie House)

The question was settled by excavating Stone-Wall milecastle 50 and turrets 49*b*, 50*a* and 50*b*; for these occurred in the one and only sector where the Turf Wall and Stone Wall ran on different lines. Conclusive proof of Hadrianic occupation was found in them all. This showed that both the Stone Wall and

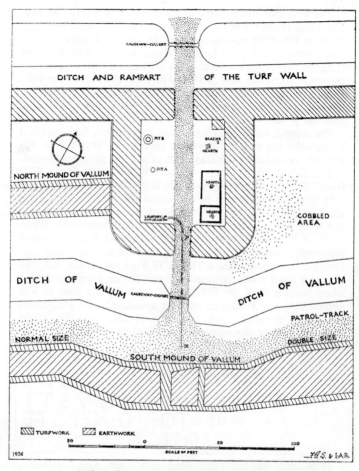

Milecastle 50 TW (High House) and the Vallum

the Turf Wall were the work of Hadrian. As for the original
length of the Turf Wall, it was ascertained in 1927 that it did
not extend east of the Irthing, where the Broad Stone Wall was
in fact its counterpart, but ran westward as far as Bowness. In
that year, the first turret on the Turf Wall was identified at Banks,

52*a*, embodied in the Stone Wall; and in 1934 the identification of turrets 49*b* TW and 50*a* TW in the Turf Wall itself followed. These turrets are of stone, 20 feet square, with plinths at back and front and without ladder-platforms. So they not only match those of the Broad Wall (pre-dating the Narrow Wall) but their design indicates that they were the counterpart of the Broad Wall turrets. In addition turrets 49*b* TW and 50*a* TW were dismantled when the Narrow Wall was built. In 1934 the sole unencumbered Turf-Wall milecastle, 50 TW, was also examined. This was found closely to resemble a Stone-Wall milecastle in plan, but it had a turf rampart instead of a stone wall, and timber gateways and barracks. Only the north gate appeared to have had a tower. The occupation was intense but very short. Then a demolition party, burying its rubbish (including a wooden writing-tablet, bracken and heather bedding, an old shoe, etc.) in pits, let fall into one of them a chip from the wooden dedication tablet of the milecastle, bearing part of the names of Hadrian and Platorius Nepos. This is now in Tullie House Museum, Carlisle. The whole text was shown by R. G. Collingwood to match that of the stone tablets from Cawfields and Hotbank. This evidence shows that the Turf Wall was Hadrianic, but in this sector was quickly replaced by the Narrow Wall, itself proved Hadrianic in 1911.

The Vallum runs close behind the Turf Wall throughout this sector. At milecastles 49 and 50 TW, it is so close that the north mound is omitted and replaced by a south mound of double size, thus proving that the Vallum is later than the Turf Wall hereabouts. At milecastle 50 TW the north mound begins again on the west, and the ditch and south mound make a southward diversion. The ditch was originally interrupted by a causeway revetted in stone, as at the forts. As the presence of a primary causeway at a milecastle is now known to be unusual, it has been suggested that this one was connected with the Maiden Way which crosses the Wall nearby, making for Bewcastle (see p. 321). This is supported by the presence of a primary causeway across the Wall ditch, another exceptional feature. Later, on the demolition of the milecastle, the causeway was replaced by a wide crossing and a new roadway which was finally blocked by embankments, restoring the ditch.

West of milecastle 50 TW, in the neighbourhood of High House, the Vallum is, as Haverfield wrote, "in astonishing preservation". The usual gaps are visible in the north mound, and

H

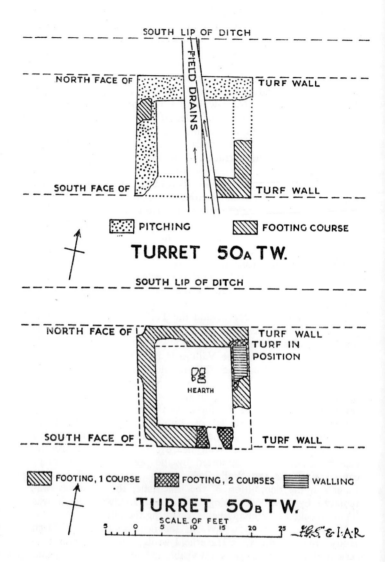

SOUTH LIP OF DITCH

FIELD DRAINS

NORTH FACE OF   TURF WALL

SOUTH FACE OF   TURF WALL

PITCHING   FOOTING COURSE

TURRET 50ᴀ TW.

SOUTH LIP OF DITCH

NORTH FACE OF   TURF WALL
TURF IN POSITION

HEARTH

SOUTH FACE OF   TURF WALL

FOOTING, 1 COURSE   FOOTING, 2 COURSES   WALLING

TURRET 50ʙ TW.

SCALE OF FEET
5   0   5   10   15   20   25   J.G.S & I.A.R

traces of causeways are to be seen in the ditch; but in the south mound, as at Shield-on-the-Wall and Wallend Common (pp. 175, 191) only notches indicate where the gaps were to have come. Gaps can also be seen notching the mound of the Turf Wall, and there are substantial causeways in its ditch.

Just before turret 50*b* a section was recorded across the ditch, Turf Wall and Vallum in 1975, when a gas-pipeline trench was cut. Although ploughing had reduced the Wall and the Vallum mounds, the Wall ditch was considerably over 30 feet in width, and a well-metalled path, 8 feet wide, still survived on the Vallum north berm, as was found a little further west in 1895.

A little beyond the site of turret 50*b* and opposite Appletree barn, a lane goes off to the south; 150 yards down this lane a section has been cut through the Turf Wall, showing its laminated structure, in blocks of whitish bleached roots and humus alternating with streaks of dark carbonised grass. Individual turves used in the structure can often be recognised.

At milecastle 51 (Wall Bowers) the Stone Wall once more rejoins the line of the Turf Wall and crosses its filled-up ditch. The milecastle is girt by a ditch as at milecastles 23, 25 and 29, though it has never been completely dug. Like milecastles 47 and 48, Wall Bowers had two stone barracks. Its south gate, of type III, had been rebuilt in the fourth century with large monolithic jambs and a massive threshold set in a deep trench. The Vallum runs some distance behind the milecastle. It displays an unusual feature, a stone-revetted causeway, which had later been replaced by a wider crossing and road across the south mound, all as at milecastle 50 TW.

It was at first supposed that the Turf Wall ended at Wall Bowers; but in 1929 it was proved to extend to Bowness-on-Solway, by the following facts. While the Stone-Wall turrets are an integral part of the Wall's structure, with wing-walls for bonding, the Turf-Wall turrets, as was proved by excavating those corresponding to 50*a* and 50*b*, were square stone towers with a plinth at back and front and the Turf Wall abutting on either side. In 1927, turrets 51*a*, 51*b* and 52*a* were found to be stone towers of Turf-Wall type, incorporated in the Stone Wall, which butted against their east and west walls with a straight joint some three feet behind their north face. Further excavation revealed actual traces of the dismantled Turf Wall in contact with them. Similar proof was then obtained at turret 79*b*, just east of Bowness.

West of Wall Bowers, at a lodge south of the road, a path leads to Coombe Crag, a freestone quarry extensively worked

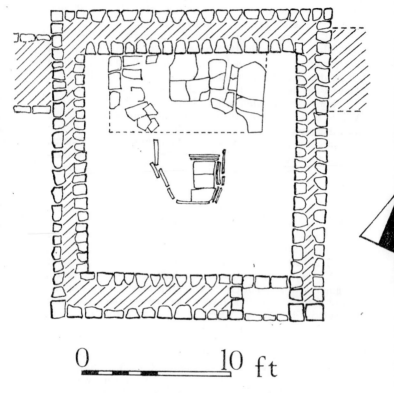

0   10 ft

Plan of Turret 51a (Piper Sike)

by the Romans. The soldiers have left inscriptions on the face of the rock, including the names SECVRVS, IVSTVS, MATERNVS, and one DAMINIUS, who added "I did not want to do it", presumably alluding to the work of stonecutting. An inscription at the foot of the cliff, reading FAVST ET RVF COS and purporting to mention Faustinns and Rufus, the consuls of A.D. 210, is a forgery, perpetrated to suggest that the Wall was built in the reign of Severus. It can be seen how relatively fresh the punching of the letters is, and how different in style from genuine inscriptions. South of Coombe Crag, at Lanerton, further quarry inscriptions, seen by Hodgson, have now vanished.

Immediately west of Coombe Crag Wood the Vallum is in its original condition for about 800 yards: there is no gap in the mounds, no causeway in the ditch, and no marginal mound. This is one of the very stretches where the Vallum can be seen entirely free from alteration.

Turrets 51*a* and 51*b* are visible on the north verge of the modern road, and in D.O.E. guardianship. Their close proximity to the Wall ditch, typical of the Turf-Wall structures, will be appreciated. Turret 51*a* (Piper Sike), was excavated in 1970 and shown to be of rather poor construction. Like 51*b* it had an

eastern door, and a substantial platform against its north wall. However, this could never have been a stair-base as it was only 8 inches higher than the associated floor. By contrast with the cooking hearths and rubbish thickly covering the whole floor of the turret, the platform had been kept clean and probably represented a living area. Occupation did not continue beyond the end of the second century. Turret 51*b* (Leahill), also contains an extremely large platform, 6 by 8 feet in size, against its north wall, but one which was never more than 6 inches higher than the floor of the turret. Re-excavation in 1958, showed that the turret had been given up in Antonine times, after only an extremely short Period IB occupation, although it had then remained standing. After A.D. 369 a rough hut had been constructed in the ruins. Amongst other finds were fragments of window glass and a merlin coping-stone, suggestive of a flat roof.

Altar to Cocidius from Milecastle 52 (Bankshead) at Lanercost Priory.

Next comes the site of milecastle 52 (Bankshead). Here in 1808 two altars were discovered, dedicated to the local diety Cocidius (now in Lanercost Priory), and in 1862 a broken slab on which had been roughly scabbled the name of Antonius Pius. One altar to Cocidius, here figured, was dedicated by soldiers of the Twentieth Legion in the years 262-6 when Aper and Rufus were consuls of the separatist Gallic Empire, to which Britain adhered. Excavation in 1934 proved the milecastle to have been exceptionally large, 76 feet 9 inches from north to south by 90 feet 3 inches from from east to west internally. Its north gate, of type III, having received new pivot-stones in the second century, was reduced to a foot-way in Period II and completely blocked late in the fourth century. The south gate, as at milecastle 51, was completely remodelled in the

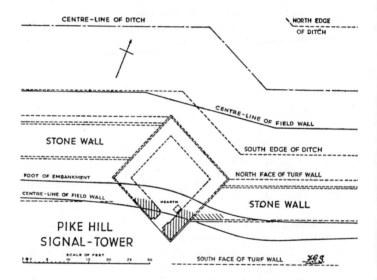

fourth century by the insertion of large stone jambs and threshold; and some of the iron strapping from the doors was found. Unfortunately, the interior arrangements are not known.

The extra large size of milecastle 52 is best explained by the remains seen on Pike Hill, the summit of the ridge occupied by the Wall. The view is extensive, embracing North Cumbria and beyond. Here stood a Roman signal-tower, 20 feet square, which was not part of the turret system of the Wall, for turret

52a lies only some 200 yards to the west. The tower is also oriented 45 degrees away from the Wall-line, while the Turf Wall, its ditch and the later Stone Wall all make a zig-zag to accommodate it. The explanation of this curious planning lies in the relation of the tower to other points. As placed, its two eastward sides face Gillalees watch-tower, Nether Denton fort, and Walltown turret (*45a*) (p. 186); its two westward sides face Boothby fort on the Stanegate and the outpost fort at Netherby. Its exceptionally deep foundations seem to denote extra height, and its purpose may well have been fast long-distance signalling, cutting out the normal patrol-signals of the Wall. Unfortunately, the tower was almost completely destroyed in 1870, when the road was drastically lowered, in spite of an attempt by the Cumberland and Westmoreland Society to save it. Excavation in 1931 revealed the one remaining corner and a ground-floor door (which contrasts with Robin Hood's Butt and Mains Rigg), as well as producing enough pottery to suggest that the tower had been constructed in Hadrianic, or possibly late Trajanic times. Two pieces of Huntcliff ware showed that some activity was still taking place on the site in the late fourth century, although a continuity of occupation until then is not assured.

Turret *52a* (Banks East), lies less than 100 yards west of Pike Hill, and is now displayed, under D.O.E. guardianship. It is a fine example of a Turf-Wall turret with the characteristic plinth visible at both front and back, and the Stone Wall abutting upon it. It stands 14 courses high, and a fallen piece of the superstructure lies just west of it. The demolished Turf Wall was found to abut against its east wall. The turret was intensively occupied until some date towards the end of the third century, after which it appears to have continued as a pent-house, with the Wall carried across it to full width.

Before coming to the brook called Banks Burn, a piece of the core of the Wall is seen. Here is the measured position of milecastle 53 (Banks Burn); but it was in fact placed on better ground, at Banks Burn farmhouse, west of the stream. Its gates were of type III and its internal dimensions $76\frac{1}{2}$ feet from north to south and 72 feet from east to west. In 1932 a fragment of the levelled Turf Wall was found inside it. Ascending Hare Hill the Wall stands 9 feet 10 inches high. The core is original, the facing a preservative measure of the nineteenth century. A centurial stone, recording the century of the *primus pilus* or senior centurion of the first cohort, found at Moneyholes, two fields further west, is placed in the north face. This is the highest piece of the Wall visible anywhere, and has been so for two centuries. "I viewed this relic with admiration", wrote Hutton, "I saw no part higher".

The road leading downhill to Lanercost Priory passes along the east edge of a ravine, in which a rock-face bears a forged inscription reading "I, Brutus, decurion in the *Ala Petriana*". It was once wrongly believed that Lanercost was a Roman site garrisoned by this unit; and the forgery was an attempt to bolster up the notion.

Lanercost Priory, an Augustinian house of 1169, is of great beauty and charmingly situated near the Irthing. Its nave is still a church, the rest is in the custody of D.O.E. Built almost entirely of red and grey stones from the Wall, it contains an altar to Jupiter, from Birdoswald, in the headway of the clearstory passage at the south-east angle of the choir. There is another, to Silvanus from Birdoswald, and two to Cocidius from milecastle 52, in the undercroft south of the church, as well as several centurial stones and fragmentary inscriptions, including pieces mentioning the Second and Sixth Legions;

*Relief of Hercules and Jupiter
(Lanercost Priory)*

also a relief showing Hercules and Jupiter. The Silvanus altar is of particular interest as it was set up "To the Holy God Silvanus by the *Venatores Banniesses*" (*Bannienses*), the Hunters of Banna; which is probably the Roman name for Birdoswald.

Altar set up by the Hunters of Banna (Lancercost Priory)

A fine eighteenth-century bridge leads over the river to Naworth Castle, the seat of the Earls of Carlisle; upstream are remains of an older bridge, once thought Roman, but in fact medieval.

About 200 yards west of Hare Hill a break in the Wall occurs, in which a turret or small quadrangular building has been situated. This building projects beyond the Wall, northwards, rather less than three feet. It is constructed of smaller stones than the Wall; the workmanship of it is excellent. It measures 14 feet 6 inches (inside measurement) from east to west. When first noticed it was full of black ashes; the discoverers took it to be a smithy. Altogether it is a peculiar building; though it has some of the features of a turret, it seems to have been built independently of the Wall.

The previous paragraph, left much as Bruce wrote it, shows how accurately he described a building which is in fact Turf-Wall turret 53*a* (Hare Hill), with the Narrow Wall brought up to its east and west sides and later covered by the medieval boundary-wall of Lanercost Priory lands. The spot has been wrongly named Moneyholes, which really lies 150 yards farther west, and where, as Bruce tells us, treasure has been sought in vain. Through the Priory Woods to the south, the Vallum runs straight westward, in good condition.

At Craggle Hill the Wall ditch is very bold. Turret 53*b*, of Turf-Wall type and built in red sandstone instead of yellow freestone, has been found here. At Hayton Gate, a track, once a drove road, crosses the Wall, approximately on the line of the Red Rock Fault, the great geological cleavage between the lime stone and the red sandstone. West of this point no limestone is obtainable anywhere near the Wall and this fact induced the change from Stone Wall to Turf Wall in the original design.

Just west of Randylands comes milecastle 54, excavated in 1934. It measures internally 77½ feet from north to south and

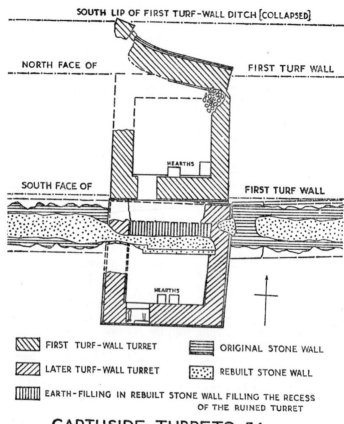

SOUTH LIP OF FIRST TURF-WALL DITCH [COLLAPSED]

NORTH FACE OF   FIRST TURF WALL

HEARTHS

SOUTH FACE OF   FIRST TURF WALL

HEARTHS

FIRST TURF-WALL TURRET   ORIGINAL STONE WALL

LATER TURF-WALL TURRET   REBUILT STONE WALL

EARTH-FILLING IN REBUILT STONE WALL FILLING THE RECESS
OF THE RUINED TURRET

GARTHSIDE TURRETS, 54A

SCALE OF FEET

$64\frac{1}{4}$ feet from east to west. Its gates, of type III, were reduced
to posterns in Period II after renewal of pivot-blocks in the
second century. Its western barrack was thoroughly excavated
and found to comprise two rooms, one fitted with stone benches,
hearth and millstone, the other empty. Beneath the stone milecastle, and on an axis a little further to the east, lay the Turf-
Wall milecastle, built in beaten clay, owing to the deficiency

of good turf. This clay construction continues in the so-called Turf Wall itself for about half a mile to the west.

After the crossing of the rivulet called Burtholme Beck, a piece of the Intermediate Stone Wall stands nearly 7 feet high; its facing-stones are gone, but the hard white mortar possesses its original tenacity. This quality of mortar is typical of the Period II reconstruction of the Wall. Here too a change in the structure of the Wall may be noted. From this point to Bowness the flag-footing is 9 feet 3 inches wide, at least, and carries a Wall 8½ feet thick, as compared with the Narrow Wall which is 7½ feet thick. This Intermediate Wall represents the replacement of the Turf Wall over the greater part of its length by an operation distinct from, and later than, the building of the Narrow Wall.

At turret 54a (Garthside) a remarkable building-sequence underlines the later building of the Intermediate Wall. As the Wall ditch approaches the turret from Burtholme Beck, it will be observed swinging northwards and taking the bottom of the northward slope. This arrangement is secondary. The older

Building-stone of a British tribal Corvée, at Howgill

ditch, still outlined in certain conditions of growth, followed the Wall to the turret, excavated in 1933, when the reason for the change became plain. There had been two turrets. The one, a Clay-Wall turret, had collapsed into the ditch, owing to unstable subsoil, after a measure of use. A new Wall, this time of turf, was then built further north, with the secondary ditch, while a second turret was built behind the old one as an isolated tower. Later came the Stone Wall, incorporating the second turret. Finally, in Period II, the later Stone Wall was built, without any turret, across the ruins of the second building. This complicated story provides ample proof that the Turf Wall here lasted for some time: its replacement in stone is of the second-century, but not immediate.

The Wall runs north of Howgill, by Low Wall and Dovecote, on its way to the King Water. In the wall of an outhouse at Howgill there is a rough inscription (shown in the woodcut) recording work by the Catuvellauni of Hertfordshire. Turret 54*b* (Howgill), at 535 yards west of turret 54*a* is a Turf-Wall turret, and some turf-work was found at its east side in 1933. Nearly due north of Low Wall are slight indications of milecastle 55, partly excavated in 1900, when it yielded later fourth-century pottery. Turret 55*a* (Dovecote), found in 1933, 528 yards west of milecastle 55, is again a Turf-Wall turret.

The Wall now becomes difficult to follow through the arable fields, but the road by Dovecote comes back to it before crossing the King Water. Immediately west of the bridge a short length of Wall is exposed, and in D.O.E. guardianship. Beyond, the ditch is seen climbing the hill to Walton, and the berm widens, doubtless because sandy subsoil threatened trouble, as at Garthside. Through Walton the general course of the Wall lies below the Centurion Inn, and milecastle 56 (Walton) is wholly obliterated. On the village green Horsley saw traces of a temporary camp. The Wall was next located at Sandysike in 1933, on deep masonry foundations near the stream. Turf-Wall turret 56*b* was also found, between the farm and the Cambeck, with traces of the demolished Turf Wall. The intermediate Stone Wall is here 9 feet 6 inches wide, across its flag footing, and it has the wide berm already noted above. Between Sandysike and the Cambeck the ditch is still preserved. The Wall then crossed the Cambeck at the modern weir, but no trace of the Roman bridge has been found, and there is no modern crossing.

An account of the destruction of the Wall hereabouts in 1791 shows unmistakably that it was the Intermediate Wall. "The breadth of the foundation was eight feet; the Wall, where entire, was faced with large stones on both sides, and the space between them filled with rubbish stone to the depth of a foot; then a strong cement of lime and sand, about four inches thick; over that a foot of rubbish, and then a cover of cement as before; these layers were succeeded by others of rubbish and cement alternately, till the interstice between the facing-stones was filled up to the top, and thus the whole became one solid connected mass." The word 'rubbish' here means broken stone or rubble.

The Vallum, of which no sign appears on the surface, was traced by excavation in 1900 in a straight line from Low Wall to a point about 300 yards south-east of the Centurion Inn at Walton, on the north edge of Crowhall wood, when it turns rather sharply to the south. Another southward turn, half a mile farther on, brought it to the south side of the fort at Castle-steads. Having skirted round the fort, it turned west again to converge with the Wall beyond the Cambeck, on whose west bank its ditch is visible.

The Roman quarries on the river Gelt, with their inscriptions, lie about four miles to the south of this point. The most famous of the inscriptions, the "Written Rock", has already been noted (p. 42). Half a mile higher up the river, on the opposite side, is the quarry face of Pigeon Crag, with the names of men from the Sixth Legion. In Cumbria, the quarries which supplied the Wall are generally further away than in Northumberland, though at Cambeck and at Bleatarn the soft red sandstone available on the spot was used.

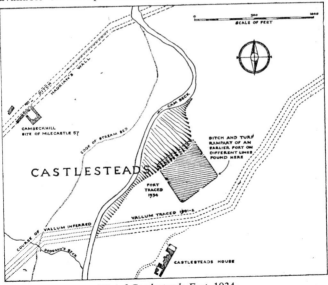

Site of Castlesteads Fort, 1934

CASTLESTEADS (CAMBOGLANNA?)

Castlesteads fort is almost 7 miles from Birdoswald. It lies on a high bluff, commanding the Cambeck valley and the important break in the mosses to the north-west which carries the modern road from Brampton to Longtown. The fort thus guards an important line of approach to the Wall and also watches the east bank of the Cambeck against raiders from the Bewcastle area. The site, however, was drastically levelled in 1791, when the gardens of Castlesteads House were laid over it.

The previously accepted name for this fort is UXELLODUNUM, but (see p. 199) if an elision has occurred in the *Notitia* the name could instead be AMBOGLANNA which the Rudge Cup and Amiens Skillet suggest to be an error for CAMBOGLANNA meaning "Crook Bank". Uxellodunum then refers to Stanwix.

Inscriptions at Castlesteads show that the Fourth Cohort of Gauls, an equitate unit, was in garrison in the second century, and the Second Cohort of Tungrians was there in the third, although presumably not at full strength, since the full unit, part-mounted and 1,000 strong, would not fit into so small a fort.

Altar of the Second Cohort of Tungrians, at Castlesteads

From east to west the fort measures 394 feet over its ramparts, and it is thought to have been originally about 400 feet square, covering some 3·75 acres. Nature itself, however, has worked against the survival of the site and the north-west front has been eroded by the Cambeck, so that the side gates now lie only 50 feet from the edge of the gorge. Assuming the whole to have faced north, about 100 feet, or a little more, of the *praetentura* has been destroyed.

Excavations in 1934 revealed the east, west and south walls of the fort, defended by a single ditch, and the east and west double gates and south-west angle tower. All had been heavily robbed, but roof-tiles occurred in a number of the towers at ground-floor level, suggesting the possibility of oven-bases, as at Birdoswald, rather than collapsed roofs. No contact has been made with any internal building, but an external bath-house was located and partly dug in 1741. Little else is recorded: however, it is known that the stone fort was not earliest on the site. Remains of a turf rampart and earlier ditch-system have been found at the south-east angle. No doubt they belong to the first fort on the line of the Wall, replacing the Stanegate fort at Old Church.

Several interesting altars and other antiquities are preserved in the summer-house, together with a few stones from other sites. The finest is an altar to Jupiter, translated as "To Jupiter, Best and Greatest, the Second milliary Cohort of Tungrians, with mounted detachment, Latin citizens, commanded by Albius Severus, prefect of the Tungrians; Victorius Severus, senior centurion, in charge of the task". This is only one of some 10 altars connected with the official worship of the state gods by the regiment in garrison.

Altar to Discipline of A.D. 209-211, at Castlesteads

An altar inscribed DISCIPVLINAE AVGVSTI is also interesting and matched by others at Greatchesters, Corbridge, Birrens and Bewcastle. Its inscription originally ended AVGGG with reference to the three emperors, Severus, Caracalla and Geta, reigning from A.D. 209-211; after the murder of Geta in A.D. 212, Severus already being dead, it was altered as we see it. The site has also yielded three altars to Mithras, although the temple from which they come remains unlocated, and altars to Belatucadrus and the Mother Goddesses; while not far from it an altar, dedicated to the north-British god Maponus by four German irregulars, was found about 1690.

Castlesteads is the only fort which stands in a southward deviation of the Vallum but is not in contact with the Wall. The engineers chose the fort-site for outlook and impregnability, while the Wall had already been taken by easier gradients to a sound crossing of the Cambeck, where rock replaces alluvial flats. Anyone seeing the Cambeck in spate will agree that the choice was right.

THE STANEGATE, CASTLE HILL BOOTHBY AND BRAMPTON OLD CHURCH

From Nether Denton west the line of the Stanegate is uncertain where it crosses the broken country, cut by tributary streams of the Irthing, in the vicinity of Naworth. East of Naworth, Pottscleugh is crossed by a very elaborate series of cuttings and embankments, in all about 350 yards long, running in from Carling Gill. The Quarry Beck, which joins the Irthing at Lanercost Bridge, is crossed in a similar fashion with deep cuttings to both east and west of Naworth Estate sawmill. These are a good example of the embanking and cutting by which Roman engineers negotiated deep ravines. West of the Quarry Beck the general course of the road was by Boothby, Great Easby and Breconhill, to Irthington.

In 1933 excavation revealed at CASTLE HILL BOOTHBY a ditch, 17 feet wide and 5-6 feet deep, containing fragments of Roman pottery, including a piece of a samian bowl. Behind the ditch were remains of a beaten clay rampart. No further excavation has taken place, but the site, situated on top of a steep bank above the Irthing, could have held a small fortlet resembling Throp and Haltwhislte Burn. Recent air-photographs have shown that much of the fort's ditches have been destroyed by landslip at the old river scarp.

From Boothby to Brampton the route of the road is not known, but just south-east of the modern Brampton-Longtown road-bridge it has again been located, running west to the Irthing. South of here, at ST. MARTIN'S OLD CHURCH, is the site of the next Stanegate cohort-fort, corresponding to Castlesteads on the Wall. The site must have had an approach road from the north, and a road cutting round towards the farm from this direction, swings to the south-west to align itself on the east gate of the fort. Another road runs diagonally from the fort's north-east corner, down the scarp to the river.

Old Church fort is situated on a steep bluff overlooking the Irthing from the east, with a good outlook. It measures 410 by 396 feet, giving an area of about 3·7 acres; sufficient for a cohort of 500. Excavations in 1935 revealed that it had been defended by a single ditch of 13 feet, behind which lay a rampart 16 feet wide, built of mixed turf and clay, laid on a cobble base. The south gate was partly excavated and found to have been of timber, like those at Haltwhistle Burn and Throp.

Much of the line of the ramparts is still visible on the ground, especially the south, west and northern sides, and the north-east angle, about the church. Nothing can now be seen of the interior, but excavation has provided the plans of several of the buildings. A granary lay inside both the east and west ramparts, each

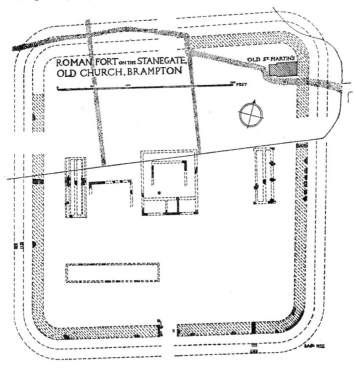

was 26 feet wide and the eastern was found to be 76 feet long. The headquarters (*principia*) lay in the centre of the fort facing north, and measuring 80 by 89 feet in size. Its courtyard, cross-hall and *aedes* were identified. To the west lay a building which was either a small-sized *praetorium* or a workshop; but only part of its plan was revealed. To the south, part of a barrack block was located. All these buildings had been constructed in clay-bonded stonework, but their upper portions were, almost certainly, of timber.

Finds from the site are few. The most spectacular is a Republican *denarius* of L. Calpurnius Piso Frugi, dated 88 B.C. Little pottery was recovered, but that which was, was said by the excavators to be "strikingly like that obtained at Haltwhistle Burn and Throp, in both fabric and type". The foundation date of the fort is still uncertain, but its occupation appears to have continued until the decision to move the Stanegate garrisons on to the Wall. Demolition then followed.

Little is known about any extra-mural settlement; but a large mass of very hard concrete lying at the bottom of the cliff, north-east of the fort, was taken in 1935 to be the remains of some substantial building, or possibly the foundations of a signal tower fallen from the cliff-top as the result of erosion.

Two other sites in the vicinity are of interest. One is the settlement at Hawkhirst to the south-east. This has produced late fourth-century pottery and, amongst other small finds, a late fourth-century cross-bow brooch, as well as a hoard of 3-4,000 third-century bronze coins. Ashlar, flagging and paving stones, as well as a series of brick arches suggestive of a hypocaust, are all recorded, together with two rectangular enclosures. Precisely what the site was is not clear, but it is usually interpreted as a Romanized native settlement of a non-military nature.   Air-survey has produced many native agricultural settlements on the surrounding ridges to the south and east.

Almost a mile from the fort, also to the south-east, in the recreation grounds of Irthing Valley School, a series of 6 tile-and two pottery-kilns was excavated in 1963. In 1964 a hoard of ironwork was discovered in a well at the same site; this consisted of agricultural and artisans' tools, fragments of furniture, general fittings and structural pieces of carts and buildings. All was worn or damaged and the whole had apparently been dumped. It is now in Tullie House Museum, Carlisle. Abundant pottery from the site dates to A.D. 120-125. This accords well with Old Church fort, suggesting that the kilns were abandoned, like the fort, when the garrison was transferred to the Wall.

From Old Church to Carlisle the line of the Stanegate is known as far as Linstock, although little is visible today over much of its length. After crossing the river it runs into Irthington on the line of the modern road. A little over a quarter of a mile west it ran through a large cutting at Buckjumping, 170 feet long and 20 feet deep, whence it made in a straight line for High Crosby. Much of the next portion has now been removed by Carlisle airport, including a Roman temporary camp at WATCHCROSS. Horsley considered this to be a permanent fort, as did other antiquaries, but excavation in 1935 showed that it was another temporary camp, about 240 feet square over the ramparts (1·5 acres in size) with three gates each defended by a traverse.

Immediately west of High Crosby, just to the south of the Carlisle road, another deep cutting is preserved, a scraggy copse growing in part of it today. On the grounds of several pieces of pottery found in the road ditches here, another intermediate post has been postulated, lying between Old Church and Stanwix. The open nature of the country, however, makes this unnecessary. Hereafter, the road has been traced to a point a little short of the M6 motorway, just north of Linstock. For the possibility of an alternative road line, running south of the Irthing and crossing the Eden at Warwick, see below (p. 243).

FROM CASTLESTEADS TO STANWIX

Returning to the Wall at Cambeck, the ditch is seen cutting deep into the red sandstone of the west bank. Cambeckhill farmhouse covers the site of milecastle 57. The ditch is also well seen west of the farm buildings at Beck, which are partly constructed of Roman stones. Turret 57a, located in 1933, is a typical Turf-Wall turret. The Intermediate Stone Wall was here 9 feet 6 inches wide across its flag footing.

Headswood occupies a commanding situation above the valley. The ditch is seen approaching it from the north-east and on its north side there is part of a Norman motte and bailey. The Wall itself, however, here lacks command northwards. About 200 yards west of Newtown of Irthington, the site of milecastle 58 is evident. At White Flat the ditch is discernible. The Wall now follows a field-path south-west of White Flat, where a long strip of the Wall, in fair state, forms a field boundary planted with oak trees.

Centurial Stone from
Old Wall at Cumrenton

Opposite Hurtleton farmhouse the Wall and Vallum are only thirty-five yards apart; the ditch of each is evident, and for a short distance the Vallum ditch is embanked through a marsh, as at White Moss, described below. At Chapel Flat the field-path ends and both works bend northward. The site of milecastle 59 (Old Wall) is a quarter of a mile beyond the turn. In the farm buildings here are many Roman stones; but a centurial stone of "The Second Legion Augusta, century of Julius Tertullianus" is now at Cumrenton farmhouse, again, built into its wall. Here, the Wall is obliterated, many hundreds of cartloads of stone having been removed, but its ditch appears between the road and the buildings.

From this point westward the works may be traced for some distance and an ancient drove-road occupies the site of the Wall. At the end of this lane, however, tall hedges and cultivated fields make the work difficult to follow. A spot called High Strand, the traditional site of milecastle 60, in 1851 yielded an altar to Cocidius, erected by the Sixth Legion and now at Castlesteads. Horseley recorded another altar from the same site.

At Bleatarn, the Wall runs a little north of the farmhouse, the Vallum immediately south of it. Between Wall and Vallum, and west of the farmhouse, a large mound carried a belvedere erected by "Nabob" William Richardson about the end of the eighteenth century. Excavations in 1895 proved Bleatarn to be the site of a quarry used for building the Wall. There is a local tradition that wooden piles used to be found in the tarn; and it is not impossible that the Wall was here carried over soft ground on a pile foundation.

On White Moss, a little further west, the Vallum ditch, as at Hurtleton, is defined by two mounds; in the marsh its steep sides would have been in danger of collapsing, and were therefore constructed by building up a mound at either side, above ground, instead of digging into the marsh. A section across the Military Way cut here in 1894, revealed a gravelled road 22 feet wide, with kerbs, axial rib and lateral ditches.

The measured position of milecastle 61 (Wallhead) is a little east of Wallhead farm, west of which the ditch of the Wall is again in good condition. South of this milecastle two superimposed marching camps are known west of Moss Side and, further south, on the west of the Eden, Roman quarry inscriptions are visible just south of the Cells, Wetheral, a beauty-spot conserved by the National Trust.

About 600 yards east of Walby, where the road turns sharply north, traces of milecastle 62 (Walby East) were once visible; and at Walby itself pools mark the Wall ditch. Here the Wall bends south and, three-quarters of a mile farther on, 500 yards west of the presumed site of milecastle 63 (Walby West), the Vallum almost shaves the Wall without changing course. Nothing is known as yet in this sector of turrets.

In Brunstock Park the lines of the Wall and Vallum ditches are visible as gentle depressions. Excavations here in 1894 confirmed the flat-bottomed section of the Vallum ditch, as found in 1893 at Heddon-on-the-Wall, and also revealed the Military Way, as at White Moss.

The measured position of milecastle 64 (Drawdikes) is opposite Drawdikes Castle, immediately west of the motorway. In 1964 a fragment of a milestone was found near the milecastle, inscribed M.P.

The site of the Wall west of Drawdikes Beck is occupied by the army, in Hadrian's Camp. Traces of foundations, and some standing stonework were uncovered here during the last war.

Tombstone from Stanwix, at Drawdikes

Immediately west of Drawdikes Castle the lines of the Vallum are well seen in Drawdikes plantation. The three large busts crowning Drawdikes Castle, connected in local story with the devil and two nineteenth-century local celebrities, are not Roman, although tradition associates them with the Wall. A tombstone from Stanwix, built into the south face of the house, is crowned by lions devouring human heads, a motif symbolic of death; its inscription may be translated: "To the spirits of the departed (and) of Marcus Troianius Augustinus; his dearest wife, Aelia Ammillusima, saw to the making (of this tomb)".

The Wall, having run straight for over a mile from near Wall-foot, turns on the crest within Hadrian's Camp, and aims for Stanwix. The line is marked by a broad footpath, running through fields and market gardens. The ditch used to be boldly developed, but is now largely filled up. One hundred and thirty yards beyond Tarraby milecastle 65 (Tarraby) was located by resistivity survey in 1976. Hereabouts an altar to Cocidius by the Second Legion was used to cover a culvert through the Wall. Fragments of an ornate dedication to Mercury have also been found. At the presumed site of turret 65*a* the south face of the Wall was found in 1975 in Tarraby Lane, but without trace of the turret. Widespread excavation in 1976, in advance of building, showed that the area between Wall and Vallum here had been cultivated prior to the construction of the Wall, and boundary ditches of fields were found. Strangely, there was no trace of the Military Way; however, it might have been rendered unnecessary by the presence of the Stanegate immediately south of the Vallum.

The Vallum runs just south of the main road from Draw-dikes to Whiteclosegate. It then crosses the road, turning southward across Knowefield Nurseries, and, entering the garden of Home Acres, must have swung still further south to avoid Stanwix fort. The Military Way runs between Wall and Vallum. Cremation burials were found south of the Vallum at White-closegate in 1936, on the same site as urns were discovered in 1872.

STANWIX (PETRIANA, originally UXELLODUNUM?)

Stanwix fort lay on the fine natural platform today occupied by Stanwix Church and Stanwix House, upwards of 8 miles from Castlesteads. The purpose of the site was to guard the Eden bridgehead and to watch the very important western route to and from Scotland. The ground falls away on all sides but the west, and there the Eden, in a wide deep valley, is close at hand. Before the ground was built over the south-eastern slope near Bampton Road and the south slope towards the Eden bridge

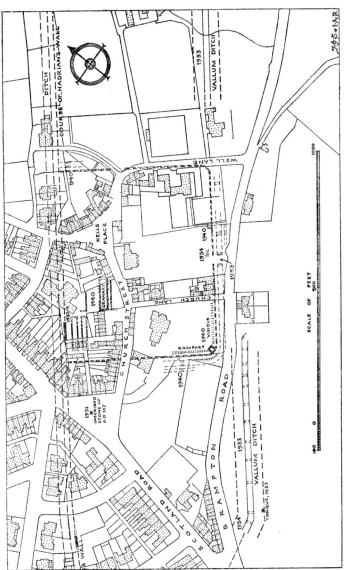

Stanwix Fort, 1940

were covered with buildings, and a road ran from the south gate of the fort, just east of Church Lane, down to the Eden a little east of the present bridge. When the piles of this bridge were being sunk a fragment of a doric column was found, shortly to be followed by a second.

The mound of the south rampart is clear in the churchyard, and the south ditch, with a break at the south gate, was traced in 1933. The south-west angle-tower, south wall and east wall were found in 1940, following the discovery of the west ditches in draining an air-raid shelter. The Wall, forming the north front of the fort, was traced in Stanwix School yard in 1932-4. The fort thus covers 580 by 700 feet, far outstripping in size (9·32 acres) the forts, covering 580 by 400 feet, designed for cavalry 500 strong or infantry 1,000 strong. It may thus be recognised as intended for a cavalry regiment 1,000 strong. This can only have been the *Ala Petriana*, the sole regiment of that size on the Wall. The unit, to give its full name, was the *Ala Augusta Gallorum Petriana bis torquata milliaria civium Romanorum*, that is, the Royal Gallic *Ala* Petriana, 1,000 strong, twice decorated with torques and made Roman citizens (all for valour on the field of battle); it was the senior auxiliary regiment of the army of Britain, and obviously a crack unit. The garrison of the fort and its name, the PETRIANA of the *Notitia*, are thus identified. The exceptional size of the garrison emphasises that this was the most important position on the Wall, the base for aggressive action against the northern tribes and the seat of the senior commanding-officer on the Wall.

A further point concerning the name arises. The Rudge Cup and Amiens Skillet give UXELLOD(UN)UM where the name of this fort would be expected, suggesting the original name of the site, before it became identified with its garrison. The meaning, "High Place", would be appropriate.

In reality, little is known of the fort and its internal arrangement. The headquarters appears to have faced east, and long, barrack-like buildings were found in the school-yard in 1934; while in 1939 a large granary, lying east and west, was found in extending the school-yard, and is marked in its pavement. A cavalry-man's tombstone was found in the wall of the old parish church about 1790, though only the dedication of the inscription is left; while in pulling down the old church a very fine relief of Victory was found, now at Newcastle. Another free-standing Victory upon a globe, also at Newcastle, came from outside the

*Sculptured upper portion
of a trooper's tombstone
from Stanwix
(Netherhall)*

fort; while in Tullie House there is a dedication set up in A.D. 167, found west of the fort in 1931.

In the low ground of Rickerby Park, north of the river, many Roman objects, washed down from the cliff, were discovered in 1934, buried 15 feet deep in river silt. They included brooches, mountings for cavalry-men's uniforms and harness, and odds and ends of metal; all had come from a bronze-founder's workshop, in use about the middle of the second century, in the suburbs of the fort.

The Vallum turns south from Knowefield Nurseries through the garden of Home Acres, and has been traced to a point just short of the south-east angle of the fort. Here it presumably deviated to avoid the fort and is so close to it that the north mound may have been omitted, as at Birdoswald. At the southwest angle a sharp turn eastwards has been traced, whence the ditch makes for the west end of the Park and turns west towards the Eden.

CARLISLE (LUGUVALIUM) AND THE STANEGATE

Roman Carlisle occupied a low hill of red sandstone south of the river Eden, with the river Caldew defining its south-western and western sides. Here, the early forts and later town lay, overlooking the bridge and the main road north. The town's name is given as LUGUVALIUM (with slight variations in spelling) in the *Itinerary*, *Notitia* and *Ravenna List*, which has been thought to mean "Strong through Lugus", or some such thing, Lugus being the name of a Celtic God, identified with Mercury. This name, however, now appears to have been in use by the end of the first century, when it referred to the fort.

The earliest units in garrison are not known for certain, but stamped tiles of the Ninth Legion suggest a legionary force of some sort, especially since the same legion is also attested at the Scalesceugh kilns, only 5 miles south. Two stones found under the *Carlisle Journal* Office record the *Ala Augusta, ob virtutem appellata* (i.e., styled Royal for valour), known to have been at Old Carlisle from the 180s onwards, and the *Ala Augusta Petriana*, later attested at Stanwix, but whose presence in Carlisle at some pre-Hadrianic date seems reasonably certain.

The earliest occupation should probably be assigned to the governorship of Frontinus (*c.* A.D. 75). Thereafter, military garrisons continued until the construction of Stanwix, across the Eden. Within this period two separate forts seem to have been built, one replacing the other, both in the area to the south of the castle. The remains consist of a great timber platform found in 1892, stretching for 220 feet from Abbey Street towards Castle Street, and partly under Tullie House. On average the structure was 40 feet wide, and it was associated with early samian. Its true nature is uncertain, but it has been interpreted both as the base for a Flavian fort rampart, and as part of a legionary building such as a store-house. More recently, in 1973-4, a second "running-structure" of timber was found further north, close to Annetwell Street, beside the Salvation Army Headquarters.

Tombstone of Aurelia Aureliana from Gallow Hill, Carlisle (Newcastle)

This consists of a timber strapping infilled with turf: both early samian and Flavian coins were associated with it. Also from this site came a mass of leather, suggesting a tannery, or some activity better associated with a military depot, perhaps, rather than a normal fort.

After the transfer of the garrison to Stanwix, Carlisle became the town of Luguvalium. By the reign of Postumus (*c.* A.D. 260), if not earlier, it appears to have had the status of *civitas* capital of the Carvetti, as attested by inscriptions from Brougham and Old Penrith. The extent of the town has been estimated at *c.* 74 acres, and its great walls were still an impressive sight when shown to St. Cuthbert, who visited Queen Eormenburga of Northumbria here and foretold the death of King Ecgfrith at Nechtansmere (A.D. 685). According to tradition the mediaeval walls stood on Roman footings, but recent excavation in the northern sector has shown that the defences there incorporate no Roman work. No plan, and few specific details have been recorded, but a prosperous market town can be visualised, of some size and wealth.

Remains of stone buildings have been discovered at various points. They include several hypocausts, one of which may have been part of a set of public baths, and the top of the arched roof of a room, found in 1794, but inadequately recorded. Earlier, William of Malmesbury noted architectural remains, including an arched structure which he called a "triclinium", bearing the inscription MARII VICTORIAE, presumably *Marti et Victoriae*, to Mars and Victory. "Stockades", recorded at many points and previously taken to be Roman work, are now thought to be more recent.

Small finds have been recovered from numerous sites and include a fine decorated bronze jug, now in the British Museum. Sculptures, too, have turned up, including groups of seated Mother Goddesses. The inscriptions are mostly dedications or tombstones. The deities honoured include Mars Barrex, Mars Belatucadrus, Mars Ocellus, the Mithraic god Cautes and the Fates. Tombstones include a prefect of the *Ala Pertiana*, Vacia, a child of 3, and three women: Anicia Lucilia, Aurelia Senicita and Aurelia Aureliana. The finest of all, however, is uninscribed. It shows a seated woman holding a fan in her right hand, while caressing her young son, who plays with a dove in her lap. Above are a sphinx and two lions, all symbols of death.

Cemeteries lie to the west, both under the Caledonian goods yard, and beyond, at Murill Hill (where the tombstone just noted was found). To the east a burial suggests a road running directly to cross the Eden at Warwick. The largest cemetery, however, lined the main road to the south-east, the modern London Road. It began as the burial place for the fort and continued in use until the fifth century. The tombstone of Aurelia Aureliana, urns, coffins and many objects were found at Gallow Hill in 1829; another tombstone, to Flavius Antigonus Papias, a citizen of Greece who lived 60 years, was recovered in 1892. Other burials are recorded, including one with a glass vessel containing bones, together with a lamp and other articles. A stone lion, devouring a ram (a well-known

Tombstone of a Lady from Murrell Hill, Carlisle (Tullie House)

funerary motif), was also found. The cemetery must have stretched from the railway station all the way to the river Petteril.

From the Petteril, below Gallow Hill, comes a milestone which probably marked the first mile south from Luguvalium. Its primary dedication is a unique epigraphic record of the British adventurer M. Aurelius Mausaeus Carausius, who ruled a breakaway empire, consisting of Britain and part of northern Gaul, from A.D. 287 to 293. He was then assassinated by his finance minister, Allectus, who himself fell to Constantius Chlorus, Caesar of the West, in 296. The milestone has been rededicated twice, once to Constantine I as Caesar (A.D. 306-7); the other text has been erased.

To the north the line of the Roman road is unknown where it passes through, or bypasses the early fort *vicus* and later town. The crossing of the Eden, on the other hand, has been deduced from the old channel of the river, south of the Sands, and the line of Scotland Road—Stanwix Bank to the north. This was confirmed when bridge timbers were recently found during the construction of the sunken roundabout south of the modern Eden roadbridge. Across the river, at Eden Bridge, a deposit of 7 *asses*, dating 70-78, was found in 1965. These have been taken to be the current pay of a legionary engaged on road building shortly after Agricola's advance north. From here the Roman road ran through the Wall and, having collected a feeder from the north

Milestone of Carausius, river Petteril, Carlisle (Tullie House)

gate of Stanwix fort, continued towards Netherby and the northern rim of the Solway basin.

The visitor should on no account omit a visit to the extremely important collection of sculpture, inscriptions, small finds and photographs on exhibition in Tullie House Museum, which includes many of those described above. The building itself stands on part of a known Roman site.

To the east the Stanegate is not known between Linstock and Carlisle, but this general line, north of the Eden, would best suit a date after the construction of the Wall. An alternative route, south of the rivers Eden and Irthing, is suggested by a burial due east of Carlisle on the obvious road line leading directly to a crossing of the Eden at Warwick. From there to Brampton Old Church any road is entirely south of the Irthing, and parallels the Trajanic arrangement of roads and posts a little further east. West of Carlisle there is evidence for the road to Kirkbride, which should probably now be seen as the western termination of the Stanegate.

FROM STANWIX TO BURGH-BY-SANDS

Just beyond the north-west angle of the fort the modern road takes the line of the Roman road north, which probably crossed the Wall by a gateway, as at Portgate (see p. 90). No trace of this, however, has been found.

The Wall runs parallel to the Vallum, with the same sharp westward turn, to the edge of the bluffs above the Eden. This is the measured position of milecastle 66 (Stanwix Bank), seen by Pennant in 1772. The ditch is visible descending the scarp near Hyssop Holme Well.

The Wall crossed the Eden below Hyssop Holme Well by a bridge. Nothing can be seen today, but Camden records "within the chanell of the river, mighty stones, the remaines thereof" and when the river was dredged in 1951, some 80-90 sandstone blocks were recorded, including cut-water pieces and a slab inscribed by "The century of Vesnius Viator". There were no voussoirs, but the centurial inscription, and sockets for butterfly-cramps cut into some of the pieces, suggest a Hadrianic date.

This site lay some 40 yards upstream from the supposed crossing-point. The Wall then ran west-south-westwards across the sewage works, where it was found in 1854, excavated in 1886 and marked with stone pillars, and finally exposed again in 1931, when a considerable stretch of its foundation was removed to the grounds of Tullie House. It is the Intermediate Wall, 8 feet 10 inches wide, on a flag footing. At the south end of the Silloth railway bridge Roman coins have been found, on the presumed site of milecastle 67 (Stainton).

Wall and Vallum draw together again on the high ground just beyond the engine sheds and run along the south bank of the river. Here, along the bluffs called Davidson's Banks, the Wall ran near the river, which probably served as the ditch. The Vallum lies close behind, and at one point four or five gaps, spaced at the usual interval of 45 yards, can be seen in its north mound.

East of the measured position of milecastle 68 (Boomby Gill) the two works diverge and the Wall keeps to the riverbank as far as Grinsdale, while the Vallum aims straight for Kirkandrews. The Wall ditch is seen crossing the road at the south-west end of Grinsdale; and here the Wall leaves the river and seizes the bluffs that overlook the river flats to the north.

About three-quarters of a mile south-west of Grinsdale, on rising ground, two small Roman camps, each with four gateways of the traverse type, were noted by MacLauchlan, who gave their dimensions as 80 yards square and 30 by 60 yards, respectively. They have recently been seen anew in air-photographs.

At Kirksteads, half a mile west of these camps, an altar was found dedicated by "Lucius Iunius Victorinus Flavius Caelianus, commander of the Victorious, Dutiful and Loyal Sixth Legion, on account of the successful operations beyond the Wall" (*ob res trans Vallum prospere gestas*). It is now in Tullie House.

LIVNIVSVIC
TORINVSFL—
CAELIANVSLEG
AVGLEGVIVI
PFOBRESTRAIS
VALLVMPR
SPEREGEST

Altar dedicated by a
Legionary Legate, after
Operations North of
the Wall
(Tullie House)

Milecastle 69 (Sourmilk Bridge) is presumed to lie a little to the west of Grinsdale, while at the Doudle Beck MacLauchlan noted a greater quantity of foundation stones than usual, although what structure they might have been is uncertain: turret 69a or a bridge? Kirkandrews church-yard, where a twelfth-century church once stood, lies south of the rectory, and is so stony that Bruce thought it might cover a milecastle. But the measured position of milecastle 70 (Braelees) is further north and the stones probably belong to the vanished church.

The Wall now follows the bluffs to Beaumont, dispensing with the ditch until it leaves them at Dolly's Brae. The Vallum runs straight, by Monkhill and Wormanby, to Burgh-by-Sands, lying south of the modern road as far as Monkhill and then north of it, until the point where the road crosses the railway beyond Wormanby. It is plainly seen in the field between the railway-bridge and Powburgh Beck.

The Ditch of the Wall is well developed at Monkhill Beck, before approaching Beaumont, and going up the hill both Wall and ditch are visible. In a wall at Beaumont, west of the village street, is part of a building-stone of the fifth cohort of the Twentieth Legion. It was fished out of the Eden in a salmon net early in the last century. In 1934, an altar was found during demolitions, dedicated to Jupiter and the Genius of the *numerus* of Aurelian Moors, Valerianus' and Gallienus' Own (A.D. 253-58). This stone doubtless came from Burgh-by-Sands, and its bearing upon the name of that fort is considered below.

The church at Beaumont stands upon a mound, which Mac-Lauchlan recognised as a motte, the early medieval castle of

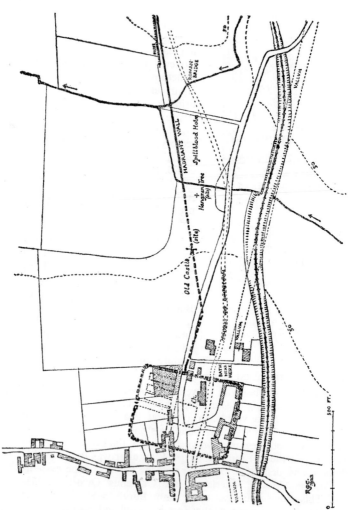

Burgh-by-Sands (broken lines conjectural)

the le Brun, or de la Ferté, family. In the western extension of the church-yard the Intermediate Wall was found in 1928: it was about 9 feet wide, its flag footing set upon a foundation of clay and cobbles a foot deep. The stones used for the core came from Stonepot Scar, north of the Solway.

The Wall turns sharply west at Beaumont, running just south of the accommodation road serving the fields north of the disused railway line. Milecastle 71 (Wormanby) was identified in 1960, close to the north-east corner of the large field where the road ends. Thence the Wall ran straight to the site of the fortified manor-house, where it turned westward, as discovered in 1950. It was noted in the modern road in 1877 by A. Mossman (an artist who did much work for Bruce) as making a sharp turn just before reaching the fort, so as to join the fort at right-angles. At Powburgh Beck the Military Way is close behind the Wall and there are traces of a culvert.

BURGH-BY-SANDS (ABALLAVA)

The fort of Burgh-by-Sands is $5\frac{1}{2}$ miles from Stanwix and was shown by excavation in 1922 to lie astride the Wall on the measured position of turret 71*b*. Only the eastern wall of the fort is known for certain, but its size has been calculated at over 500 by 400 feet, giving an area of between 4·5 and 5 acres. The function of the fort was to guard the southern end of two important Solway fords, the Peat Wath and the Sandwath, favourite routes for mediaeval Border-raiders at low water.

The site of turret 71*b* seems to lie just at, or just within, the east gate of the fort, which was found in the south-eastern corner of the new church-yard, north of the road running through the village. Traces of robbed barrack-blocks also occurred in the same area.

An altar found in 1934 at Beaumont, as noted above, shows that in the third century the fort was garrisoned by a *numerus* of Aurelian Moors, who were also there in the fourth. The name of the fort is ABALLAVA, as recorded by the *Notitia*, meaning "Orchard". A relic of a cohort is a fragmentary second-

Dedication to Hercules and the Emperor, at Burgh-by-Sands

century altar, dedicated to Hercules and the deity of the Emperor, which is now built into a stable at Cross Farm. Inscriptions also attest the presence of the *Ala I Tungrorum* and the First Cohort of Nerva's Own Germans, part-mounted and 1,000 strong, in the second century. At some date before A.D. 241, when the unit concerned is known to have been at Papcastle, a *cuneus* of Frisians was stationed at Burgh, and remained there long enough to take the title *Aballavensium*.

The area to the south-east, around the vicarage, contained *vicus* buildings, and much pottery has been found there. In 1823 a sculpture of Mercury was found in or near the fort bath-house, which was destroyed in making the canal-bed that later carried the railway line, now itself dis-used. The Vallum approached the fort from east and west in such a way as to suggest that it must have made a deviation, though its course has not been traced, and the railway has probably carried it away.

South of the fort fragments of the tombstone of one Julius Pi[ ]linus . . . a Dacian tribesman . . . , were found with bones, pottery and coins; no doubt marking the site of a cemetery. Three altars to the god Belatucadrus are known from the fort, and one to the goddess Latis.

The village church, built almost entirely of Roman stones, is a rare specimen of a fortified Border church. Its west tower is an early fourteenth-century pele-tower, with walls 7 feet thick and an original iron grille, or yett, shutting it off from the nave. The east tower, blocking an original east window, is thought to be the late medieval vicarage.

North of the village lies Burgh Marsh, where Edward I was encamped, waiting for a favourable opportunity to cross the Solway, when death seized him on 7 July 1307. A monument erected in 1685 marks the spot where local tradition placed his tent.

FROM BURGH-BY-SANDS TO DRUMBURGH

From Burgh fort the Wall runs slightly south of west for a quarter of a mile to the site of milecastle 72 (Fauld Farm), identified in 1960. In the surface of a lane running north from the main road beyond this point, the facing-stones of the Wall may be seen, and the ditch is visible in the fields. Turret 72*a* lies in the measured position at West End and its site yielded pottery. At the lane west of the police station the Wall turns

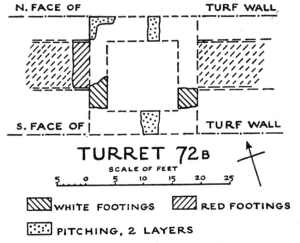

N. FACE OF   TURF WALL

S. FACE OF   TURF WALL

TURRET 72B

SCALE OF FEET

5   0   5   10   15   20   25

⬛ WHITE FOOTINGS   ⬛ RED FOOTINGS

⬛ PITCHING, 2 LAYERS

and runs west-north-westward to Watch Hill, north of Dykesfield. Turret 72*b* was identified in 1948 at the north-east corner of the field north of Rindle House. It was a Turf-Wall turret, projecting four feet north of the Stone Wall. Milecastle 73 (Dykesfield) was then found at the correct measured position. It is $62\frac{1}{2}$ feet from north to south and $60\frac{2}{3}$ feet from east to west, but its gateway type remains unknown. East of the milecastle traces of the levelled Turf Wall were found in 1934. The Intermediate Wall, 8 feet $8\frac{1}{2}$ inches wide, on a flag footing, then runs straight down to the marsh at Dykesfield. The Vallum at Burgh-by-Sands has been traced from the low ground behind the Greyhound Inn to the west end of the village, and it then runs, faintly visible, through the fields to Dykesfield, about 50 yards north of the modern road.

The Wall, when last seen both at Dykesfield and Drumburgh, is making straight for the opposite side of the marsh, over two miles away. It was once thought that it might have skirted the marsh by way of Boustead Hill and Easton; but the location of milecastle 73 makes it clear that the straight course across the Marsh fills the correct distance to milecastle 76. The marsh is probably due to post-Roman transgressions, as at Skinburness. Milecastles 74 (Burgh Marsh) and 75 (Easton) are now lost without trace.

The Wall, deeply buried in the marsh silt, emerges east of Drumburgh village. Its line crosses the disused railway-siding 150 yards west of the road-bridge over the railway. The site of milecastle 76 (Drumburgh) is marked by a low mound 223 yards east of Drumburgh fort. Here the Wall is running almost due west, and excavation in 1899 traced it up the hill to the fort. It is the Intermediate Wall, 9 feet 7 inches wide across the footing. The berm and ditch were here found to be some 24 feet wide and 26 to 29 feet wide respectively.

DRUMBURGH (CONGAVATA)

Drumburgh fort occupies a bold knoll with excellent outlook over the flatter lands to east and west and the Solway shore to the north. Raiders intending to use the Stonewath or the Sandwath fords could be well observed and on occasion interrupted. The site lies four miles west of Burgh-by-Sands and was linked by a Roman road with Kirkbride. Early antiquaries placed a fort on the top of the hill, but did not agree about its size; and were in fact deceived by the deep ditch of the medieval grange occupying the crest.

Excavation in 1899 revealed a stone fort, whose north-west angle was bonded with the Intermediate Stone Wall. Immediately within this angle, part of a buttressed granary was found, in a position where normally the interallum road would be expected. In 1947 it was shown that the stone fort lay within a slightly larger fort with levelled clay rampart, measuring 270 feet from north to south by 316 feet from east to west, that is just under 2 acres in size, over its ramparts. This earth-work fort had been added to the Turf Wall, and faced east. The stone fort presumably dated from the building of the Intermediate Stone Wall, but neither its date nor its size was ascertained. Pottery attested an occupation continuing after A.D. 369.

Drumburgh is omitted from most name-sources, but the *Notitia* calls it CONGAVATA, and gives its garrison as the Second Cohort of Lingones. However, there can only have been a vexillation of this unit in so small a fort, albeit one including the headquarters staff. Very few inscribed stones have been recorded, and only one is of interest: a building-stone which reads PEDATVRA VINDOMORVCI, that is a length of Wall built or repaired by Vindomorucus. This stone falls into place with the records of work by British *civitates* already noted.

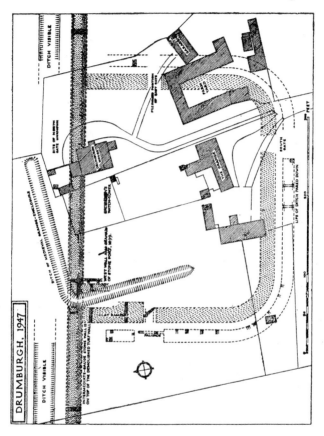

   Drumburgh Castle, south of the village street, is a fine old
Cumbrian manor-house. It was fortified in 1307 by Robert le
Brun, but the present house was built by Thomas, Lord Dacre
under Henry VIII. Leland noted that at "Drumbuygh the Lord
Dakers father builded apon old ruines a pretty pyle for defens
of the contery . . . The stones of the Pict Wal were pulled down
to build Drumbuygh. For the Wal ys very nere yt". The house
is in fact almost entirely built of Roman stones.

Inscription of
Vindomorucus, Drumburgh
(British Museum)

FROM DRUMBURGH TO BOWNESS-ON-SOLWAY

As the road leaves Drumburgh, the Wall is visible on its south side, and turret 76*a* was found in 1948, just east of Drumburgh schoolhouse, and 320 yards from the fort. At the school the road turns north-west, while the Wall goes straight on along a hedge line, and then itself turns sharply north, to meet the road again before the railway bridge. Beyond the disused railway it can be traced west of the road. Along the Solway shore, the Wall runs south of the road to Port Carlisle. The ditch of the Wall is here omitted. Milecastle 77 (Raven Bank) was located in 1973 just south of the Glasson road-junction. It had been well robbed, but some of its foundations remained. North of the milecastle the Stone Wall was sectioned and found to be 8 feet 5 inches wide. Almost 16 feet in front of it the Turf Wall was found, 9 feet wide and still 10 inches thick.

When the canal was dug, in whose bed the Port Carlisle railway later ran, remains of an interglacial forest were discovered near Glasson, and foundations of the Wall lay on piles three or four feet above the level of its trees. Some of the piling timber was used for the jetty at Port Carlisle and the president's chair of the Society of Antiquaries of Newcastle upon Tyne is also made of it.

Just west of Glasson, north of the accommodation-road to Kirkland, the Vallum reappears and remains bold until it runs close behind milecastle 78 (Kirkland), identified in 1934. Sections cut across the Vallum revealed the typical flat-bottomed ditch and turf-kerbed mounds of normal proportions. East of Glasson its line is taken by a deep drain, almost as far as the sharp turn in the Wall west of Drumburgh School.

At Kirkland, Horsley observed turret 78*a*, rediscovered in 1948, 100 feet north-west of Kirkland farm-buildings, in the south hedge of the road. At the beck south-east of Port Carlisle traces of the Military Way are seen; and over the door of Hesket House, formerly the "Steam Packet Hotel", is a fragmentary altar, retaining the words MATRIBVS SVIS MILIT[s], dedicated to the *Deae Matres* by a contingent of soldiers. Beyond this, the modern road and the Wall run out again to the sea-shore, the Wall now running a little north-east of the road; and where it hits the shore there is a mound called Fisher's Cross, in which Roman coins have been found. One was seen by MacLauchlan.

The line of the Wall may be traced from this point nearly all the way to Bowness. From Fisher's Cross it runs at first almost due west, swinging south of the road. Excavation in 1930 revealed the Wall-foundation $9\frac{1}{4}$ feet wide. MacLauchlan noted at an angle 150 yards west of Fisher's Cross, signs of milecastle 79 (Solway House). Here, on the old sea-shore, no ditch existed and the Turf Wall had been built upon a substantial sea-bank.

The milecastle was excavated in 1949. In its Turf-Wall phase it had been of short-axis type, measuring internally $48\frac{1}{4}$ by $40\frac{1}{2}$ feet in size, with a staircase-ramp in the south-eastern corner. Two posts of the south gateway survived, giving a width of just under 10 feet. No building was found in the eastern portion of the interior, only cooking hearths. The Stone-Wall replacement measured internally $57\frac{1}{2}$ feet both ways, giving a square over-all plan, not found in Stone-Wall milecastles. The gateways were of type II or III, but only the solid cobble foundations of the piers remained. These were identically massive, at both the front and back, showing that the gate superstructures had been identical at both gates. Later they had been reduced to posterns, and the towers possibly demolished. A timber-framed building had stood in the eastern area of the stone milecastle.

The date of the replacement of the Turf-Wall milecastle was clear. Hadrianic-Antonine pottery types were found, showing that the early structure had continued throughout the reign of Hadrian. Antonine pottery was absent; and as a rebuilding is unlikely at the very moment of the abandonment of Hadrian's Wall, it must have occurred as part of the re-occupation under Marcus, that is, about 162/3.

On leaving the milecastle, the Wall curves to the north, aiming for Bowness. The Wall, when first seen here by Bruce, was several feet high and gunpowder had to be used to bring it down. Horsley reported it hereabouts 10 feet high. Excavation 110 feet east of the milecastle in 1949 revealed it as 8 feet 7 inches wide, upon footings 9 feet 2 inches wide, rebuilt in the hard white mortar of Period II; and 245 yards west of the milecastle a massive fragment still stands. Turret 79*b*, excavated in Jeffrey Croft in 1934, proved to be of Turf Wall type; thus showing that the Turf Wall, of which the actual turfwork was last identified at milecastle 79, continued all the way from the Irthing to Bowness.

The Vallum is seen in the fields west of Port Carlisle. After a southward turn, due south of the village, it runs north of Acremire Lane straight from Bowness, but visible remains

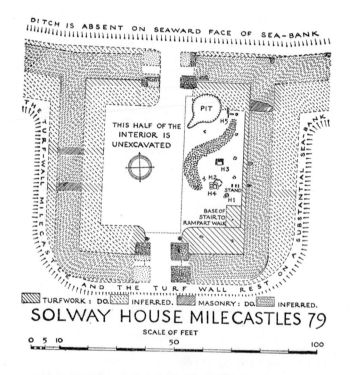

DITCH IS ABSENT ON SEAWARD FACE OF SEA-BANK

THIS HALF OF THE INTERIOR IS UNEXCAVATED

PIT

THE TURF-WALL MILECASTER

AND THE TURF WALL REST ON A SUBSTANTIAL SEA-BANK

H5
H3
H2
H4   STAND   H1

BASE OF STAIR TO RAMPART WALK

TURFWORK : DO. INFERRED.   MASONRY : DO. INFERRED.

SOLWAY HOUSE MILECASTLES 79

SCALE OF FEET

0 5 10   50   100

terminate two fields east of Jeffrey Croft. The ditch, however, has been traced as far as Jeffrey Croft, where it turns sharply southwards as far as Acremire Lane. Nothing further is known of its course, nor of how it ended at the coast. Local tradition places the Military Way just behind the Wall as it approaches Bowness.

BOWNESS-ON-SOLWAY (MAIA)

Bowness, the west terminal fort of the Wall, stands on a sea-cliff a little over 50 feet high, rising steeply from the shore and commanding lower ground in every direction. The cliff forms a rounded promontory, as its name implies, where the estuary ends and the Irish Sea begins. Here, a little east of the fort, was the Stonewath or Bowness Wath, the lowest ford on Solway, used by John Wesley in 1766. Camden observed, in Holland's words: "I marvailed at first, why they built here so great fortifications, considering that for eight miles, or thereabout, there lieth opposite a very great frith and arme of the sea; but now I understand, that at every ebbe the water is so low, that the borderers and beast-stealers may easily wade over". The late Sir Ian Richmond recorded that he himself had seen youths walk across the river from Scotland. Bowness was accordingly chosen as the western end of the Wall.

Altar to Jupiter for the Emperor's well-being, at Bowness-on-Solway

The name of the fort was MAIA ("The Larger", or some such term), given as *Mais* on the Rudge Cup and Amiens Skillet. It is omitted from the *Notitia*. Its third-century commander was a tribune, implying a milliary cohort of infantry, perhaps part-mounted. Its outlines are known, although they may for the most part only be made out with difficulty now, as so much of the fort is overbuilt. An ancient mound, known as Rampire, or Rampart Head, lies just outside its east rampart. The west rampart is marked by a re-cut thirteenth-century ditch; and its south-west angle appears faintly. The south rampart was traced by excavation, in 1930, just north of the church-yard. At the same time, by fixing the position of the axial west gate, it was shown that the north rampart lay beyond the present edge of the sea-cliff, and has perished by erosion. The computed size of the fort is 710 by 420 feet, covering over 7 acres, and making it the second largest on the Wall. The road south to Kirkbride lay some distance west of its present successor, which fixes the position of the south gate, showing that the fort faced west.

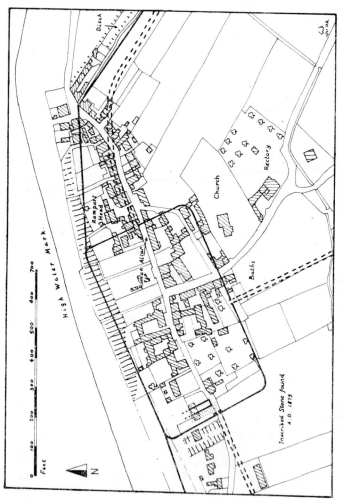

The Site of the Fort at Bowness-on-Solway

The fort's west gate was located in 1930 in Mill Field, and in 1967 its western rampart was found. In 1973 larger scale excavations produced traces of the original west rampart of turf and clay, and the four post-holes of a timber gate-tower. Some evidence for timber internal buildings was also recovered. Later, the tower had been rebuilt in stone, in a slightly different position, and a stone fort wall constructed on footings 4 feet 7 inches wide. Inside the fort, a narrow stone building was erected. This was later replaced by a second stone building, 22 feet 8 inches wide, almost certainly a barrack, which in its turn was either demolished or fell into ruin, so that only its footings remained. For the subsequent history of the fort there was little evidence, although part of a later building survived, in the form of a timber sill-beam.

No precise date could be given to the stone rebuilding, although the second stone period was assigned to the third century, and some late-fourth-century pottery was recovered. Apart from the initial timber period the structural sequence does not appear to have been so very different from that recovered at Halton-chesters and Rudchester, although at Bowness there was no evidence for a destruction by fire at any date in the fort's history.

Excavation in 1976 beside the Police House produced three superimposed barracks of second-century date, running north-south. These had been demolished at the end of the second century and not replaced until a small fourth-century building was erected on the site. This produced pottery and a coin of Gratian (A.D. 367-383).

A large and prosperous civil settlement lay south of the fort, where traces of it can still be seen, lining the road to Kirkbride. A trench across this area in 1938 produced a gold *ligula* and other Roman material. The bath-house lay between the ancient and modern roads, opposite the church-yard. Occupation of the civil settlement continued at least until A.D. 367.

Among inscriptions from the fort, one, now very damaged, is seen over a stable door in the main street of the village. It is a small altar to Jupiter, for the welfare of the Emperors Gallus and Volusianus, by Sulpicius Secundianus, tribune of an un-named milliary cohort, and dates to A.D. 251-253. Another is part of a larger inscription erected to a pair of third-century emperors, now not identifiable. A third, and still more interesting stone, now at Carlisle, commemorates a trader's vow as he set out upon a venture. The words are in verse, of which the beginning must be supplied, as here in brackets:

> [*Matribus deabus aram Ant*]*onianus dedico*:
> *Sed date ut fetura quaestus sunppleat votis fidem*:
> *Aureis sacrabo carmen mox viritim litteris.*

Someone, called perhaps Antonianus, sets up an offering, and adds, "grant that a profitable return may add surety to my vows, I will presently hallow my poem one by one with letters of gold". The final sentiment is inspired by Virgil (*Ecl.* vii, 35-6). No trace of gold, however, is visible today on the stone.

KIRKBRIDE

Four miles south of Bowness the village of Kirkbride sits on a low ridge overlooking the river Wampool, and Moricambe Bay. Part of the site lies under the church of St. Bride, the Rectory, and Bank House farm, as older records and excavations in the 1960s and '70s have shown. Unfortunately, the remaining area has been heavily ploughed, so that there is now little left of the interior of the fort. Excavations in 1976 picked up the north and east ramparts, near the north-eastern corner, where the ditches and some trace of the rampart survived. Indications suggest a size of over 5 acres as likely for the whole. Internally, structural remains discovered consist mainly of timber construction trenches, with one instance of clay and cobble, and road surfaces, together with furnaces, which may have been used to work lead after the dismantling of the site buildings.

An altar to Belatucadrus was discovered in the nineteenth century, and also samian sherds with *graffiti*. Pottery from the recent excavations dates to the period A.D. 80-120/5, suggesting a fort contemporary with the Flavian and Trajanic Stanegate posts further east. Later occupation may be indicated by the discovery of an *antoninianus* of Tetricus I (A.D. 270-4).

Whether Kirkbride was the western terminal of the Stanegate system is still uncertain, although likely, as the date of its occupation agrees. To the north-east a road has been traced to Drumburgh. It runs a little north of the track of the disused railway line, and is known from the Wampool crossing as far as the access road to Walker House. No direct link with Bowness has yet been found, but recently the road to Carlisle has been traced.

CHAPTER IV

THE DEFENCES OF THE CUMBRIAN COAST

No account of the Wall is complete without a description of the western shore defences. Although the Solway cannot be forded beyond Bowness it can easily be crossed by boat, and no fortification of the isthmus would be effective which did not provide against this potential danger. Accordingly, the Romans continued a chain of posts from Bowness to Moresby, consisting of a regularly-spaced series of milefortlets and towers, whose spacing closely corresponds to turret-intervals; with a series of forts interjected amongst them. South of Moresby, the forts continued to Raven-

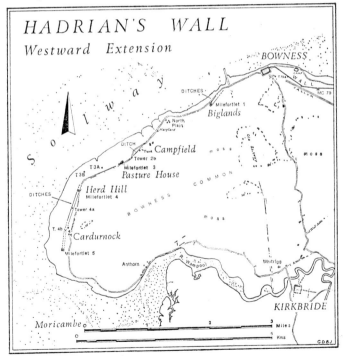

glass. It is thus clear that the Romans treated the Cumbrian coast as they treated the banks of the great frontier rivers, such as the Danube, providing it not with a continuous barrier, which was unnecessary (except in the first sector), but with regularly-spaced cohort-forts and watch-posts for patrols, to prevent any attempt at a landing (see also pp. 33-6).

FROM BOWNESS TO BECKFOOT

At Wallsend the Wall continued to a point below low-water mark on the Tyne; a similar sort of continuation existed at Bowness. MacLauchlan observed that "the old inhabitants point out, at about 250 yards from the north-west angle of the station, a spot where a quantity of stone was dug out of the beach many years since, for building purposes, and the line of it was followed for some distance under the sand, without arriving at the end of it. The direction of these remains, as pointed out by the old people, would fall in with a continuation of the north front for about 100 yards, thence down a natural ridge, well suited to a line of defence, . . .". Reginald Bainbrigg wrote in 1601: "the fundacions of the picts wall may be sene, upon the west skar at a lowe water, covered with sand, a mile and more within the sea, wher the people gett fishe". Many antiquaries noted the submerged postglacial forest.

Precisely how far, or even where, the extension of the Wall ran is not now known, for no trace of it has been found in recent times, but it has been suggested that it was of sufficient length to have accommodated turrets 80*a* and *b*. The ease with which the Eden channel can be crossed at low tide has already been noted, and even beyond Bowness the estuary offers little problem to small boats putting out from the Dumfries shore. This necessitated the continuation of posts at least as far as Moricambe, which has been called the true western termination of the Wall. Whether the first two towers to the west of Bowness were really turrets 80*a* and *b*, or free-standing towers 0*a* and*b*, is unknown, for they have not been located, and erosion may have removed them as it has removed others further south.

Beyond Bowness, a pronounced raised beach runs south of the modern road for some distance, but after almost a Roman mile it begins to flatten, and milefortlet 1 (Biglands House) lies on what is no more than a low rise. The fortlet's ditch is visible from the road, encircling a gently swelling hump in front

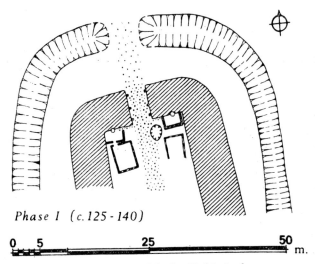

Phase I *(c. 125 - 140)*

```
0    5              25                    50
                                              m.
```

Plan of Biglands Milefortlet, Hadrianic phase

of the farm and recent bungalow. Excavation in 1974-5 showed the fortlet to have been something like 115 by 95 feet over the ramparts, and produced structural evidence for three periods of occupation, all of second-century date. The defensive ditch had been some 14 feet wide and 4½ feet deep, within which lay a rampart, initially 20 feet thick, but widened in the third period to 30 feet. The north gate, facing the estuary, was originally 12 feet wide and surmounted by a tower carried by 6 solid posts. This tower had been rebuilt in the second period, after demolition, but was not replaced in period three, when the entrance way was narrowed. Inside the fortlet two small timber buildings originally lay, one on each side of the central roadway, to be replaced in the second period by a single building on the west side. Behind the north rampart were two areas of cooking fires. The internal arrangements of the third period have not survived. The occupation of the post did not outlast the second century.

Approaching the milefortlet from the north-east, and running at an oblique angle to the coast and the road, a pair of ditches was discovered from the air in 1975. The northern, where sectioned east of the fortlet, had been dug through gravel, and probably measured some 4½ feet in width. Subsequently it had been re-cut, slightly further north, on two occasions. The southern ditch, sectioned a little further east, was a single-period cut of about the same width, with a drainage gully at the bottom. Some 2½ feet south a stakehole survived. The ditches were approximately 50 yards apart.

Beyond the milefortlet nothing is known of the system for a little over a mile. Towers 1a, 1b, and 2a, and milefortlet 2 have most likely been lost to coastal erosion, for no trace of any has been found. Milefortlet 2 (North Plain) is estimated to have lain east of High West Scar, at a point now 400 yards into the Solway, and tower 2a at a point just beyond Maryland Farm, to the right of the road. Tower 2b stood in the second field beyond Campfield Farm, on a shingle bank (raised beach) above the flood plain, 200 feet south of the road and 110 yards east of the Campfield Drain. Local accounts speak of several loads of stone being taken from a building here, and today little trace of the tower survives, although it responds to air-photography. In 1975 a ditch was recognised 7½ yards to the north of the tower, which excavation showed to have been 3½ by 1½ feet in size, and re-cut at least once. The matching rear ditch has still to be located. Chancellor Ferguson noted a paved causeway running from Bowness as far as Campfield, this site; probably the service road for the tower and fortlet system. This too was visible from the air in 1975.

Continuing along the Cardurnock road, milefortlet 3 is situated immediately east of Pasture House Farm and partly under the road. It was first noted in 1880; recently turfwork has been identified, and a slight rise is still visible in the field. At the farm the upper part of the gable end of a brick-built out-house contains smallish square stones, said to have come from towers 3a and b. Tower 3a stood on a lower seaward ridge in the second field west of the farm and, when found in 1880, it was still a well-marked mound. Since then quantities of dressed stone, and some pottery, have been removed, as already said, although as recently as 1945 stonework, including facers, was visible in the plough. Tower 3b was also discovered in 1880 and robbed in the same manner. It stood close to the coast, over the brow of the second field beyond the last tower, and is recorded as being about 19 feet square externally, 13 feet internally. Its north wall had collapsed outwards and extended some 9 feet from the floor.

Much pottery was recovered, including a late first-century stamped amphora handle.

The last tower was particularly low-lying and close to the shore. We now change direction and turning inland a little reach Herd Hill, a stable sand-dune ridge. In the adjacent field to the west, about 100 yards south of the sandpit, turfwork of mile-fortlet 4 was seen in 1945. In the sandpit itself, abundant Hadrianic pottery has been found, all from cremations, and a black band is still visible in the eroding pit section, where local children play.

CARDURNOCK, MILEFORTLET 5

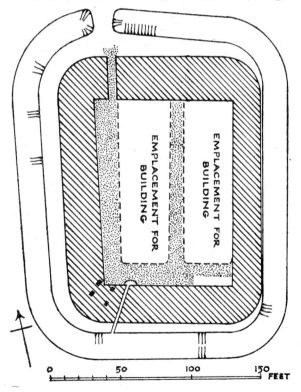

EMPLACEMENT FOR BUILDING

EMPLACEMENT FOR BUILDING

0   50   100   150 FEET

Here, too, a pair of linear ditches was visible from the air in 1975, running from milefortlet 4 to tower 4*a* and a short distance beyond, as far as the Pow Drain. These were some 35 yards apart, that is, noticeably less than at Biglands. A section showed that the forward ditch had been re-cut several times, and had had what appeared to be a palisade slot in its outer side. The rear ditch had been re-cut twice.

The ridge of Herd Hill continues south to Cardurnock village, running west of the road. Tower 4*a* (Pow Drain), lies halfway between these points in one of a series of narrow strip-fields, a little north of the Drain: 4*b* is immediately west of Cardurnock. At each site sandstone fragments have been seen in recent times.

The last post on the north side of Moricambe lay south of Cardurnock village. This is milefortlet 5 (Cardurnock), which was destroyed in 1944 shortly after excavation, for an extension of Anthorn airfield. With it we come to the end of the first stretch of towers and milefortlets, that is those apparently established and maintained as a western extension of the Wall proper. Cardurnock fortlet sat on a slightly elevated ridge with an excellent view: north-west it commanded the Scottish coast, especially the mouth of the Nith, while to the south it communicated with the Grune, and Beckfoot fort 8 miles down the coast. The special purpose of this post is indicated by its size: measuring 178 by 142 feet over its ramparts it had an area of three to four times that of a normal milefortlet. The rampart was turf-built, 21-19 feet broad, breached by a single narrow gateway and surrounded by a ditch 17 feet wide which was interrupted by a causeway opposite the entrance. The gateway, as the causeway across the ditch, was placed towards the western end of the north rampart. This, and the north-south alignment of the fort, at first appears strange, but both are explained if they relate to the linear ditch system, known a little further north. Inside, two timber barracks, measuring 110 by 28 feet, were carefully constructed with a side-drain and raised timber floors. A gravelled surface ran between them, and to the south and west, communicating with the entrance-way, while a 14 foot square timber tower stood at the south-western angle, instead of above the entrance. This position is explained if the tower was a look-out rather than a signal-structure, for the south-west angle commands a better view of the flats of Moricambe than does the north gateway.

In detail this post is so different from the normal milefortlet that it is probably better seen as a fortlet, for perhaps a *centuria*. Occupation, too, continued for longer than usual. Periods IA and IB are both attested by pottery, as well as a later reoccupation which ran through the mid-fourth century, continuing after A.D. 369 without a break. At some date the fortlet was reduced in size when two of its sides were contracted, bringing it down to 144 by 120 feet. A new entrance-way was provided, but the old barracks were not replaced. This reduction is attributed to Period IB, but could, perhaps, equally well fit the fourth-century reoccupation of the site.

To the south stretch the flats of Moricambe, watery at high tide, expanses of mud at low, crossed by the channels of the Wampool and Waver rivers, and backed by the Lakeland hills. The area's appearance in Roman times was probably very similar to what we see today: the most recent opinion is that milefortlets 6, 7 and 8 never existed, neither on some vanished ridge, nor spaced around the shores of the inlet. To the east is Kirkbride (see p. 258), and south across the water lies Grune Point and a new stretch of the coastal system: one apparently laid out northwards from Maryport fort, and one where the towers and milefortlets show signs of deliberate demolition in Period IB as well as, in some cases, earlier damage through wind erosion.

No tower has been found on the Grune Point, nor the sand and shingle ridge which forms the peninsula. Milefortlet 9 (Skinburness) is reached from the unsurfaced road on the eastern

Altar to the Mothers of the Fates, from Milefortlet 9 (British Museum)

side of the headland. It lies in the field beyond the last cottage, where it is visible as a low mound, partly under the northern hedge. The outlook is good: not only does the fortlet communicate north and south, but it looks directly at Criffell, the mouth of the Nith and the site of Wardlaw fort, across the Solway Firth. A small altar dedicated "To the Mothers of the Fates" was found here in 1866, and air photographs suggest a strong post, perhaps matching Cardurnock, with an annexe or temporary camp on its southern side.

From here to Silloth the coast is covered by ribbon development and no posts are known for 3 miles. By measurement, milefortlet 10 lay at East Cote, 11 at Silloth and 12 on the golf course north-west of Blitterlees. Here, excavation following fieldwork confirmed the presence of turfwork, but the milefortlet has unfortunately been badly damaged by both sand-working and wind erosion, so that little was recovered except traces of a rampart 28 feet wide. Second-century pottery was found, as well as one fragment dated to the late third or early fourth century.

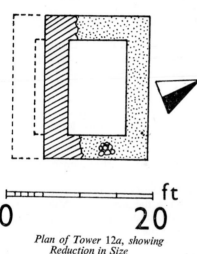

Plan of Tower 12a, showing Reduction in Size

Towers 12*a* and *b* lie in a line extending south from the milefortlet, and parallel with the coast. No. 12*a* was found in 1963 south-west of the old Isolation Hospital, on an isolated hillock of sand which rises 10 feet above the ridges of the raised beach. Its south wall had collapsed in Roman times, probably as a result of wind erosion, and a new wall had been built, giving dimensions of 19 by 14½ feet. Early in Period IB the tower had been demolished: none of the pottery recovered was later than the reign of Hadrian. Tower 12*b* is at the southern end of the golf course, behind Bloomingheather. In 1955 it was found to be 11½ feet square, internally, with an entrance in its north-eastern corner. Four courses of good masonry survived and abundant traces of occupation were found, including 5 hearths, all under wind-blown sand. Later, the tower had been reduced to 8½ feet in size, probably after damage caused by wind erosion, and three courses of inferior wall in reused stones remained. The only pottery found was Hadrianic.

Wolsty milefortlet, no. 13, has not been located, and it too has probably been destroyed by erosion. Beyond Heather Bank a low dune ridge begins, to the east of the road. Tower 13*a* lies just south of Cunning Hill, an unenclosed part of this ridge. In 1954 excavation showed it to have been 20 feet square externally, with an internal platform. It, too, had been demolished, but an almost mint condition coin of Hadrian, and Hadrianic pottery, survived. Wolsty tower, 13*b*, also stands on this ancient dune ridge, in particular in the second field beyond the Abbey Town road junction. Excavation in 1880 showed that only the lower courses of stonework remained, giving a tower 20 by 20 feet externally and 12½ feet square internally. Its entrance lay to the south-east and a "rough pavement" 6 by 4 feet in size was found in the angle of the opposite wall, almost certainly a platform. In 1963 Hadrianic-Antonine pottery was collected after fresh ploughing.

The sites of milefortlet 14 (Beckfoot) and tower 14*a* are still to be discovered. Possibly they lie under the houses of the straggling hamlet of Beckfoot. Pottery has been found in the dunes hereabouts.

BECKFOOT (BIBRA)

The next known post is Beckfoot fort, which lies east of the road, on the measured position of tower 14*b*, a bungalow squatting on its north-western corner. The name of the fort is given in the *Ravenna List* as BIBRA (which may be corrupt, but appears to mean "Brown River") and an inscription from the site records a Prefect of the Second Cohort of Pannonians. The site lies on a slight rise with an outlook to the north as far as Silloth, and beyond, while to the south Maryport is visible, 9½ miles away. Across the Firth the Scottish shore is still only 7½ miles distant.

The existence of a fort here was preserved in the name Castlefields, recorded by Whellan, and excavation located it in 1879-80, when the towers and gates were found. The rampart-wall was traced at the same time, and shown to be standing in places two courses high. The outline of the fort can be seen quite easily in the field south of the bungalow, particularly its western rampart and south-western angle. Its dimensions are 405 by 283 feet at maximum (two sides being of unequal length), giving an area of almost 3·25 acres, or enough to have accommodated a quingenary cohort. Of the fort interior only part of one building has been excavated, but a remarkable series of air photographs taken in 1949 gives the outline arrangement. This shows not only the headquarters, commanding-officer's house and other buildings

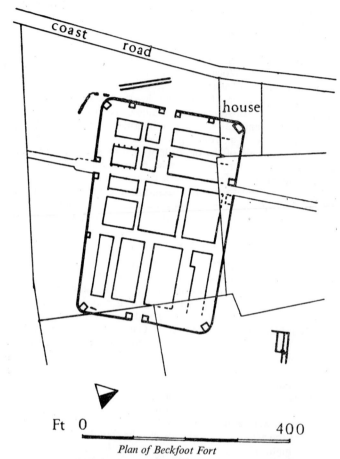

Plan of Beckfoot Fort

of the central range, but an unusual situation in the *praetentura*, which seems to contain store buildings in addition to two barracks. Not everything visible appears to belong to the same period. Finds, for the most part, have not been recorded, but an altar (uninscribed) and a figure of Victory were noted by Joseph Robinson, while a coin of Constantius II (A.D. 337-61) attests a fourth-century occupation.

LIAPRAEF·C·OH·II·PANNON·FECIT

Inscription of Second Cohort of Pannonians from Beckfoot (Netherhall)

A few traces of extra-mural buildings have been noted, including part of a large structure to the north-east, which may have been a bath-house. In 1975 air-photographs showed part of the field-system of the *vicus*. A cemetery is known some 500 yards south-west of the fort, exposed in the dune face above the beach. Finds have been made on various occasions and include material from a complete cremation (now in Tullie House Museum, Carlisle), cinerary urns and stone cists. The pottery runs from Hadrianic times down into the late fourth century. A fire-damaged, late disc-brooch has also been found, as well as a fragment of a tombstone, probably of the fourth century. The position of the cemetery suggests that it began as the burial place of milefortlet 15, but the late pottery shows that it continued in use, serving Beckfoot fort.

FROM BECKFOOT TO MARYPORT

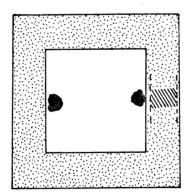

ft

0   10

Plan of Tower 15a (Bank Mill

After Beckfoot fort the modern road runs due south for a short distance, passing to the east of the measured position of milefortlet 15 (Beckfoot Beach), which has not been found— unless residual traces of turfwork in the seashore section indicate its almost total erosion by the waves. Tower 15*a* (Bank Mill) lies on a dune-shaped hillock some 20 feet high, nearly due west of the Newtown road junction. The site is within 80 yards of the shore and is accessible from the track to the beach. The tower was excavated in 1954, and found to be 20 feet square externally, with a door in its north-eastern corner. The original sill showed wear, and had been raised, apparently to prevent drifting sand. Hadrianic pottery was found, and an early demolition was argued by the excavator. Red sandstone fragments were visible on the site in 1975.

Tower 15*b* is as yet unlocated. The measured position of mile-fortlet 16 (Mawbray) is marked by a little ridge, or hill, just north of Mawbray road end. The mile fortlet is now seriously eroded, but rampart material was found in 1969, and later enough evidence was recovered to show that the milefortlet had had a rear entrance, the timber posts of which had been withdrawn from their sockets, indicating dismantlement. Fragments of Hadrianic-Antonine pottery were recovered. Recent sand-digging and the dumping of rubbish, however, threatens what is left of the site.

Immediately south comes a scatter of farms and cottages, marking Old Mawbray road end. Beyond this lies the Jordan beck and a large abandoned sandpit, which has claimed towers 16*a* and *b*. One wall of Cote How, 16*a*, was seen in 1934: in 1937

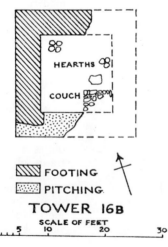

FOOTING

PITCHING

TOWER 16B

SCALE OF FEET

excavation in advance of final destruction produced facing stones and a cobble foundation. Hadrianic pottery, two spearheads and a possible merlon cap-stone from the superstructure of the tower were also recovered, this last being of particular interest. The next tower, 16*b*, also lay in the sandpit, towards Dubmill Point. Remains of two periods were found in 1954, the upper consisting of a mass of clay, suggestive of a rebuild, as at tower 12*b*. Below this, part of the original tower survived, built of red sandstone and measuring 12½ feet square internally, with a stone platform in its south-western corner. Finds included hearths, three iron spearheads and Hadrianic pottery. One fragment of amphora was inscribed "At Esuris (a town in south-eastern Lusitania) III *congii* II *cyathi* (when) vessel (is) full; unsalted . . ." e.g. nearly 17½ pints or 9·94 litres. A little further on, the road turns south-east at Dubmill Point. At the bend Milefort 17 (Dubmill) was discovered from the air in 1976. It lies mostly east of the modern road and measures some 50 yards across its ditches. An entranceway is visible to the east as a causeway in the ditch. The western side is partly obscured by the road.

The traveller now reaches the broad sweep of Allonby Bay, with Allonby village in the foreground. Beyond, the dark scarp of Swarthy Hill rises to over 100 feet, to fall and pick up again as the less conspicuous ridge of Brown Rigg. Finally, the bay ends 6½ miles away with the plateau crowned by Maryport fort. The first 3 miles of coast are devoid of known posts. At Heather Bank, milefortlet 20 (Low Mire) has been found on the low hillock just north of the farm entrance.

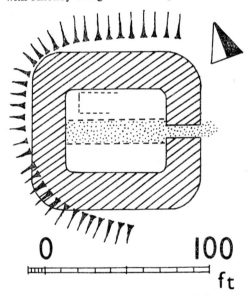

Plan of Milefortlet 20 (Low Mire)

It is of long-axis type, measuring 48 by 60 feet internally, with its entrance at the rear. Excavation produced traces of a wooden building on the north side of the central roadway and Hadrianic-

Antonine pottery, glass and nails, with one early fourth-century pot rim lying beside a hearth well above the earlier levels.

On measurement, tower 19*b* would lie at Mealo House and 20*a* by Blue Dial; conspicuous for its silo. All of these are on a low ridge: thereafter Swarthy Hill starts its steep climb. Tower 20*b* has been located a short distance before its summit in the field north of the triangulation point. In 1962 portions of its south and west walls were uncovered, revealing two courses of sandstone slabs. Milefortlet 21 (Swarthy Hill) lies well south of the summit, under the southern boundary of the field beyond the triangulation point, where it would not have been visible at ground level from the previous tower. It appears to be of long-axis type with a front entrance, but no excavation has taken place.

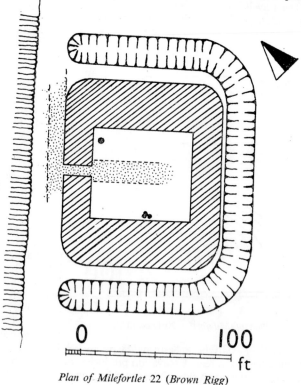

0   100
ft

Plan of Milefortlet 22 (Brown Rigg)

The next tower, 21*a* (Saltpans) was noted by a sandpit worker south of Cross canonby road end, during its destruction "just before the last war".

Tower 21*b* has been found on the northern slope of Brown Rigg. Ploughing has denuded it, removing the floors, but in 1962 two courses of walling still survived at one point. Its overall dimensions were 20½ by 21 feet. Brown Rigg now rises to its full height: a little to the south of its summit milefortlet 22 (Brown Rigg) was found in 1962, close to the scarp edge, and crossed by a field boundary. Its dimensions are 103 by 113 feet externally, 68 by 58 internally, and it is of long-axis type, with a horse-shoe shaped ditch, and western entrance. Excavation showed the rampart to have been 31 feet wide and still to be standing 2½ feet at highest: it also recovered Hadrianic pottery. There was no trace of later occupation.

With this we reach Maryport golf course, where the next tower, 22*a*, has been detected as a rectangular stony mound in the fairway. About here the modern road diverts from the line of the Roman road, the latter running straight on, past tower 22*b* (Club House) where pottery has been noted in a sandpit. It then climbs the steep hillside, making directly for the north gate of Maryport fort. If the next milefortlet, 23 (Bank End), occurred at the expected position, it has been lost to cliff-slip, here responsible for considerable indentations in the coastline. Tower 23*a* has not been located, but on regular spacing it would lie exactly half way between milefortlet 23 and Maryport fort, while tower 23*b* would fall exactly at the north-western angle-tower of the fort. This, and the similar coincidence of tower 24*a* with the fort's south-western angle, force the conclusion that north and south of Maryport the system was laid out by measurement from the fort.

MARYPORT (ALAUNA)

The fort occupies a prominent position on the slightly hog-backed, cliff-girt plateau north of the modern town, with an excellent outlook on all sides. To the north Brown Rigg, Swarthy Bank and Allonby Bay are all visible, with Silloth Mills on the distant skyline. South, Risehow Bank is in full view, while across the Firth the Scottish coast is still only 12-14 miles away, and under good conditions the Isle of Man may be seen. Nothing of pre-Hadrianic date has so far been found on the site and the only possible exception, a tombstone which appears to be earlier, was discovered north of the fort. A fragmentary building inscription, considered to mention Hadrian, is probably one of the fort's original dedications.

The site's name is given as ALAUNA in the *Ravenna List*, and is no doubt derived from the ancient name of the river Ellen. Ample epigraphic evidence attests the fort's garrisons. The earliest was the First Cohort of Spaniards, part-mounted and 1,000 strong. This unit may have been doubled in size from 500 at some date prior to A.D. 130. The most noteworthy of their commanders was M. Maenius Agrippa, who took part in Hadrian's British Expedition, and later became successively

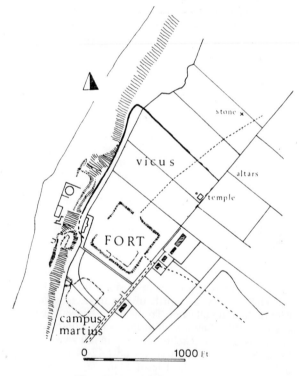

Plan of Maryport Fort and vicus

Prefect of the British Fleet and Procurator of the province. Under Pius the garrison was the First Cohort of Dalmatians, 500 strong and part-mounted, who were replaced before the end of the century by the First Cohort of Baetasians, Roman citizens. These were moved to Reculver early in the third century. Third century building inscriptions record vexillations of the Second and Twentieth Legions, especially under Gordian III, but Maryport's later garrison is unknown.

The fort measures some 535 by 520 feet across the ramparts, giving an area of 6·5 acres. It is defended by a triple ditch system and a stone-faced rampart. The sites of all four gates are known, showing that the principal one faced the sea. Today nothing is visible except the fort platform, which has suffered much from continued stone robbing. However, some earlier discoveries were spectacular: the vaulted strongroom of the *principia*, 10½ by 12 feet in size, was twice uncovered. In 1787 the north gate was cleared and found to be of good quality ashlar: an entire fallen arch survived there, but was removed. A year later an elegant internal bath was uncovered. The *principia* well has

Altars to Jupiter and Victory from Maryport Parade ground (Netherhall)

also been located, and when the east gate was cleared its sill showed heavy wear from cart wheels, 5 feet 10 inches in gauge. Much of this stonework, however, was removed following discovery. More recently, in 1966, an area excavation was carried out in the north-eastern portion of the fort. This established that the rampart was a stone-faced earth bank 26 feet wide. Internally, the buildings proved to have been three or four periods of barracks, or similar accommodation. All has been badly robbed, but nowhere was there any sign of violent destruction between the successive periods. Occupation of the fort began in the second century and continued until the late fourth, as witnessed by a coin of Honorius (probably 398-402) and others of a Theodosian date (388-402).

Outside the fort important discoveries have also been made. The early parade ground lay to the north, and in 1870 no less than 17 altars were found, buried in a series of 57 pits, some 350 yards from the fort. Though no attention was paid to the general contents of most of the pits the altars have certainly been well studied. They are official dedications, almost all to Jupiter Optimus Maximus, which had been set up on the parade ground by the second-century garrisons of the fort, as part of the army's regular annual religious obligations. Later they had all been buried, and the area became the third-century *vicus*.

Intensive digging has been carried out, revealing buildings, mostly strip-houses 20 by 40-50 feet in size, lining the road north from the fort. Some contained amounts of iron slag and much coal, attesting industrial activity. Two buildings were different from the rest. One was circular, 34 feet in diameter, the other rectangular, 46 by 25 feet in size with a square apse projecting from its rear wall. The pair have been called a bath-house, two mausolea, and temples (two altars being found nearby). A spectacular discovery made some distance north of the fort is a stone shaft and base, phallic in shape, 5 feet high with a human face carved on one side and a serpent on the other. Close by was a pavement 13 by 6 feet in size, covering four burials, and a portion of a second serpent.

J. B. Bailey noted a continuous mound, 8-9 feet wide with a ditch on its outer side, running from the south-western corner of the fort north along the cliff edge for some 450 yards, before turning south-east (to exclude the area where the second-century altars were buried), and then south-west to head again towards the fort. In all it enclosed some 30 acres. Excavation has pro-

Inscription for the Safety of Antoninus Pius, Maryport (Netherhall)

duced a Roman building and probable third-century pottery below this bank, and it has been dismissed as post-Roman, but on no sound evidence: equally well it could have been a late defence for the shrunken remains of the *vicus*. Air photography has shown that the strip houses run considerably further north than this enclosed area.

East of the fort there appear to have been less buildings, although it has been suggested that the bath-house lay on this side. The road to Papcastle (Derventio) has been traced from the south-east gate of the fort as far as the Ellen, and thence across Netherhall Park, and away east. Apparently the main road south also left by the same gate, to turn and run under the modern Camp Road. Immediately south of the fort lay the "Campus Martius", the later parade ground, a levelled area some 300 by 300 feet in size, with a mound of boulder-clay 12 yards wide and 35-40 yards long at its western end. Known locally as "Pudding Pie Hill" this was the tribunal, or saluting base, from which troops could be addressed or drilled. One almost certain and one possible dedication for the safety of the Emperor, from the equivalent tribunal to the north of the fort, have been found. This parade ground and its tribunal survived until 1921-2 when the area was built over, during which operation a column or statue base, of heavy mortar, was found at the point where the road passed the parade ground.

Further south still, in the loop of the Ellen, other remains have been recorded. These include wooden piles once seen in the river bed which Bailey suggested could have been part of a trestle bridge, and a wall which might have been Roman. Across the river foundations and remains are known, including the possible line of the road, and a large enclosed area, first recorded by Camden. This consisted of a "massive wall" on the west and south sides, defending an area 125 yards square which contained cobbled paving. The true nature of this, and even its date, are uncertain, but it could be the remains of an early fort or, perhaps more likely, a harbour installation or late defence, some 3 acres in size.

Tombstones suggest that the cemeteries lay well outside the settlement, four examples have been found at the Ellen crossing 900 yards to the east and at the Barney Gill 1,500 yards north of the fort. They include monuments to Ingenuus son of Iulius Simplex, aged 10 and Julia Martina aged 12; also to Julius Marinus, a centurion of 40, Spurcio who was 61 and Morirex who lived to the age of 70.

The very fine and important collection of stones from Maryport, built up by the Senhouse family over several centuries, is still at Netherhall, but unfortunately it is only rarely visible at present, and that by prior arrangement. However, there are plans for a modern museum and public display.

SOUTH OF MARYPORT

On strict spacing from Maryport fort, tower 24*b* lies under the town, and milefortlet 25 on Castle Hill, a prominent headland within a loop of the river Ellen. Thereafter, the next milefortlet position (26) is on Risehow Bank, an ancient sea cliff.

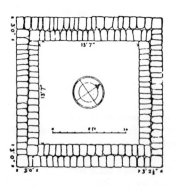

In 1969, traces of it were located, together with Roman pottery. From the site the low hill of Maryport is conspicuous to the north, while Workington blocks the horizon to the south, heavy with industrialisation. Across the Firth, Criffell and the coast of Kirkcudbright are visible 15 miles away. Tower 26*a* (Risehow) is another of those discovered in 1880, and remains the most

Plan of Tower 26a (Risehow), 1880

southerly known. It was found 150 yards south of Risehow Bank summit, when foundations for coke ovens were being dug. It measured about 20 feet square with walls 3 feet thick, and had a floor of cobbles covered with clay.

South of here the site of no milefortlet or tower is known with certainty, but the latest schedule places them thus: 27 Flimby and 28 St. Helen's. In 1929 a Roman quernstone was found on the south side of Tottergill, which may be an indication of the site of tower 28*b*. On measurement, milefortlet 29 would lie at Siddick, where previously marshes extended well inland, across the line of the modern main road. This makes it likely that the milefortlets and towers lay to the east, on the rising ground, which would place tower 29*a* on Oyster Bank and 29*b* under the fort of Burrow Walls. The next milefortlets have been calculated to lie at North Side (30) and John Pier (31); thereafter, the area is more densely covered by modern buildings, and sites less easy to pick. Further milefortlets are suggested at Harrington Parks (34), Catgill (35) and Lowca (36) with Moresby fort on the position of tower 36*b*. On such a spacing milefortlet 42 would lie on St. Bee's Head.

BURROW WALLS

The site of Burrow Walls is not an impressive one today: it is crossed by a railway embankment, and it looks out on to the Siddick marshes, while between it and the sea are the signs of active and derelict industrialisation. The fort is situated 5 miles south of Maryport and 5¾ miles north of Moresby, in each case about half the normal spacing for coastal forts, which suggests that Burrow Walls may not have been an original part of the system. The fort lies on an old cliff top, slightly higher than the marshy area of the coast, which most likely remained little changed from antiquity until the coming of modern industry.

The ancient name of the site is probably unknown, although it has been suggested that it was the Gabrosentum of the *Notitia*. Against this, the garrison of Gabrosentum is given as the Second Cohort of Thracians, which unit is well attested at Moresby. The garrison of Burrow Walls is unknown.

In 1852 Roman pottery and 5 altars were found here, one of which survives today. It is an undated, and incomplete dedication inscribed ". . . and for their children Aurelius and Secundus". It was not until 1955, however, that modern excavation took place

K

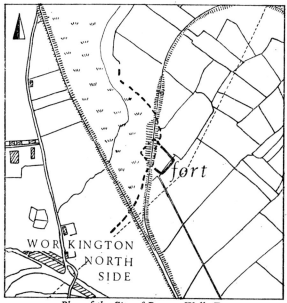

Plan of the Site of Burrow Walls Fort

and the nature of the site was confirmed. The fort measures 292 feet by an estimated 450 feet, which would give a size of a little over 3 acres, approximately a third of which has been lost to erosion. The excavation showed that the rampart wall had been robbed, and only its clay and cobble foundations survived, 8-10 feet wide. Two ditches, 16 and 18 feet wide, lay outside the rampart, and immediately inside it on the north-eastern and south-western sides, a late ditch was found, 15 feet wide. This contained a considerable amount

Altar Fragment from Burrow Walls
(*British Museum*)

of fourth-century pottery: nothing of earlier date has so far been recovered from the site. The probable position of the north-east gate is indicated by a road approaching the fort, but this is the limit of our knowledge. The two pieces of upstanding stonework on the site, lying within the Roman ditches, are mediaeval in date, although they reuse Roman facing stones.

MORESBY (GABROSENTUM?)

The fort at Moresby lies on a low, flat hill-top overlooking the sea to the west and the Lowca beck to the north; to the east the slope is more gentle. In antiquity the site probably appeared more imposing than it does today; but it must always have had the appearance of lying in a slight saucer with higher land on three sides. To the north the outlook could never have been further than Lowca Hill, where milefortlet 36 and tower

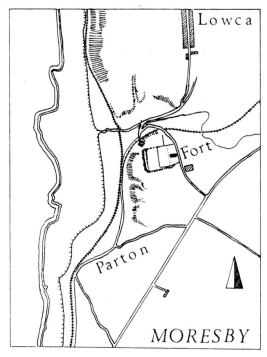

36a must have lain. To the south the headland of St. Bees is clear, 5 miles away. Today, the churchyard of St. Bridget occupies almost half of the fort platform, with the church, built in 1822, sitting immediately outside the east gate.

The name of the fort was probably GABROSENTUM, given in the *Notitia* as the base of the Second Cohort of Thracians. This unit is attested at Moresby by two inscriptions, one of which is probably of third-century date. The name means "Goatpath", applicable to the site and its sea cliffs. Alternatively, if Gabrosentum is Burrow Walls (see p. 279), this fort was Itunocelum. The Thracian cohort was 500 strong and part-mounted, as was the Second Cohort of Lingones, which is assumed to have been an earlier garrison at Moresby, on the strength of an altar found in Harrington church, almost 3 miles to the north.

The fort measures 440 by 358 feet over the ramparts, giving an area of about 3·5 acres; enough to accommodate an equitate cohort comfortably. Its long axis runs east and west, and it has been calculated from the positions of the north and south gates that it faced the sea, as the other coastal forts do. Nothing is now visible, except the fort platform, but nineteenth-century excavations recorded that subterranean walls were still standing three to four feet high, and portions of some buildings were exposed. More recently, from the location of small hypocaust pillars recorded during grave-digging, it has been suggested that the commanding-officer's house lay on the north side of the fort. Finds, and records, however, have been few, although

Hadrianic Inscription of A.D. 128 or later, Moresby (British Museum)

when the new church was under construction it was noted that it stood 15-20 feet east of the fort's east gate. An inscription of the Second Legion was found in the church foundations, dedicated to Hadrian, who is honoured as "Father of his Country", a title he did not take until A.D. 128. In 1860 the north wall and gate, the north-west angle and parts of the south gate were found, but little else is recorded. Coins show that the occupation continued into the early fourth century.

The *vicus* is recorded to the south, where conspicuous remains were once visible, and Roman material was found when the telegraph poles were erected on the site. A small statue of a horned god is in Tullie House museum, and Camden records an altar to Silvanus. In 1962 a fragmentary tombstone was discovered 600 yards to the south-east. Excavation in the church-yard extension in 1951 showed that the area immediately north of the fort had contained no buildings. A single fort ditch only was found there. At the foot of the cliff to the west, a small natural harbour existed until it was destroyed by the railway in the nineteenth century.

SOUTH OF MORESBY, AND RAVENGLASS (GLANNIBANTA)

We have now passed the most southerly fort known definitely to have been part of the Hadrianic system. South, sites of towers and milefortlets are theoretical, but the system is usually taken to run as far as St. Bees' Head. At that point the coastline swings south-east and thereafter faces the Isle of Man and the Irish Sea, instead of the Solway Firth and the coast of Galloway. Here then, is the logical conclusion of any watch-system planned

Altar to Hercules and Silvanus (Haile Church)

to prevent intrusion from the north and north-west. The forts, on the other hand, continue (see p. 36) with a missing site near the mouth of the Eden. This is the Iuliocenon of the Ravenna List, which is the Tunno-celum of the *Notitia*, more correctly perhaps Itunocelum (Eden Head). The *Notitia* gives the garrison as the First Cohort of Hadrian's Own Marines. An altar in nearby Haile church unfortunately only mentions a vexillation, with no record of the unit concerned. A hoard of Roman coins, including at least one of Commodus, was discovered late in the nineteenth century at Braystones, and a small deposit of Hadrianic and Diocletianic pottery has been found at Warborough Nook, a short distance to the south. Although neither is in itself conclusive, each is a pointer towards a site in the vicinity.

The next fort south, RAVENGLASS, was previously considered to have faced inland, and as such has usually been omitted from the coastal sequence. However, arguments in favour of its inclusion have already been put forward (see p. 36). The *Notitia*, listing the fort as *per lineam valli*, gives its name as GLANNIBANTA and its garrison as the First Cohort of Morinians, a unit originally recruited from the sea-faring tribe living around Calais and Boulogne. In the light of the *Itinerary* and *Ravenna List*, the actual form of the site's name appears to have been GLAN-NOVENTA, that is, The Forum, or Market, on the Bank.

RAVENGLASS   *GLANNAVENTA*

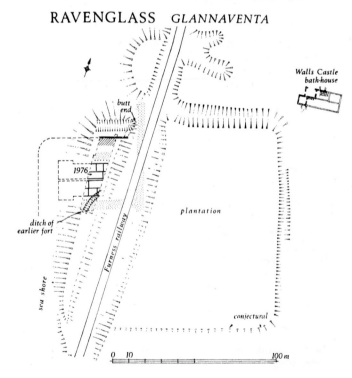

Walls Castle bath-house

butt end

1976

ditch of earlier fort

plantation

Furness railway

sea shore

conjectural

0   10   100 m

Ravenglass lies on the estuary of the Esk, near to its mouth and its confluence with the Mite and Irt rivers. The site possesses a good outlook to the west, sited as it is on a bluff above the present river channel, which has eroded much of the fort's western side. In antiquity, however, the river quite possibly entered the sea a little further south, which would leave the fort well placed, lying above the peaceful anchorage a short distance inland from the coastal dunes.

Very little is known of the fort, today bisected by a railway cutting, mostly over-planted by a fir thicket and partly eroded by the sea. Excavation was carried out in the 1880s, but the site was found to have been heavily robbed, although much Roman building material still appears in the sea-cliff as erosion advances. General finds include a first-century mortarium fragment, second and third-century pottery and a gold coin of Theodosius I (A.D. 379-95). Lengths of rampart and ditch can be made out, with difficulty, in the thicket, suggesting the whole originally to have been *c*. 150 yards square, or some 4 acres in size, the seaward portion of which is now badly eroded.

In 1976 excavation between the railway and the sea produced the outline history of the site. This began in pre-Hadrianic times with an early fort of unknown size and shape lying apparently a little to the south and east of the later defences. No details of this are known, but after a period of abandonment it was replaced by a new fort constructed on a noticeably different alignment. This continued in use from the reign of Hadrian until about A.D. 400, with periods of abandonment in the mid-second and first half of the third century. Although over a hundred feet of the fort has been lost to sea erosion excavation suggested that it had in fact faced seawards, and produced a large rectangular oven of second century date and two early fourth-century barracks of timber, running east-west. These were 28 feet wide, with verandahs. In the late fourth century they were rebuilt as simple rectangular structures no more than 23 feet in width. The whole had been defended by a 23 feet wide turf rampart with a stone facing-wall, and an external V- shaped ditch of 20 feet.

A short distance north of the fort Roman material has been observed in the sea-cliff, while some 30-40 yards north-east is Walls Castle, the fort bath-house. This survives as parts of four rooms with upstanding walls, door-ways and traces of 5 windows.

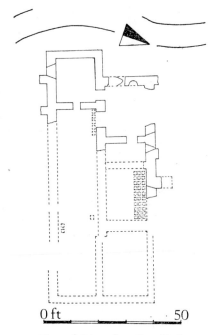

Plan of Ravenglass Fort Baths
(Walls Castle)

Excavations in 1881 produced a fuller plan, but no real interpretation of the building. It also produced various finds including window-glass, arch voussoirs and necked tiles, probably from water-pipes, but just possibly rib-vaults from the heated rooms. This building is one of the most upstanding pieces of Roman masonry in northern Britain, but not today very intelligible either to the specialist or the layman. The surrounding fort *vicus* is thought to have been of considerable size.

No inscriptions survive today from the site, although one was found in 1881, which the workman who found it threw into the sea, because its letters were "English in shape".

CHAPTER V

THE OUTPOST FORTS TO THE NORTH

To succeed, the Wall was dependent upon forward patrol and advance warning of any rising storm to the north. This was achieved by a system of outpost forts: initially Bewcastle, Netherby and Birrens, later augmented by Risingham and High Rochester, and at its fullest also including Newstead and Cappuck (see pp. 36-8).

FROM CORBRIDGE TO RISINGHAM

Unlike the western outpost forts, the eastern lie on a single road, the great Roman arterial route into Scotland known today as Dere Street, which for part of its length is now under the modern A68. In spite of this, however, much of importance and interest has survived along its line, including as remarkable a group of marching camps as is to be found anywhere in Britain, or beyond.

North of Corbridge Roman site the road runs under the western edge of Corchester School playing field. A short distance to the north the Corbridge bypass motorway crosses its line. Here, in 1974, excavation revealed an aqueduct channel crossing the Roman road, and cremation burials. North of the Cor Burn the *agger*, or bank of the road, is clearly visible as a mound 30 feet wide, running for some 150 yards, to the west of Stagshaw road. Beyond this the two converge, to remain more or less on the same line while ascending Stagshaw Bank.

Beyond the Fox and Hounds Inn lies "the stinted pasture" of Stagshaw Common. At its northern edge, just before Fairhill Cottage and a small stream, there is an indistinct rectangular earthwork to the west of the road, some 1·25 acres in size, with two entrances. Although no excavation has taken place, there is no apparent reason why this could not be a Roman camp. North, the modern road has been diverted from the ancient line for the Errington Arms roundabout, where Dere Street and the Military road cross. The Roman gateway of Portgate now lies to the south-west of the intersection (see p. 90).

A little over a mile north the road turns west at Bewclay (Beuklay). Here, the eastern branch road, known as the Devil's

287

Causeway, leaves Dere Street to run via Low Learchild to Berwick. For the next four miles the modern road lies on top of Dere Street, until the two diverge at the approach to the Swinburn, or Dry Burn, leaving the line of the Roman road clearly visible as it approaches the stream. Beyond, it continues north, to be regained by the modern road, which turns through two sharp angles to do so. Three miles further north, on the ridge beyond Waterfalls farm and to the east of the road, an uninscribed Roman milestone has been re-erected. It was found at the roadside, south of the modern twelfth milestone from Corbridge, when the road surface was being lowered, and stands in its present position as a bleak memorial to the Earl of Derwentwater's share in the 1715 Rising. A mile beyond, the two roads part company again at Four Laws, where the A68 takes an easier descent into the valley of the Rede, via Ridsdale and West Woodburn.

Here, Swinehill Camp lies 90 yards west of the road, on a small hillock, with a stream on its northern side. It is almost square, 515 by 540 feet in size, giving an area of about 6 acres, with gates in its north, east and south sides, each protected by an internal *clavicula*. Both ditch and rampart are well-preserved for much of their length. A short distance north, in Vickers' testing range, under the lee of the hill and close to Four Laws farm, 7 circular stone platforms line, and partly overlie, the Roman road. These have been interpreted as a series of signal-beacon platforms, similar to examples on the Syrian frontier, and arranged to communicate with the Wall some 8 or so miles south. Recent excavation of one platform, however, has cast doubt on this interpretation. The line of the Roman road now crosses Chesterhope Common to drop past High House into the Rede valley and the fort of Risingham. At points on the descent the *agger* is still visible. A mile south of the fort Hunter and Wallis both recorded a fallen Roman milestone, 8 feet long, by the roadside.

At Parkhead, on the A68 and near a large modern quarry, the legs of a figure are still to be seen carved on the rock face. This is the famous Rob of Risingham, probably in origin a native hunting god, who was recorded by Horsley and other antiquaries before being wantonly destroyed, as Hodgson tells us, "to prevent the curious from trespassing over a few yards of barren land and from enjoying the pleasure of visiting "the man of stone" who for so many ages had been the talk and

Rob of Risingham, at Parkhead

wonder of the neighbourhood". Horsley's drawing and Hodgson's description preserve for us a figure about four feet high with an ansate panel 29 by 20 inches above his head. The god holds a bow and a small animal, possibly a hare, in his hands and is dressed in a tunic and cloak, with a square block or altar opposite his right knee.

RISINGHAM (HABITANCUM)

The fort is low lying, and occupies a slight mound overlooking the river Rede, and Chesterhope Burn. In size it measures 400 by 450 feet, or just over 4 acres, and it is heavily defended by ditches, still visible on two sides. To the north the rampart is eroded by the river, but otherwise the platform remains. Under a low sun the outlines of what are possibly Roman buildings can be seen in the interior, and in places they give a plan not unlike the chalets found in fourth-century Housesteads. On the other hand, the buildings in question could be the remnants of a long post-Roman village. The name of the fort is given as HABITANCUM on an altar set up by Marcus Gavius Secundinus, a consular beneficiary on duty there.

The visible remains are those of the third and fourth centuries and represent an extremely finely built fort, originally facing south. The walls were constructed of excellent sandstone ashlar, based on a chamfered plinth and backed by a clay bank some 30 feet thick. Angle-towers are indicated by fallen stones with feather-broached decoration. The principal gate of the fort was the south, which has yielded a Severan inscription, now in the Museum of Antiquities, Newcastle, recording that it was restored from the ground, with the walls, after they had collapsed through

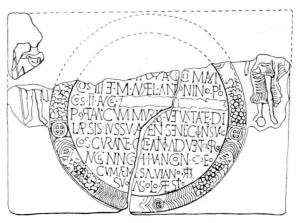

Inscription of Alfenus Senecio, South Gate, Risingham (Newcastle)

age, by order of the governor Lucius Alfenus Senecio, the work being carried out by the First Cohort of Vangiones, part-mounted and 1,000 strong, commanded by Aemilius Salvianus. It is dated to A.D. 205-8. The gate is exceptional in that it was a single portal with projecting, 7-sided towers, built of feather-broached masonry on particularly deep foundations. Nothing is known of the other gates of this period.

Later, the fort was replanned to face west, and the visible west gate is a single-portal gateway inserted into the earlier wall in the early fourth century. A north gate can be expected, but is not now to be seen. Whether there was ever an east gate is uncertain. In the fourth century the eastern tower of the south gate was rebuilt with four faces instead of 7, suggesting perhaps that it had collapsed after a period of disuse, later still the passage-way was narrowed to a mere postern.

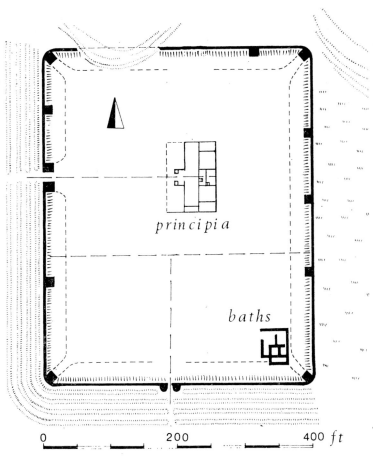

Plan of Risingham Fort

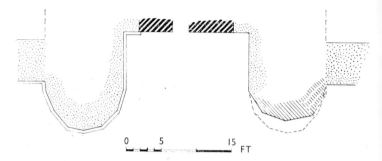

Risingham South Gate, dotting is Severan, light shading early fourth century, dark shading last period

Internally, the late headquarters was partly excavated in 1840 and 1849. The remains are still faintly recognisable on the ground and consisted of the cross-hall and *aedes* of a building facing west. The *aedes* contained a raised dais across its rear portion and apparently some provision for the safekeeping of the pay chest. In front of it stretched the basilica or cross-hall, with its tribunal to the south. To the north the steps of the pay-office window still survived. Outside the entrance doorway of the cross-hall stood two bases, large enough to have carried life-sized statues, no doubt of the Augusti Diocletian and Maximianus. The only other internal building known is the earlier bath-house, which occupied the south-eastern angle of the fort. It was excavated in 1839-42, but its plan is not immediately intelligible. However, it did produce two notable altars dedicated to Fortune, one to Fortune the Home-Bringer by Julius Severinus, the Tribune attested on a stone now at Jedburgh.

The only trace of pre-third-century occupation so far recovered is a layer of ashes and broken Antonine pottery found below the west rampart; but an extremely fine and elaborately decorated building inscription was set up in Antonine times to the Spirits of the August Ones by the Fourth Cohort of Gauls, part-mounted. Neither Flavian nor Hadrianic occupation is attested.

In addition to the Gauls (later at Chesterholm) we know that a detachment of a Cohort of Nervians built at the fort, also, that the third century garrison consisted not only of the First

*Frag. recording
a* Numerus *of*
Exploratores
(Elsdon)

Cohort of Vangiones, already mentioned, but a *Numerus Exploratorum* or Unit of Scouts, and a detachment of *Raeti Gaesati*, or Raetian Pikemen. All of these last three units are mentioned on a single inscription, an elaborate profession of corporate devotion, 18 feet 9 inches long, set up under the governor Gaius Iulius Marcus (whose name was later erased) to the Emperor Caracalla and his mother Iulia Domna, in the year 213. Fragments of the text were found in the headquarters building in 1849 and are now to be seen in the Museum of Antiquities, Newcastle. They match similar professions of loyalty from High Rochester, Netherby, and forts on the Wall (see p. 7). As the thousand-strong Vangiones, alone, would have found the fort a tight fit, it is clear that most of these troops must have been engaged on duties away from their base, perhaps outstationed, perhaps continually patrolling and policing the area in advance of the Wall.

As already noted an early fourth-century rebuilding and reorganisation took place at Risingham. That fort perished in flames, as the red calcined threshold of the west gate vividly attests. A further rebuilding followed, but after the disaster of A.D. 367 the reforms of Count Theodosius saw the final abandonment of the outpost system.

Numerous religious dedications survive; in addition to Jupiter Optimus Maximus and Fortuna, Mars Victor, Jupiter Dolicenus, Hercules Invictus, Diana and the Mother Goddesses are all represented. The figure of Rob of Risingham has been mentioned: Mogons and Cocidius also received dedications, the latter on an altar showing him as a hunter accompanied by deer in a forest glade. This altar is now walled up in a byre at Townfoot Farm, East Woodburn. A more substantial dedication is an

*Altar to the Nymphs
by the wife of Fabius
(Newcastle)*

altar which was set up about a mile south of the fort, at a spring. It bears the inscription "Warned by a dream the soldier ordered her who is married to Fabius to set up this altar and revere the Nymphs". The stone is now in Newcastle.

The *vicus* area is not known, but ample tombstone evidence attests civilians, mostly children: Satrius Honoratus aged 5 years and 8 months, Aemilianus aged 10 years, the daughter of Blescius Diovicus aged 1 year and 21 days, Iuliona almost 17 and Aurelia Quartilla aged 13 years and 4 months, were all remembered, as well as the standard bearer Iulius Victor and a soldier, name now lost, of the Fourth Cohort of Gauls.

FROM RISINGHAM TO HIGH ROCHESTER

At Risingham the road crosses the Rede. Traces of the bridge masonry were recorded by Hodgson at the meeting of the Rede and the Chesterhope Burn. These consisted of stones dowelled and dovetailed together, with dowels and cramps of oak. A "milestone" or marker-bollard from the bridge end now stands in the garden of the Grey Horse Inn at West Woodburn.

Traces of the road have been found north of the river in recent times. After passing under Woodhouse it again falls in with the A68, where, a short distance higher up the hillside, at the crossing of an old drove road, a Roman milestone has been re-erected by the Redesdale Society in the field to the west. Further north, at the road junction for Corsenside, Dere Street is again free of the modern road, as it runs under Dikehead. Investigation there in 1973 showed that the surface was lacking, and most of the surviving make-up material was of post-Roman date. A mile and a half further, just beyond the Old Town junction, the modern road makes a further detour past Troughend Hall, while Dere Street runs straight, under Dunns Houses.

The next marching camp lies at Dargues, with Dargues farm occupying its south-eastern corner. It is not quite square in shape, the two clearest sides measuring 1,014 by 665 feet. This gives an area of about 15 acres, which it has been calculated would be sufficient for 7 cohorts, that is, most of a legion. Each side has a gate with an internal *clavicula*, the whole facing on to Dere Street.

Beyond, where the modern road turns sharply to the right, Blakehope fort lies immediately to the east of the road, its ditches and ramparts clearly visible, with gates to the north and west. In size it measures 390 by 440 feet across the ramparts, or a little under 4 acres, with an annexe to the south, enclosing Blakehope farm. Limited excavation in 1955 showed that the rampart had been of turf, and had at some time been completely reduced by fire. Any internal buildings had been of timber, and the only pottery recovered was of late first or early second-century date. Also in 1955 air-photography showed that the whole lay within a large, early marching camp approximately 720 by 930 feet in size.

The siting of the fort was probably to guard the crossing of the Rede at Elishaw, some distance to the west of the modern bridge, where Wallis recorded remains in the form of stones with iron cramps in them, and melted lead. Beyond, the Otter-burn-Newcastle road joins the A68.

At Bagraw farm the modern road cuts across the next marching camp, which had to adopt rather unusual proportions to fit the available level space. It measures 1,497 and 1,575 feet along its longer sides by 539 feet along the shorter, giving an area which it has been calculated would accommodate a legion. Later, the northern half had been divided off by a cross-rampart and ditch, enclosing an area of about $9\frac{1}{2}$ acres, or approximately half the total. The later east, west and south entrance-ways survive, each protected by an external straight traverse. This camp occurs at the point where Dere Street is crossed by the A68, thereafter it runs to the east of the modern road, making directly for High Rochester.

HIGH ROCHESTER (BREMENIUM)

The fort of High Rochester lies $8\frac{1}{2}$ miles north of Risingham and is approached by a minor road from Rochester village. At the junction, the porch of the old school-house is decorated with Roman stones, including guttering and large roughly-dressed balls, usually described as *ballista* (catapult) missiles. A nearby house has an illegible altar built into its front wall.

The ancient name of the fort was BREMENIUM ("The Place of the Roaring Stream") given by *Ptolemy* and the *Itinerary*, and substantiated by the name of the Unit of Scouts which formed part of the third-century garrison. The site lies in a strong position: it occupies the end of a ridge with the ground falling away especially steeply to the north and west, so providing a clear view over the Rede valley and beyond. In size it measures 485 by 445 feet, giving an area of just over 5 acres.

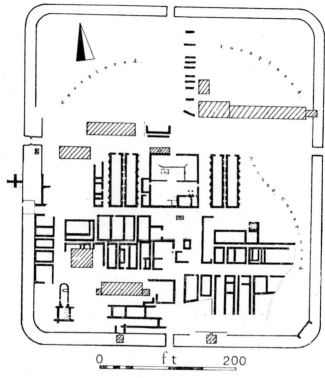

Plan of the Fort of High Rochester

Inscriptions attest the second-century garrison to have been the First Cohort of Lingones, part-mounted and 500 strong. In the third century the fort held the First Cohort of Loyal Vardullians, Roman citizens, part-mounted and 1,000 strong, with the Unit of Scouts of Bremenium under command. Vexillations of the Sixth and Twentieth Legions are recorded, and a stamped tile of the Sixth is known, but the legionaries were most probably employed on building operations rather than in permanent garrison.

The original foundation was of first-century date, and two Flavian periods are represented, both turf and timber, the second following quickly on the first. There does not appear to have been a Hadrianic outpost here, and it was not until the Antonine reoccupation of lowland Scotland that the site was again fortified, this time by a stone defensive wall with a backing bank of earth. The contemporary buildings, too, were of stone. An inscription mentioning the governor Quintus Lollius Urbicus (139-143) records the First Cohort of Lingones as the garrison at that date. Thereafter, the fort remained occupied following the abandonment of Scotland in the early 160s. The remains visible today are substantially those of the third and fourth centuries, with the remnants of a recent village still standing within the walls. Excavation in the 1850s has given us a plan of some two-thirds of the fort interior, which was truly remarkable for its time but leaves many questions of date and purpose unanswered, although later, limited work in 1935 did settle some of these problems.

Approaching the fort from the south the visitor notices the rampart and ditches, still visible to right and left of the road:

Altars recording the Scouts of Bremenium (*Newcastle; Trinity College, Cambridge*)

the south gate survived until 1810 when it was taken down by the local Presbyterian minister, along with much of the walls from the south-west tower, as far as the middle of the east side. The visible remains to the left of the road are the side walls and rear, blocked doorway of an interval-tower between the south-west angle and the south gate. All the wall facings have been removed. At the corner large blocks, robbed from the wall and angle-tower, are visible. To the east the outline of the south-east corner and the east rampart can be seen, but little is known of the defences, or the gate, on this side. At the north-east corner the fort platform is upstanding, with the modern field wall turning on the angle: the ditches, too, are clear. Most of the north rampart has been robbed, although some stonework can be seen at the central gateway, on the east side of the approach to the modern field gate. Originally, the north gate was like the west gate, but in its later period, it has been argued, it could not have carried towers, for immediately behind the stone walls closely-packed buildings stood upon the levelled rampart-backing; a common late-Roman feature.

The north-west angle is particularly high, but here again it is mostly the rampart backing which survives, although at the angle-tower the remains of a facing of massive masonry are still visible, and the ditches are pronounced. Stonework of this type originally graced the entire defences of the later period, but excavation of the west wall has shown that much has been robbed away. The west gate, however, remains at once the most visible and the noblest part of the fort's perimeter. It is a single portal, recessed $7\frac{1}{2}$ feet, with the northern impost and its moulded cap and springer still in place. The moulding is richer than anything on Hadrian's Wall, but in keeping with contemporary decoration at Rising-ham. The gate was flanked by towers some 13 feet broad, constructed with their lower portions at least, of massive masonry. The rear blocking is modern.

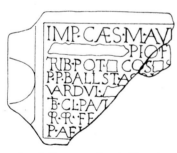

Inscription recording ballistaria
(*Newcastle*)

Internally, the defences were provided with interval and angle-towers in the usual manner. In the third century they were augmented with *ballistaria* or gun platforms, as recorded on inscriptions of A.D. 220 and 225-35, and attested archaeologically in 1935. These consist of a massive packing running back 32 feet from the fort wall, solidly faced and substantial enough to carry very large *onagri* (literally "mules"), that is, high-trajectory machines which could hurl missiles of considerable size over the ramparts to break up any massed attack upon the fort. Elsewhere, in the late period buildings were placed immediately behind the rampart, on its levelled backing. Such are known behind both the west and the north ramparts, the latter dating to the fourth century.

The Principia *Strong-room, High Rochester*, 1852

No interior buildings are now to be seen but ample remains have been found and planned. They comprise a central range of headquarters building, granaries and commanding-officer's house, running east to west, with barracks and associated buildings to the north and south. The whole faced north. The plan is no doubt third century, or earlier, in origin, but many late characteristics are visible in the barracks, suggesting that much of what was recorded dates from the fourth century. The headquarters building consisted of the usual arrangement of forecourt, with a 70 ft. frontage, opening from the main cross street. Behind lay a cross-hall 18 by 74 feet in size with side doors, as at Chesters.

On the south side of this was the normal range of administrative offices, clerical on one side and financial on the other, one of the latter being heated by a hypocaust. The *aedes*, when excavated, contained an unusual feature: at the foot of the stairs of the sunken strongroom a sliding stone door still survived, complete with two pairs of small iron wheels. The room itself was some 8 feet square by 6 feet deep. Flanking the headquarters were two double granaries, one per side. This is twice the usual complement from a fort, but it may represent the requirements of a milliary unit, part-mounted, with attached Scouts. To the west lay another building, probably the commanding-officer's house, occupying the area between granaries and rampart.

The central range faced on to the main east-west street (*via principalis*), which connected the lateral gates of the fort. Behind it lay a minor street and, running north-south, the main road to the south gate (*via decumana*). The plan of buildings in this area, as preserved, shows several rows of small detached rooms similar to the late barrack provision at Housesteads (see p. 146) and Greatchesters. In other areas, such as the south-east angle, the interpretation is uncertain, while the south-west angle is occupied by the bath-house, here, as at Bewcastle and Risingham, internal. Two other things can be seen: one is the arrangement of buildings immediately behind the rampart wall, already noted, the other is that some buildings have been allowed to spread right across the principal southern street. Both of these suggest

Water Nymphs, High Rochester (Newcastle)

that we are dealing with a fourth-century arrangement rather than a third. The northern area of the fort is mostly unexplored.

Religious dedications include many recording the official state religion, such as the Imperial Cult, Dea Roma and the Standards of the Unit. Three altars to Minerva, patroness of a guild probably connected with the regimental administration, were found in a building to the west of the south gate. Hercules and probably Mithras (the Unconquered God) also received dedications, as well as Silvanus Pantheus and native or local deities. An impressive, if somewhat roughly carved slab, now in Newcastle, shows a water nymph with her two attendants.

Tombstones mostly record serving soldiers or their families, including a legionary of the Sixth and a centurion of a Cohort of Dalmatians or Dacians. One stone, now in the north aisle of Elsdon church, records Rufinus, tribune of the Vardullians, who died at High Rochester aged 48½ years, having commanded two previous units and who, in the interim, had been Sub-curator of the Flaminian Way and Corn Doles, and Sub-curator of Public works, at Rome. It was set up by his wife Iulia Lucilla, of senatorial rank. The return of Rufinus to a military command after his two civil posts is not unparalleled: had he survived he would probably have gone on to a procuratorial position. This stone was found in 1809, across the stream opposite the north-eastern corner of the fort, with another, not recorded. Clearly there had been a cemetery at this point, lining Dere Street. Another cemetery is known further south, where Dere Street crosses the hillside 750 yards south of the fort. There, the remains of three tomb-bases were found in 1850. Two were square and one round, this latter still stands two stone courses high. It was originally possibly conical in shape, capped perhaps by a pine-cone ornament, symbolic of the after-life.

FROM HIGH ROCHESTER TO CAPPUCK

North of High Rochester village lies the Redesdale artillery range. Most of the antiquities there are marked by metal posts topped by a white star, and permission must be obtained from Redesdale Camp before a visit is undertaken, in case firing is in progress. Just across the Sills Burn are the two superimposed marching camps of Birdhope, 25 and 7½ acres in size respectively. The smaller, and later of the two, is particularly well preserved.

North again lie two small camps of Sills Burn North and South, the one square, the other oblong. West of these is Bellshield, on the rim of the Sills valley. This camp is to a certain extent obscured by recent fieldbanks, but it can still be seen to have been large, some 40 acres in extent. Continuing north, we reach Silloans Camp, which is bisected by Dere Street, and at a little over 1,220 by 1,700 feet in size is even larger than Bellshield. The position of the side entrances shows that it faced north.

All of these temporary camps lie on or about a straight stretch of Dere Street, now covered by the range road, which runs directly to Featherwood. Beyond a double bend at Featherwood

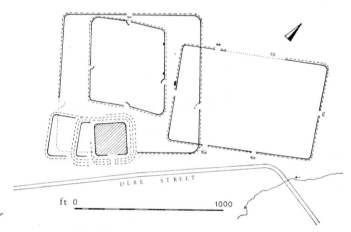

Plan of Temporary Works and Fortlet (*Chew Green*)

is Foulplay Head, with two more camps, each over 40 acres in size. The next stretch of the road has intermittent side ditches, terracing or cuttings, and quarry pits. It runs along the ridge to Harden Edge, where the Coquet valley and the complex of CHEW GREEN unfold themselves before the traveller. This complex consists of three marching or temporary camps, with a small fortlet and attached annexes, all superimposed and crowded "on to the restricted space, until the site became one of the most complicated and remarkable in the Roman world". Although few of these works were probably connected with the Wall system, their exceptional nature demands their inclusion here.

The steep descent to Chew Green still displays the terracing and cutting by which Dere Street swings down to cross the Coquet. Beyond the camps the road *agger* is particularly conspicuous After passing the site the road turns north, crosses the burn, and steeply climbs the hillside, to reach the modern border fence at the site of the small signal station of Brownhart Law. This lies just north of the fence, and measures 54 by 41 feet in size with a turf rampart, 15 feet wide, and ditches. Both entrance-way and ditch causeway face the road. Whether the post was part of a long-distance signal system is now uncertain: to the north-west Rubers Law is visible, down Hind Hope, but to the south posts would be necessary to signal across the ridge of Thirl Moor, and others to communicate via Rochester and Risingham with the Wall.

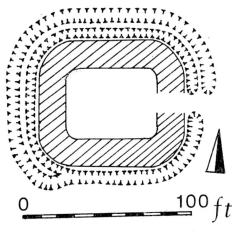

Plan of Signal Station, Brownhart Law

Beyond Brownhart Law, quarry pits, terracing, side ditches and the road *agger* are all visible at numerous points over the next several miles. For the first length of something over half a mile, Dere Street becomes the Pennine Way, where it skirts the steep valley of the Hindhope Burn, before swinging west near the summit of Blackhall Hill. A mile further on it passes Woden Law, to the south, where a native hillfort is invested on three sides by Roman practice earthworks, no doubt constructed by troops on manoeuvres.

North of Woden Law the road drops directly to the Kale Water, which it crosses at Tow Ford. Beyond, it falls in with the modern road and turning beside the school, makes for Pennymuir. In the vicinity lies a group of temporary camps which have been seen, amongst other things, as the base for the troops who constructed the investing works on Woden Law. Between the school and Pennymuir crossroads two superimposed camps lie to the west of the road, the larger of which is some 42 acres in size, that is, large enough for two legions on the march. Inside the south-east corner is a smaller, later camp of *c.* 9 acres. To the east is the corner of another camp, now mostly destroyed, while a fourth, of a little over 13 acres in size, bestrides the Hownam road, to the north.

Beyond the crossroads Dere Street continues as a straight green track, which runs by Trestle Cairn and Five Stanes, before passing to the east of Cunzierton Hillfort. Numerous quarry pits mark this length of road, and its *agger* is intermittently well preserved. Two hundred yards north of Five Stanes it measures 27 feet in width, and its side ditches are conspicuous.

On Whitton Edge the traveller reaches the Hownam-Oxnam by-road, and turning west continues to Shothead crossroads, where the ancient and modern ways again part company. Dere Street has now assumed a direct bearing on the Eildons, which it holds for the next 11 miles, as far as the outskirts of St. Boswells. From Shothead to Cappuck the road is a "green road", delineated by turf banks and hedgerows, some of considerable age. At Cappuck a fortlet is situated on the east bank of the Oxnam water, the crossing of which it was clearly built to defend.

CAPPUCK (EBUROCASLUM?)

The name EBUROCASLUM, given in the *Ravenna List* as lying between Newstead and High Rochester, refers to "Yew Trees", and so fits Cappuck better than Chew Green. The remains of the fortlet are now scarcely discernible, but excavation has shown that they comprised four structural periods. The first, dating from the initial occupation of the site under Agricola, consisted of a fortlet 290 by 218 feet in size, with a clay rampart and north-facing gateway, defended by a single ditch. In later Flavian times the rampart received an external thickening, and a new larger ditch. Excavation has shown that the timber buildings of this period were destroyed by fire; their plan and nature, however, have not been ascertained.

A fragment of an inscription of the Twentieth Legion is most probably to be associated with the next fortlet, which dates from the Antonine reoccupation of the Scottish Lowlands. This was a new construction, 303 by 260 feet across its ramparts, which

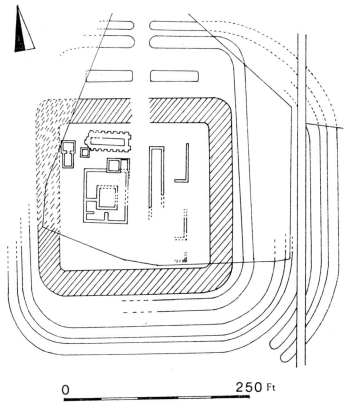

0   **250** Ft

Later Antonine Fort at Cappuck

were raised over the earlier remains. The external defences
consisted of a pair of ditches, and the principal internal buildings,
at least, were of stone. These were an officer's house, a sub-
stantially-built granary, a small detached bath-building and at
least one barrack. Later, this fort was reduced in length to 252
by 260 feet and its ditch system again altered. Modification of
the internal buildings is also attested. The date of its final
abandonment is not known, but it seems likely that it continued
to be held well after the mid-160s, and a date of about 180 has
been suggested (see p. 6).

Inscriptions of the Raetian Pikemen and First Vardullians
(Jedburgh Abbey)

Two inscriptions built into Jedburgh Abbey (some 2½ miles distant) are of interest here. One is to Jupiter Optimus Maximus, dedicated by a detachment of Raetian Pikemen under the tribune Julius Severinus, the other was set up by the First Loyal Vardullians under Gaius Quintus Severus. There is no reason for thinking that the Julius Severinus was other than the tribune who completed the third-century bath-house at Risingham (see p. 292), which implies that either Cappuck, or some other nearby post, was held throughout at least part of the third century as an outpost of the Wall, or was perhaps even the *locus Segloes* of the *Ravenna List* (see p. 7).

FROM CAPPUCK TO NEWSTEAD

Crossing the Oxnam Water at Cappuck ford, Dere Street makes a minor change of direction, but still keeps its alignment on the Eildon Hills. Beyond the Jedburgh-Crailinghall road it is conspicuous as a flat-topped mound 31 feet in width. At various points on Ulston Moor the road's make-up can be seen, while at others it is heavily worn by use, a state of affairs which continues all the way to Jedfoot.

Between the A698 and the Ancrum-Roxburgh highway all trace of the road is lost, so that we know nothing of its crossing of either the Jed Water or the river Teviot. It next picks up in Divet Ha' Wood, beyond Woodside, and at various points the *agger* is well defined, measuring over 20 feet in width. Crossing a side-road, it then runs between Harietsfield and Down Law.

Hereabouts it collects a pair of turf dykes, but in some stretches it still remains in very good condition; this is particularly true in Whinny Plantation. The road then climbs to Lilliard's Edge, the site of the battle of Ancrum Moor (1545), the summit of which bears clear traces of the cutting, 12 feet deep and 25 feet wide, which took the road. It continues the same line to Forest Lodge, where the A68 again joins it, the two roads having been separated ever since High Rochester. Hereafter, Dere Street is for the most part fairly well preserved as a mound 25 feet wide, with flanking turf dykes, as far as the outskirts of St. Boswells. Here the road vanishes as it passes under the railway embankment, and little is known of its actual approach to Newstead fort, by way of Newtown St. Boswells and Eildon village.

The summit of Eildon Hill North carries the second largest hillfort in Scotland, which was once a major centre of the Selgovae. Lying on the western end of the summit, however, are the remains of a Roman signal station. These consist of 6 postholes, indicating a timber tower $11\frac{1}{2}$ by $10\frac{1}{2}$ feet in size, placed within a circular defensive ditch, 7 to 16 feet wide, and entered from the north by a paved causeway. A Flavian date has been assigned to this post, although the only dateable find was a *dupondius* of Trajan (minted A.D. 116-7). At any date the almost total field of vision, for 15-20 miles around, would make this point of particular importance as both the watch-post for Newstead fort, and a signal-post in a larger system. Whether or not this latter really existed has already been questioned, but the peak of Rubers Law is clear almost exactly 12 miles to the south. That hill-top has not only a view to Brownhart Law, but has produced large numbers of Roman building stones of standard size. Any Roman building there is likely only to have been a signal station: thus messages from Newstead could, on a clear day, be sent quickly to Chew Green, if not beyond.

NEWSTEAD (TRIMONTIUM)

The Roman fort of Newstead occupied an important position, and on more than one occasion it was the key post for the whole system north of the Wall. Its ancient name is supplied by the *Ravenna List* as TRIMONTIUM, "the Place of the Triple Peaks", an obvious reference to the Eildon Hills. Its garrisons are known only in part, altar dedications recording a detachment of the Twentieth Legion and the *Ala Augusta Vocontiorum*, the Royal Cavalry Regiment of Vocontians.

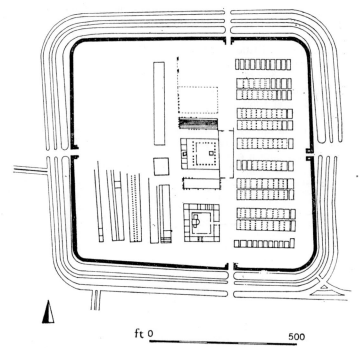

ft 0 _____ 500

The Later Antonine Fort, Newstead

The site lies at the crossing of the river Tweed, below the triple peaks of the Eildons: in modern terms it straddles the B6361 road, between Broomhill and Newstead, with the disused North British railway cutting across the southern and eastern sides of the complex. Nothing is visible on the site today except a modern inscription, but its role as a late second-century outpost of the Wall warrants its inclusion in this volume. The earliest Roman features are the remains of a series of marching camps, two of which, known in full, are just over 40 and a little under 50 acres in size. These were succeeded by a complex of forts each of which was accompanied by at least one annexe which was usually modified in succeeding periods, until the south, west and eastern sides of the fort were surrounded by a network of abandoned and modified enclosures.

The first permanent fort, built during Agricola's northern campaigns, was quite exceptional in its plan. At each of its four gates, centrally placed, the rampart was staggered so as to expose attackers to fire from the right. This type of arrangement is extremely rare, but it displays characteristics of Agricolan forts elsewhere in Scotland. Two ditches completed the defences, while a 7-acre annexe to the west and another of 20 acres to the east seem to be contemporary. The fort was 655 by 705 feet in size, giving an area of 10·6 acres, which is unusually large. The interior layout, like the garrison, is unknown, although the one building traced by excavation has been identified as a timber stable.

The first fort was replaced soon after A.D. 86 by a second and even larger one, 760 by 820 feet, or 14·3 acres in size. The rampart was thickened to a huge 43 feet in width, and has been estimated to have stood at least 28 feet high. This indicates a post of exceptional strength, as would befit the main defensive site remaining in south-eastern Scotland after the withdrawal from the Highland line. A single ditch, well over 16 feet wide, defended the rampart. Again, little is known of the garrison, except that one double barrack, probably legionary, has been excavated in the *retentura*, while another in the *praetentura* appears to be of auxiliary size. Stone foundations suggest stone sill walls now supported the timber buildings.

Externally, the eastern annexe was modified, while we know that the western annex now, if not earlier, received a *mansio* and a bath-house, suggesting that Newstead was an important road-post. The southern annexe of 14½ acres probably belongs to this period, while some half mile to the south of the main fort, just north of the Bogle Burn, a small post 180 feet square has produced fragmentary Flavian samian ware.

The second Flavian fort perished by fire, almost certainly the result of enemy action, for not only were its internal buildings burnt, but various pits have been found to contain occupation debris, including damaged weapons and armour, the most conspicuous pieces of which are visored parade helmets worn by cavalry troopers on ceremonial occasions. The date of this disaster is usually taken to be the same as that which ended the contemporary fort at Corbridge, early in the reign of Trajan.

The first Antonine fort on the site was also large, 14·7 acres, with a broad stone wall facing a 36 foot rampart. Two ditches completed the defences. Inside the fort the headquarters was altered, now to face east, and a granary has been identified on either side of it. To the south was the commanding-officer's house while a large, but unidentified building or pair of buildings lay in a comparable position to the north. An altar dedicated by G. Arrius Domitianus, a centurion of the Twentieth Legion, came from a well in the headquarters, along with both legionary and auxiliary arms and armour.

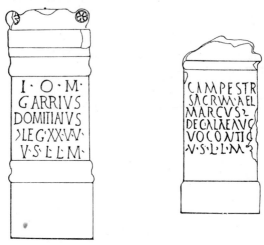

Altars set up by the Twentieth Legion and the Vocontians (*Edinburgh*)

The *praetentura* has been found to contain 12 barrack blocks, again probably for a legionary vexillation, while the *retentura* was divided from the rest of the interior by a cross-wall with central gateway, built of masonry rather inferior to the rest of the fort. No *retentura* barracks definitely belonging to this period have been found, but Sir Ian Richmond suggested that the enclosed area would have contained a cavalry regiment 500 strong, the *Ala Vocontiorum*. The eastern annexe received some modifications, while the western bath-house was provided with a defensive bank of its own, cutting it off from the *mansio*.

The shortest of periods of abandonment, only, separated the last period from the next, for virtually no silt had accumulated in the first Antonine ditches before they were filled at the start of the next period. A new triple ditch system was then provided. The size of the fort remained the same, but its rampart was extended backwards across the *intervallum* road to an unparalleled 54 feet. No doubt it was of corresponding height, creating again an exceptionally large and impregnable stronghold. Within the fort the dividing wall was dismantled and stables were built, east-west, across the whole of the *retentura* area. The 12 barracks of the *praetentura* continued in use. It has been suggested that all of this was provision for the 24 *turmae* of a milliary *Ala*, but as only one such unit is known to have been stationed in Britain, and it is believed to have lain at Stanwix at this time, its presence at Newstead is unlikely.

That cavalry was the garrison in this period, however, is suggested by the addition of a huge cross-hall 50 by 160 feet in size, which was constructed across the *via principalis* directly in front of the headquarters building. The *principia* itself received modifications, including a sunken strongroom below its *aedes*, but no other radical changes seems to have occurred in the central range. Outside the fort further modification of the annexes occurred.

The only inscribed stones from the site are a series of altars, mostly recording the Twentieth Legion, although one records the Vocontians. No building inscription, unfortunately, is known, but a remarkable collection of tools, implements, weapons and armour has been recovered from pits, mostly to the south of the fort. The finds are now on permanent exhibition in the National Museum, Edinburgh.

NETHERBY (AXELODVNUM? later CASTRA EXPLORATORUM)

The western Roman trunk road, running north from Carlisle, has already been described as far as Stanwix (see p. 242). Its line north is known beyond the Wall, continuing to the east of the A7-M6 intersection. At Blackford the two converge and remain together as far as Westlinton. Beyond, the Roman road must have turned slightly east to make for Netherby, where it branched, one arm running via Gilnockie to Broomholme, which may have fitted into the Trajanic-Hadrianic frontier-system, the other making for Birrens, the most westerly outpost fort.

The site of NETHERBY is low-lying, overlooking the River Esk from the east. Its name is given in the *Itinerary* as CASTRA EXPLORATORUM, the Fort of the Scouts, which tells us some-

L

Inscription Recording a Cavalry Drill-Hall
(Tullie House)

Relief of a Genius, Netherby
(Tullie House)

thing of the third-century garrison. However, it almost certainly had an official name, and the *Notitia* puts the known third-century garrison of Netherby at Axelodunum, which is traditionally amended to Uxellodunum and taken to be Castlesteads. The First Cohort of Spaniards, however, is not amongst the three units attested at Castlesteads, and the *axelo-*portion of the *Notitia* name could well relate to Netherby, situated on the Esk. The Uxellodunum of the Amiens Skillet, by contrast, appears to refer to Stanwix.

The early garrison of the fort is not known, but in the third century, an altar tells us, it held the First Aelian Cohort of Spaniards, part-mounted and 1,000 strong; as well as, presumably, a detachment or unit of Scouts.

The fort itself was known only to the earliest antiquaries, and little of it has been recorded. The original house, or castle of Netherby occupied its centre, but from the early eighteenth century, or even earlier, improvements began, which gradually transformed the building and its surroundings into the residence and park we see today. The *vicus* lay to the north and west and there is more than the suggestion of a harbour on the river. In the *vicus* the bath-house was found in 1732 and recorded. It is of the normal Hadrianic plan, as Benwell and Chesters (see p. 117), with a cold room and bath, warm and hot rooms and hot dry room; all noted. In the cold room an altar to Fortuna was found, dedicated by Marcus Aurelius Salvius, tribune of the Cohort of Spaniards.

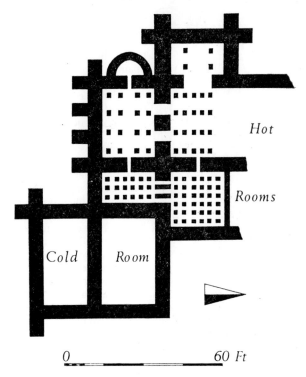

Plan of Netherby Fort Baths, 1732

The site may have had a Flavian occupation, we do not know. An inscription to Hadrian, recording the Second Legion, confirms that an original outpost fort lay here, while a fragment mentioning the Emperor Commodus as consul implies something occurring in the year 177. Later, in 213, the garrison set up a dedication "Out of Common Duty and Devotion" to Caracalla and Julia Domna, under the governor Gaius Iulius Marcus, matching those found elsewhere (see p. 7). In 219 detachments of the Second and Twentieth Legions were here, probably assisting in building operations, and a slab of 222 records the completion of "the cavalry drill-hall, long since begun, from the ground" by the Spaniards, commanded by the same Marcus Aurelius Salvius who dedicated to Fortuna in the baths. This hall most probably stood in the centre of the fort, across the two principal streets, as did a similar one at Haltonchesters in the third century. Later, the inscription was reused as a drain cover, suggesting alterations sometime during the fourth century.

Tombstone of Titullina Pussitta
(Tullie House)

Altars are dedicated to Jupiter Optimus Maximus, Apollo, Cocidius (which may be a stray from Bewcastle), Silvanus, Mogons Vitris, Mars Belatucadrus, and other local deities. The one definite tombstone records Titullina Pussitta, a Raetian lady aged 35 years and 8 months. Several pieces of sculpture come from the site. One is a most impressive figure of a Genius, found before 1725, another is part of a decorated relief showing a Pegasus in flight, a third of a Celtic horned god, while two others show a further Celtic deity with a wheel, cornucopia and altar. All, along with several other stones, are now in Tullie House Museum.

BIRRENS (BLATOBULGIUM)

Birrens fort lies 1½ miles east of Ecclefechan. The *Itinerary* places it and Netherby next to each other, implying that the normal route from Birrens to Carlisle lay via Netherby. If this was the case the line of that road has not been found; but an alternative is known, branching from the Carlisle-Netherby road and running by way of Blackbank (close to the battlefield of Solway Moss) and Gretna Green. From there General Roy recorded that the road ran on to Birrens: "for many miles together the vestiges of it are distinctly to be seen". Today, the modern road overlies this line in part.

The fort lies on the north side of the Mein Water, which has eroded its southern rampart. A minor road to Middlebie runs along the east side of the site, and the main line from Carlisle to Carstairs Junction brushes the south-west corner with an embankment and viaduct.

The ancient name is given in the *Itinerary* as BLATOBULGIUM, meaning either "the Floury Hollow (or Hillock)", or "the Flour Sack", the latter referring either to well-stocked granaries, or perhaps, the shape of Burnswark Hill to the north-west. The

Altar showing the Fort Aedes, *Birrens (Edinburgh)*

visible remains are those of the Antonine forts, with an enclosure lying to the west. The earliest garrison is not known, but in the first Antonine Period it was probably the First Nervan Cohort of Germans, part-mounted and 1,000 strong, and in the second the Second Cohort of Tungrians, part-mounted, 1,000 strong, citizens with Latin Rights. A detachment of this unit was serving in Raetia from 121/5 to 153, and during that time it recruited Germans into its ranks. The dedications to the deities of these Germans set up after the detachment's return, make up one of the most interesting groups of altars from the site.

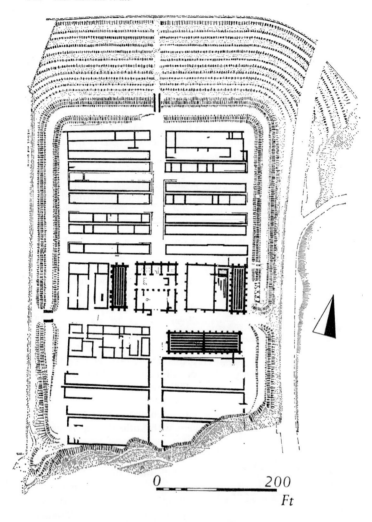

The Antonine Forts at Birrens

The earliest fort was Flavian in date and small; not larger than 1·32 acres it has been calculated. Its west ditch and north-west corner have been found under-lying the south-west portion of the visible platform. This was replaced by a larger fort dated by Hadrianic pottery and, possibly, a missing inscription which Thomas Pennant recorded, commemorating Hadrian and the Second Legion. An outpost here might seem far west, but if the

Altar to Harimella, Birrens
(Edinburgh)

purpose of the original outliers of the Wall was to control the northern edge of the Solway basin, a western blocking fort was necessary, and Birrens, some 8 miles from the coast and covering the all-important Annandale route north, is crucially placed. The Hadrianic fort was some 464 by 390 feet in size, giving an area of 4·2 acres, with turf ramparts and timber buildings, except for the central range which was of stone. A western annexe appears to have been attached.

With the Antonine advance into Scotland the Hadrianic fort was demolished and replaced by a longer stone fort measuring 550 by 385 feet, that is 4·9 acres in size. This is basically the fort platform to be seen by the visitor today. The defences were a ditch system and turf rampart set upon a stone base, at least 18 feet wide. To the north 6 ditches can still be traced, with a central causeway. On the north, east and west sides the rampart is still upstanding, with gaps for three gates, but to the south, river erosion has removed almost all trace of the defences.

Internally, the buildings were of red standstone, and very well constructed, suggesting legionary work. The arrangement was normal: the central range consisted of a headquarters building, commanding-officer's house and two granaries, along with an additional building of unknown purpose. To the north lay two narrow store-buildings and at least 6 barracks, three on each side of the central roadway (*via praetoria*). Each had a double central wall, so that at first glance they appear more like a pair of narrow sheds than a barrack. The two most northerly buildings seem to have been larger than the others, but this is probably the result of their being rebuilt at a later date. All these barracks were laid out at right angles to the long axis of the fort. To the south of the central range lay an additional double granary, the two sections placed endways to each other; also, what may have been workshops, a hospital or possibly more officers' accommodation. South again were four more barracks, and two narrow store-buildings. The whole faced south.

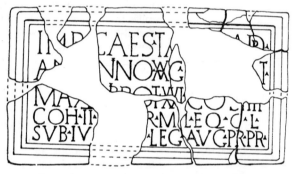

Inscription of Julius Verus, Principia, *Birrens* (*Edinburgh*)

This fort was destroyed by fire, which, in the words of its most recent excavator, Professor Anne Robertson, "seems less likely to have been Roman and orderly, than savage and wayward". The site was then extensively rebuilt in A.D. 158, under the governor Julius Verus (as an inscription records), when the Second Cohort of Tungrians, 1,000 strong and part-mounted came into garrison. The internal buildings were in some cases much modified, but their arrangement and number remained basically the same as before. Alterations were visible in the central range, too, with modifications to the commanding-officer's house, and extra granary provision. In all of this, however, the workmanship was of such inferior quality that it can certainly be attributed to auxiliary craftsmen. The rampart was cut back and a new turf face added.

The Antonine occupation of Scotland effectively ended in the early 160s, but Birrens, as a handful of other sites, was maintained as an outpost of Hadrian's Wall until towards the end of the second century (see p. 6). A date in the early 180s, during the governorship of Ulpius Marcellus, has been proposed for the final abandonment of the site.

West of the upstanding fort platform, air-photography and slight surface indications show what is either another Flavian fort or, more likely, the annexe attached to the Hadrianic and Antonine forts. It lies on a slightly more north-west/south-east axis than the fort, with its south-western corner brushed by the railway embankment and its southern sides removed by river erosion. In 1731 Sir John Clerk recorded "long buildings which I take to have been stables for horses" running north-south in the eastern part of this annexe, and more recently pieces of third-century pottery have been picked up in the river bed opposite it. These, and third-century coins attributed to the site, may indicate a more complex history than usually accepted. One possibility is that Birrens was the *locus Maponi* of the *Ravenna List* (see below). North of the annexe what has been called a *mansio* has been seen on air photographs, while a small fortlet lies to the south.

The Goddess, Brigantia, Birrens (Edinburgh)

Many altars come from the site. These include the usual official dedications to Jupiter Optimus Maximus. Another, to Imperial Discipline, shows a front view of the *aedes* of the headquarters with its doors closed, carved on the capital. Mercury is honoured by a group of worshippers, and one Amandus set up a very fine statue to the goddess Brigantia. Perhaps the most interesting altars are those erected by the Raetians, recruited while part of the cohort was serving at Eining, on the Danube. These are dedicated to the goddesses Harimellae, Ricagambeda and Viradecthis by men of the Vellavian and Condrustian districts. The only definite tombstone is that of Afutianus, son of Bassus, centurion of the Tungrians, set up by Flavia Baetica, his wife.

Beyond Birrens the road is known via Middlebie, almost to Lockerbie. At Burnswark it passes the well-known native hill-fort, with two Roman practice camps and a fortlet at its foot, once thought to be actual siegeworks. From the summit an extensive view is gained south, to the Solway and Bowness, and west to Criffell and Galloway, beyond.

A little west of Lockerbie is Lochmaben. Either here, or at the Lochmaben Stone, on the coast south-west of Gretna, the *locus Maponi* of the *Ravenna List* most probably lay (although it could just have been at Birrens fort itself). This was a meeting-place for local tribes and the Roman troops and officers responsible for maintaining peace and order in an area which then, as later, was often a frontier and usually a debatable land.

THE MAIDEN WAY AND GILLALEES BEACON

From Birdoswald the northern extension of the Roman road known as the Maiden Way has been traced across the fells to Bewcastle. North-west of Birdoswald it crosses the eastern edge of Midgeholme Moss, where for the first half-mile its course is unknown. It then passes an area of recent forestry planting and makes for the King Water west of Snowdon Close, although the precise point where it crosses the stream is uncertain. There-after, traces of it have been found at frequent places as far as Spadeadam. The Reverend J. Maughan, who first recorded it, described the countryside it crossed as often singularly bleak and wild, with little to arrest the attention, except now and then the whirring of a startled brood of grouse, the melancholy whistle of the plover, or the solitary scream of the curlew. Good lengths survive on Waterhead Fell, near Highstead Ash, where its grass-grown *agger* has been noted. There, some 500 yards west of the farm, and by Spadeadam, it was found to be 16½-17 feet broad and edged with large, roughly-squared kerbstones.

The next stretch takes the road across the area called "the Gillalees Beacon", where it keeps to the east of the highest point. Just above the 950 feet contour, but still screened by higher ground to the north, it passes the site of Robin Hood's Butt (Little Beacon Tower), which is visible from Birdoswald fort to the south, is a small cairn-like mound. This has, in fact, been found by excavation to be a stone-built tower approximately 19 feet square externally and 13 feet internally with walls, now covered by earth, standing perhaps 4 feet at highest. The whole is surrounded by a ditch with a causeway to the east, the side of the Maiden Way. The size, the ditch, and the apparent absence of a doorway at ground level all make this a close parallel to Mains Rigg. Discreet signals from it would be seen at Birdoswald or on the Wall, but not by an enemy to the north, so that a surprise intercepting move could be prepared in terrain well adapted to ambush.

East of Gillalees Beacon good stretches of the road survive, and intermittent traces of it are visible as it passes the tower; further north it crosses the highest point, and begins its descent via High House. Maughan described the fellside in its higher reaches as an inexhaustible field for botanists, especially among the mosses. North again, the road has been found to be 15 feet wide and its *agger* is visible for good stretches, where it passes to the west of Oakstock. Half a mile or so south of Bewcastle it turns slightly north-west, on a low ridge from which the traveller would gain his first close view of the fort. On this ridge top an altar was found, dedicated to Cocidius by Annius Victor, a legionary centurion. The road then makes for the east gate of the fort.

BEWCASTLE (FANVM COCIDII?)

The modern visitor will most probably arrive by way of Askerton Castle and first see the bold, if small plateau of the fort, with its church and castle, as he crosses the fell ridges to the south. The site lies in the valley of the Kirk Beck, on the western edges of the Solway Basin, with the Bewcastle Fells and their southern continuation sheltering it to the east. It does not command an extensive view, even to the west, and must always have been something of a remote outpost.

In addition to the Roman fort, the plateau contains the medieval castle of Bewcastle and the well-known, and rightly famous Anglian cross-shaft, which stands in the churchyard. This is of early eighth century date and depicts on its face John the Baptist and the Agnus Dei (upper figure), Christ standing on beasts, and John the Evangelist (lower figure). The sides are decorated with interlace, scrollwork and chequer pattern. On the face is the badly damaged text of a memorial inscription asserting that three people (whose names are damaged) set up a slender "Victory monument" in someone's memory. The whole finishes with a prayer formula. Other inscriptions mention Christ (twice)

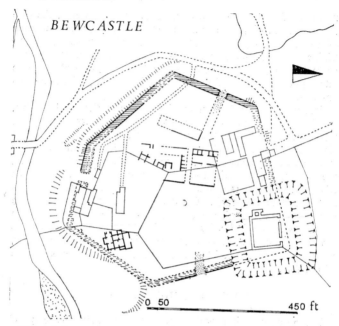

Plan of the outpost fort at Bewcastle, showing the buildings, and defences, of third-century date, together with the Hadrianic bath-house, east of the church. Modern buildings and boundaries have been superimposed.

and a female name. The traditional dating of the cross, to King Alcfrith (died *c.* 670) is now considered to be too early.

The Roman name for Bewcastle is uncertain. BANNA is often accepted as a possibility, the name appearing on the Rudge Cup, but the site had strong connections with the god Cocidius, and the FANUM COCIDII of the *Ravenna List* is probably better. An early garrison may just have been all or part of the First Cohort of Dacians, and in the third century it may have been occupied by the First Nervan Cohort of Germans, part-mounted and 1,000 strong.

The fort is exceptional in that it occupies the whole of the available plateau, which gives it an irregular 6-sided shape, and an area of almost 6 acres. An inscription found in the churchyard, but now lost, records Hadrian and the Second and Twentieth Legions, implying a Hadrianic outpost fort here, which is supported by the Hadrianic plan of the bath-house excavated in 1956.

Limited excavation was carried out in front of the churchyard and Demesne Farm in 1937, and behind the churchyard in 1954 and 1956. This has given us some idea of the unusual layout of the fort interior, although, with the exception of the baths, very little is known about it in Hadrianic and Antonine times. The principal buildings encountered in front of the church-yard were of third-century date and consisted of the headquarters building and commanding-officer's house. The headquarters was 72 feet wide and 100 feet long and, perhaps unexpectedly, faced east. It contained the usual forecourt and cross-hall with *aedes* and administrative offices behind. In the strongroom cellar were the collapsed remains of the burnt shrine above, including a stone base for a full-sized imperial statue and coins dated to A.D. 268-73 : also, two silver plaques dedicated to Cocidius. Other fragments represented mortaria, which had been used as hanging-lamps. These had been smashed, no doubt in the first moments of destruction as the desecration and pillage began. A damaged altar to Imperial Discipline was also found in the filling.

South lay the commanding-officer's house, a single block at least 88 by 78 feet in size. This and the headquarters faced on to the principal cross-street of the fort (*via principalis*) which ran from a north gate behind the farm, to a south gate excavated by Maughan under the rectory garden. The position of the fort's principal gate (*porta praetoria*), aligned on the entrance-way of the headquarters building, can be seen as a gap in the east rampart. The arrangement of buildings in the eastern part of the fort, the *praetentura*, could have been reasonably symmetrical within the space available, with the exception of the internal bath-house which lies in a south-eastern position, partly under the churchyard wall.

The baths consisted of a normal Hadrianic-plan building which had continued in use, with modifications, until the early fourth century. To the north lay the entrance and the first room of the system, the changing room (H). This was large, but not primary to the building. South, came a small vestibule (A) and the cold room (B), with cold bath (b). Further south lay

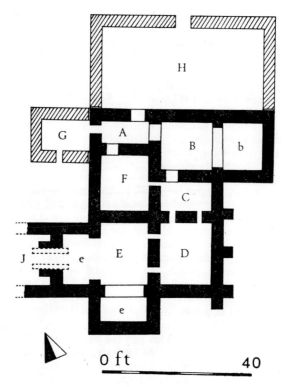

Plan of Bewcastle Baths

the warm (C, D, F) and hot (E) rooms, with hot baths (e), and the principal furnace (J) to the west. Also on the west, and partly under the churchyard, was a hot dry room (G) which, like the changing room, had been added to the building. In the final period, after violent destruction, the baths had been abandoned and a building resembling a barrack block built on their site.

The *retentura*, or area to the west of the central range, must have been less regular. The western gate lies north-west of the headquarters and the street between the two (*via decumana*) ran obliquely. A barrack or stable was excavated in the south-western section, and found to have been planned with its long axis at

Altar to Holy Cocidius, Bewcastle (Tullie House)

right angles to this street. What buildings could be fitted into the north-western portion is uncertain.

Of the gates, the southern was found by Maughan and the western excavated in 1937, when it was found to be a double portal with large jambs front and back, but with no guardchambers. Its construction, as that of the associated fort wall, matched the third-century work within the fort. Outside, lay a ditch 10 feet wide.

From all of this it was clear that the hexagonal fort was a single third-century creation; the plan of the earlier post is not known and, indeed, only the bath-house, fragments of pottery and slight traces of timber buildings belonging to it have so far been found.

After the destruction of the third-century fort, encountered in the headquarters building, the site was levelled and the fourth-century re-building was carried out. Stone-robbing has taken its toll of this period, but its buildings clearly lay on a different alignment from the earlier ones, and were of a different nature from those just described. At this date the earlier rampart backing was removed, probably to accommodate additional buildings, as at contemporary High Rochester. Later still, the early fourth-century buildings were destroyed, and rebuilt. At that date the older fort wall was totally removed and replaced by a new structure of very massive, roughly dressed, fresh stone slabs, set back some 9 feet from the outer face of the earlier wall. Pottery from the last period displayed none of the characteristics of the late fourth century, showing that the final abandonment of the site was carried out by Count Theodosius, who dismantled the outpost system after convicting its garrisons of treason and complicity in the Barbarian Conspiracy of A.D. 367. The earlier destruction may have occurred in A.D. 343 when we know there to have been trouble on the frontier.

Finds from the site are few: the silver plaques and one altar dedicated to Cocidius have been mentioned; three other small

Two Silver Plaques from Bewcastle Strongroom (*Tullie House*)

altars are dedicated to the same god, and one panel each to Jupiter Optimus Maximus and Jupiter Dolichenus. A seated mother-goddess with fruit in her lap is, like the other finds, now in Tullie House Museum. Neither *vicus* site nor tombstones have been recorded.

*   *   *

The traveller who has seen the antiquities just described has journeyed far, but he will have learned something of the great frontier of Hadrian, of its complexities and of its history. But perhaps more; he will have seen something, in sun or driving rain, or even under snow, of the noble frontierland through which the Wall runs, and for this, no less than for the antiquities themselves, he should give thanks, for each is one of our greatest heritages.

⬧DIS⬧
CVLTORIBVS
HVИS⬧LOCI
VSLLM

APPENDIX

BIBLIOGRAPHY

The purpose of this bibliography is to give references to original first-hand accounts of excavations or discoveries on the line of the Wall. It is not intended to be an exhaustive list of all literature upon each site.

ABBREVIATIONS

AA[1 5]   =*Archaeologia Aeliana*, series 1-5.

B[1 3]   =Bruce, *Roman Wall*, ed. 1 (1851); 2 (1853); 3 (1867), the first page number is for the standard size volume, the second (in brackets) for the larger, folio volume.

Brit.   =*Britannia* (1970 onwards).

CW[1 2]   =*Transactions of the Cumberland and Westmorland Archaeological and Antiquarian Society*, series 1-2.

DUJ   =*Durham University Journal*.

H   =Horsley, *Britannia Romana* (1732).

JRS   =*Journal of Roman Studies*.

LS   =Bruce, *Lapidarium Septentrionale* (1875).

M   =MacLauchlan, *Memoir written during a Survey of the Roman Wall* (1858).

MW   =MacLauchlan, *Memoir written during a Survey of the Watling Street* (1852).

NCH   =*Northumberland County History*.

OS[2]   =Ordnance Survey *Map of Hadrian's Wall* on a scale of 2 inches to the mile, ed. 2, 1972.

PSAN[1 4]   =*Proceedings* of the Society of Antiquaries of Newcastle upon Tyne, series 1-4.

PSAS   =*Proceedings* of the Society of Antiquaries of Scotland.

R   =Roy, *The Military Antiquities of the Romans in North Britain* (1793).

RHW   =E. Birley, *Research on Hadrian's Wall* (1961).

RIB   =R. G. Collingwood & R. P. Wright, *The Roman Inscriptions of Britain* (Oxford, 1965).

Rox.   =Royal Commission on the Ancient Monuments of Scotland, *Roxburghshire* Vols. I and II (1956).

SWS   =S. N. Miller, *The Roman Occupation of South-west Scotland* (1952).

WMW   =F. G. Simpson, *Watermills and Military Works on Hadrian's Wall* (ed. G. Simpson, 1976).

ANCIENT GEOGRAPHICAL SOURCES

The Antonine Itinerary: O. Cuntz, *Itinerarium Antonini; Itineraria Romana*, vol. I (Leipzig, 1929); *Brit.* p. 71 *et seq.*

The Notitia Dignitatum: O. Seeck, *Notitia Dignitatum* (Berlin, 1876).

The Ravenna List: *Archaeologia*, xciii 1.

The Rudge Cup: AA⁴ xii 310.

The Amiens skillet: JRS xli 22.

SOUTH SHIELDS

General account: H 286, 449, B² 293, PSAN² ix 215, RHW 152.

Excavations: AA² x 234, AA⁴ xi 83, *South Shields Arch. & Hist. Soc. Papers* I pts. 7, 8, 9, II pts. 1, 5, JRS lvii 177, lviii 179.

Seals: AA⁴ xi 101.

Small finds: AA⁴ xiii 139, xxvi 89.

Late coins: AA⁴ ix 91.

Animal bones: AA⁴ xlix 135.

Tombstones: AA⁴ xxxvii 203.

THE TYNE TO WALLSEND

Tynemouth: B³ 307 (243), AA² xvi 78, AA⁴ xlv 33.

Jarrow: B³ 308 (244), AA² x 195, RHW 157, *Brit.* vi 234.

Hadrianic war-memorial: AA⁴ xxi 93, RIB 1051.

South bank of Tyne: AA⁴ xxxviii 47.

WALLSEND

General account: H 135, M 6, B³ 88 (70), PSAN³ v 209, NCH xiii 485, RHW 159.

Excavations: *Brit.* vii 306.

Wall to Tyne: PSAN³ ii 278.

Vicus: Hodgson, *Hist. North.* II iii 168, NCH xiii 495.

FROM WALLSEND TO NEWCASTLE

General: H 136, M 7, B³ 94 (75), NCH xiii 493-501, *Brit.* v 410.
Milecastle sites: AA⁴ xxxviii 40.
Military Way: AA⁴ xliii 77.

NEWCASTLE UPON TYNE

General account: H 137, M 10, B³ 98 (78), NCH xiii, 501, RHW
    161, WMW 169.
Sculpture: LS no. 15.

FROM NEWCASTLE TO BENWELL

M 11, B³ 106 (84), NCH xiii 515-21.
Wall at Mining Inst., JRS xliii 110.
Ditch in Westgate, AA⁴ xi 227-233.

BENWELL

General account: H 138, M 12, B³ 107 (84), NCH xiii 521-527,
    RHW 163.
Excavation reports: (1926-1927) AA⁴ iv 135-192, v 46-74; (1937)
    AA⁴ xix 1-43 (1959), AA⁴ xxxviii 233.
Inscription of Hadrian: AA⁴ xix 19, RIB 1340.
Baths: Brand, *History of Newcastle*, i 607.
Praetentura: AA² iii 47.
Vallum causeway: AA⁴ xi 177. Pottery: AA⁴ xxxiii 142.
Temple of Antenociticus: AA⁴ xix 37, RIB 1327-8.
Mansio: AA⁴ v 52.

FROM BENWELL TO RUDCHESTER

Denton: B³ 119 (93), NCH xiii 529, AA⁴ vii 145, xl 135.
Wall ditch: AA⁴ xxxvi 55.
    Turrets and milecastle: H 138, M 14-6, NCH xiii 527-40.
Vallum inscriptions: West Denton, AA⁴ xiv 227, JRS xliv 105,
    RIB 1362-5.
    Ditch, West Denton, AA⁴ xl 135.
Milecastle 9: B³ 123 (96), AA⁴ vii 152.
Milecastle 10: B³ 123 (97).
Throckley hoard: AA⁴ viii 12.
Milecastle 11: B³ 124 (97).
Milecastle 12: AA⁴ iv 121.
    Turrets 12*a* and *b:* AA⁴ viii 322.
Heddon inscriptions: RIB 1388-9.
Vallum at Heddon: AA⁴ xl 142.

Milecastle 13: M 16, B³ 125 (98), AA⁴ viii 319-22.
   Turret 13a: AA⁴ viii 322.
Wall and culvert: *Brit.* vii 308.

RUDCHESTER

General accounts: H 139, M 15, B³ 125 (99), RHW 165.
Excavation reports: (1924) AA⁴ i 93-120, (1972) AA⁵ i 81-6.
Course of Vallum: CW¹ xv 178.
Wall-ditch below fort: CW² ii 391.
Gold and silver coin hoard: AA³ viii 219.
Mithraeum: AA⁴ xxxii 176.
Sculpture: LS No. 82.

FROM RUDCHESTER TO HALTONCHESTERS

Wall with moulded plinth: AA⁴ i 103.
Milecastle 14: M 16, B³ 129 (103), JRS xxxvii 168.
   High Seat: M 90.
   Turret 14a: Horsley, map.
Milecastle 15: H's map, B³ 130 (102).
Milecastle 16: H 141, M 18, B³ 130 (102).
Welton milestone: AA⁴ xvi 255, RIB 2298.
Milecastle 17: H 141, M 19, B³ 131 (103), AA⁴ ix 256.
   Change of construction from type A to B: AA⁴ ix 258, plate
      xliii.
   Turrets 17a, b: AA⁴ ix 257.
Milecastle 18: M 19, B³ 131 (103), NCH xii 21, AA⁴ ix 257.
   Turret 18a: AA⁴ ix 198, 258.
   Turret 18b: JRS 1 214, AA⁴ xliii 88-107.
Milecastle 19: M 19, B³ 131 (104), AA⁴ ix, 205, 258, x 98, xiii 259,
      RIB 1421.
   Turret 19a: AA⁴ x 98.
   Turret 19b: AA⁴ x 99, AA⁵ iii 222.
Milecastle 20: M 19, AA⁴ xiii 259.
Milecastle 21: M 19, B³ 132 (104), AA⁴ xiii 259.

HALTONCHESTERS

General accounts: H 105, 142, M 22, B³ 133, NCH x 468, RHW
      170.
Excavation reports:
   North third of fort: AA⁴ xiv 151-171.
   South-west quarter: AA⁴ xxxvii 177, xxxviii 153; JRS li 164,
      lii 164.
   Western extension: PSAN⁴ vii 132-4.

Inscription of Hadrian: AA⁴ xiv 161, RIB 1427.
N.W. Baths: Hodgson, *Hist. North.* II iii 316.
Course of Vallum: NCH x 468, WMW 159.
Tombstone: AA⁵ iii 212.
Sculpture: LS no. 102-3.

HALTONCHESTERS TO PORTGATE

Milecastle 22: H 143, M 23, B³ 139 (109), AA⁴ viii 317.
Portgate: M 23, H 142-3, PSAN³ ii 283, AA⁴ xlv 208.

CORBRIDGE AND THE STANEGATE

General accounts: B³ 339 (268), NCH x 474, DUJ xxxiv 144, RHW 149, AA⁴ xxxvii 1.
Early excavations: AA² vi 18, AA³ iii 161, iv 205, v 305, vi 205, vii 143, viii 137, ix 230, xi 279.
Recent excavations: AA⁴ xv 243, xvii 85, xxi 127, xxviii 152, xxx 239, xxi 205, xxxiii 218, xxxvii 59, xlix i, plus many annual reports in JRS and *Brit.*
Pottery and glass: AA⁴ xxvi 172, xxvii 60, xxxiii 116, l 205, 217.
Hoard of armour, etc.: AA⁴ xlvi 115.
Silver and gold: LS 338, JRS xxxi 100, NCH x 515, AA⁴ xiii 310, xxvi 139, AA³ v 351, viii 210.
Town: AA⁴ xi 158, xiv 95, xxxvi 227.
Religion and sculpture: AA⁴ xxi 127-224, LS no. 649, p. 454.
Inscriptions: RIB 1137, 1147-9, 1151.
Bridge over Tyne: NCH x 457, AA⁴ xlv 17.
Stanegate East of: AA⁴ l 224, RIB 2296.
Washing Well site: *Brit.* ii 250.
Stanegate West of: AA⁴ xix 194, RIB 2297, NCH X 461.
Shorden Brae Mausoleum: AA⁴ xxxix 37.
Red House baths and site: AA⁴ xxxvii 85, *Brit.* vi 230.
Hexham stones: B³ 343 (271).
Site at Wall: RHW 149.

FROM PORTGATE TO CHESTERS

Turrets 22*a, b*: AA⁴ viii 317.
Milecastle 23: H 143, M 24, B³ 139 (110), AA⁴ viii 317, RIB 1426.
Turrets 23*a, b*: OS.
Milecastle 24: H 143, M 24, AA⁴ viii 317.
Turrets 24*a, b*: AA⁴ viii 317.
Milecastle 25: H 143, M 25, B³ 141 (111), AA⁴ viii 317.
Turrets 25*a, b*: AA⁴ viii 317.

Fallowfield inscription and quarries: M 24, CW² lxviii 22, RIB
  1442.
Milecastle 26: H 143, M 25, B³ 142 (112), AA⁴ viii 317; quarry-
  wedges found, AA⁴ xxxvi 313.
  Turret 26a: AA⁴ viii 317.
  Turret 26b: AA² viii 134, ix 22f.
Milecastle 27: M 26, B³ 144 (113), AA⁴ viii 317, AA⁴ xxxi 165.
Bridge over North Tyne: AA² v 142, vi 80, xvi 328, B³ 144 (113),
  PSAN² ii 178, WMW 44.

CHESTERS

General accounts: H 143, M 27, B³ 149 (117), RHW 172.
Principia: PSAN³ iv 134.
Praetorium: AA¹ iii 142.
East gate: AA² vii 171.
South gate: AA² viii 211.
Barracks: AA² xiii 374.
Inscriptions of Antoninus Pius: RIB 1460-1.
Inscriptions of Ulpius Marcellus: RIB 1463-4.
Inscription of Severus: AA⁴ xvi 241, RIB 1462.
Inscriptions of Elagabalus: RIB 1465-6.
Baths: AA⁴ viii 219.
Vicus: AA⁴ xxxvi 228.
Sculpture: LS no. 149-50.
Relation of fort to Wall and Vallum: PSAN² ix 307, PSAN³ ii 284,
  CW² i 84, iv 240, PSAN³ x 216, AA⁴ xxxvi 230.
Relation of fort to Wall and turret 27a: PSAN⁴ x 274, JRS xxxvi
  134.
Chollerton: PSAN³ iii 322, PSAN³ x 105, NCH iv 263-4.

FROM CHESTERS TO CARRAWBURGH

Milecastle 28: H 144, M 32, B³ 165 (131).
  Turrets 28a, b: OS.
Tower Tye temporary camp: AA³ v 262.
Milecastle 29: H 145, M 33, B³ 166 (131).
  Turret 29a: AA² vii 256, AA⁵ i 97.
  Turret 29b: AA³ ix 56.
Wall ditch on Limestone Bank: AA³ ix 63.
Camps on Walwick Fell: AA³ ix 70.
Milecastle 30: H 145, M 33, B³ 167 (132).
Gaps in Vallum north mound under Military Way: CW² xxii 417.
  Turrets 30a, b: AA³ ix 55.
Milecastle 31: M 35, B³ 168 (133).

CARRAWBURGH

General accounts: Gordon, *It. Sept.* 74, H 145, M 34, B³ 169 (133), RHW 175.

Excavations: PSAN² x 161, AA⁴ xlv 1, l 81.

Relation of fort to Vallum: CW¹ xiv 415, xv 175; DUJ xxix 97, JRS xxv 203.

Inscription of Iulius Severus: RIB 1550.

Baths: Bruce, *The Wall of Hadrian, two lectures* (1874) 17, AA² xxiv 19.

Coventina's Well: AA² viii 1, 20: coins from, *ibid.* 43.

Mithraeum: AA⁴ xxix 1.

Air-photograph of *vicus:* AA⁴ xxxvi 244 pl. xxv 1.

Shrine of the Nymphs: AA⁴ xl 59.

Sculpture: LS no. 930.

THE STANEGATE, NEWBROUGH AND GRINDON

Stanegate at Chesters and Tyne: M 27, AA² ix 217, xi 131, AA⁴ xiii 201, xvi 140.

Stanegate to Newbrough: AA⁴ xxxvi 316.

Newbrough: B² 59, PSAN⁴ iv 163, RHW 147.

Stanegate and Grindon: M 30, 36, 41, RHW 147.

FROM CARRAWBURGH TO HOUSESTEADS

Milecastle 32: H 145, M 35, B³ 173 (136), *Brit.* iii 308.

    Turrets 32*a*, *b*, 33*a*: OS.

Browndykes camp: M 35.

Milecastle 33: B³ 173 (136), AA⁴ xiii 262-3.

Vallum near 33, M 90.

    Turret 33*b*: AA⁴ l 145, *Brit.* ii 291 No. 10.

    Turrets 33*b*-35*b*: JRS xxxviii 84.

Milecastle 34: H 146, M 35, B³ 174 (137), JRS xxxviii 84.

    Turret 34*a*: AA⁵ i 99.

    Turret 34*b*: OS.

Milecastle 35: H 147, M 37, B³ 176 (139), JRS xxxviii 84.

    Turret 35*a*: AA⁴ xliii 151.

    Turret 35*b*: JRS xxxviii 84.

The Black Dyke: M38, 42, AA³ xix 121-168.

Queen's Crag: JRS li 194 no. 10.

Milecastle 36: H147, M 37, B³ 178 (140), JRS xxxvii 168, WMW 70.

    Turret 36*a*: PSAN³ v 66.

Knag Burn Gateway: PSAN¹ i 186, M 92, AA⁴ xiv 172.

HOUSESTEADS

General accounts: H 148, M 38, B³ 179 (141), RHW 178.

Excavation reports: AA² xxv 193, AA⁴ xxxviii 61, xxxix 279, xl 83, xli 37, xlix 95.

North gate: PSAN¹ i 234.

East gate: PSAN² ii 204, AA⁴ vi 171.

West and south gates: AA¹ 1 267, AA⁴ xiv 179, 183.

N.E. angle-tower: PSAN³ iv 96, WMW 125.

Relation of fort to turret 36*b*: PSAN⁴ x 274.

Barrack blocks 13-15: AA⁴ xxxix 279, xl 83, *Brit.* vi 232, vii 309.

Praetorium: AA⁵ iii 17.

Latrines and S.E. angle: WMW 133, 147.

Water supply: WMW 143.

Hospital: AA⁵ iv 17.

Inscriptions: AA⁴ ix 233, RIB 1612, RIB 1613.

Vicus: AA⁴ ix 226, x 85, xi 185, xii 204, xxxix 301, xl 117.

Baths: AA¹ i 263, PSAN¹ i 48.

Mithraeum: AA¹ i 273, AA² xxv 255, AA⁴ xl 105.

Shrine of Mars Thincsus and the Alaisiagae: AA³ xix 185, AA⁴ xl 121.

Limekiln: PSAN³ iv 96, WMW 152.

Coin and gold rings: AA¹ iv 274, AA⁴ xlvii 39.

Sculpture: LS no. 230-43.

Vallum at fort: AA⁴ ix 225, xi 188.

BARCOMBE, CHESTERHOLM AND THE STANEGATE

Barcombe: M 41-2, AA⁴ xliv 71, xlvii 183, RHW 147.

Crindledykes milestones: AA² xi 130, AA⁴ xvii 116, RIB 2299-2305.

Thorngrafton coins: B³ 419 (334), AA² iii 269, CW² liv 57.

Milestones E. and W. of site: M 43, PSAN ³ v 184, RIB 2308.

Stanegate E. of fort: M 41-2, AA⁴ xiv 185.

Fort, General accounts: Hodgson, *Hist. North.* II iii 195; H 148, M 40.

　　　Name of fort, AA³ xii 201, B³ 210 (166), AA⁴ viii 182, RHW 146, 184.

Excavations of 1930: AA⁴ viii 182; of 1931, AA⁴ ix 216, of 1932-5, AA⁴ xiii 218.

Recent excavations: AA⁴ xlviii 97, annual reports *Brit.* i-iv.

Principia: AA⁴ xiii 221.

Inscription of Caracalla: JRS xxiv 218.

Tablets: *Brit.* v 360, 471.
Textoverdi: RIB 1695, AA⁴ xi 138, JRS xxxviii 56.
Stanegate W. of fort: M 43, JRS xxix 202.

From Housesteads to Greatchesters

Milecastle 37: H 148, M 40, B³ 201 (159), AA¹ iv 269, PSAN¹ i 47,
   plan, AA⁴ viii 311; Excavation, AA⁴ xi 103, WMW 119,
   RIB 1634.
   Turrets 37*a*, *b*: PSAN³ v 66, OS.
Milecastle 38: M 40, B³ 208 (164), AA⁴ xiii 263, *Surtees Soc.* lxxx
   134 (inscription), RIB 1637-9.
Native village, Milking Gap: M 43, AA⁴ xv 303.
Vallum west of Housesteads: CW¹ xv 356.
   Turrets 38*a*, *b*: PSAN³ v 66.
Milecastle 39: M44, B³ 225 (178), PSAN¹ i 46, AA⁴ xiii 268,
   WMW 81.
   Turrets 39*a*, *b*: PSAN³ v 66, WMW 98, 110.
Wall at Steelrig: CW² xiii 307-8, AA⁴ viii, pl. lviii 1, WMW
   76, 109, 114.
Milecastle 40: M44, B³ 227 (179), CW² xiii 318, WMW 86.
   Turrets 40*a*, *b*: OS, JRS xxxvii 168.
Milecastle 41: M44, B³ 228 (180), JRS xxxvii 168.
   Turrets 41*a*, *b*: AA⁴ xlvi 69, WMW 108.
Milecastle 42: M44, B³ 229 (181), AA¹ iv 54, AA⁴ xiii 269, AA⁴
   xvii 116, RIB 1666-7.
Vallum and Mil. Way: WMW 116.
Cawfields milestones: AA² ix 211, AA⁴ xvii 117, RIB 2306-7.
Watermill: PSAN³ iv 167, WMW 32.
   Turrets 42*a*, *b*: OS, WMW 80.

Haltwhistle Burn and the Stanegate

Temporary camps: PSAN³ iii 219, vii 125, AA³ v 259, JRS xxix
   202.
Stanegate beyond fortlet: H 150, M 46.
Fell End milestone: AA⁴ x 103, RIB 2309.

Greatchesters

General accounts: H 150, Gordon *It. Sept.* 78, M 45, B³ 232 (183),
   RHW 188.
Excavations: AA² xxiv 19, PSAN³ ii 287.
Relation to the Wall: AA⁴ ii 197. Relation to milecastle 43: JRS
   xxx 161, 163-4.

Aqueduct: M 45, B² 225, JRS xxxv 80.
Hoard of jewellery: *Archaeologia* lv 179, AA⁴ l 282.
Inscription of Hadrian: B³ 236 (183), RIB 1736.
Sculpture: LS no. 281.

FROM GREATCHESTERS TO CARVORAN

Vallum at Cockmount: JRS xxx 164.
　　Turrets 43*a*, *b*: OS.
Milecastle 44: M 47, B³ 239 (188).
　　Turret 44*a*: OS.
　　Turret 44*b*: AA² xxiv 13, AA³ ix 56, 69.
Milecastle 45: M 47, B³ 240 (189).
　　Turret 45*a*: AA² ix 234, x 58, AA³ ix 68, CW² xiii 302, JRS
　　　　1214, AA⁴ xliii 162.
　　Turret 45*b*: AA² ix 234, x 57, AA³ ix 69.

CARVORAN

General accounts: H 151, Gordon, *It. Sept.* 79, M 48, B³ 241 (190),
　　RHW 144, 192.
North Gate: *Brit.* iv 275.
Baths: *Archaeologia*, xxiv, 352.
Relics visible 1859: AA² iv 146.
Coin of Constans: PSAN⁴ ii 22.
The Carvoran *modius:* AA³ xiii 85, AA⁴ xxxiv 130.
Hadrianic inscription: RIB 1808.
Late-Hadrianic Building-records: PSAN⁴ ix 250, RIB 1816,
　　1818, 1820.
Cult of Vitiris, Collingwood & Myres, *Roman Britain and the
　　English settlements²* (1937), 272, Map IVc.
Vallum at Carvoran: AA⁴ xxxi 82.
Teutonic spear-head: AA⁴ xxvi 142.

FROM CARVORAN TO BIRDOSWALD

Milecastle 46: PSAN³ iv 167.
Wall and ditch: AA⁴ xxxvii 211.
Milecastle 47: H 152, M 51, B³ 251 (198), AA⁴ xiii 270, RIB 1852.
　　Turrets, 47*a*, *b*: OS.
Rose Hill: B³ 251 (198).
Milecastle 48: H 152, M 53, B³ 252 (199), CW¹ ix 163, CW² xi 390.
Gilsland, Wall and Vallum: M 90, CW¹ xiii 467, xiv 397, CW²
　　xiii 390, xxviii 385.
Willowford camp: M 52.
　　Turrets 48*a*, *b*: CW² xxvi 429, WMW 64.

Centurial stones: CW² lv 320, RIB 1859-62.
Bridge over the Irthing at Willowford: CW² xxvi 429, WMW 59.
Milecastle 49: M 53, B³ 253 (199), CW¹ xv 352, 374, CW² lvi 18.
Vallum here: CW² lvi 24.
Turf Wall hence to Birdoswald: CW¹ xv 183, 347, 367.
Centurial stones: JRS xlviii 152 no. 10, xlix 136 no. 5, l 237,
    no. 12.

BIRDOSWALD

General accounts: H 152, Gordon, *It. Sept.* 80, M 54, B³ 253
    (199), RHW 143, 196.
Possible name of fort: CW² xviii 223.
Excavations: 1850, AA¹ iv 63; 1852, *ibid.* 141; 1859, AA² iv 249;
    1896, CW¹ xiv 413; 1897, CW¹ xv 174, 180; 1898, CW¹
    xv 345; 1927, CW² xxviii 380; 1928, xxix 306; 1929,
    xxx 169; 1930, xxxi 122; 1931, xxxii 141; 1932, xxxiii
    246; 1933, xxxiv 120.
Relation of the fort to turret 49aTW: PSAN⁴ x 274.
Vallum causeway: CW² xxxiii 247.
Inscriptions of Severus and Constantius: CW² xxx 199, JRS
    xix 214; RIB 1909, 1912.
Coin-hoards: CW² l 69, liv 56.
Tombstone: JRS lii 194 no. 21.
Sculpture: LS no. 417-21.

THE STANEGATE, THROP AND NETHER DENTON

Glenwhelt, Chapel Rigg and Crooks camps: M 49.
From Tipalt to Poltross Burn: M 49-51, CW¹ ix 163.
Throp fortlet: M 52, CW² xiii 363, RHW 143.
Stanegate W. of Throp: CW² xiii 381.
Mains Rigg signal tower: CW² xxix 314, RHW 143, *Brit.* iii 308.
Nether Denton fort: CW¹ i 88, CW² xiii 385, xxxiv 152, RHW 141,
    recent air-photographs.
High Nook: CW² lxxiv 14.
Stanegate west of here: CW² xiii 385, xxxvi 188.

BIRDOSWALD TO CASTLESTEADS

Wall west of Birdoswald: CW² xiii 301.
    Turret 49b: Hodgson, *Hist. North.* II iii 279, PSAN¹ i 236,
    CW² xiii 303.
Milecastle 50, turrets 50a, b: M 56, CW² xiii 312, 307, 309.

Turf Wall, discovery of: M 56, CW¹ xiv 186, 399; general account of, JRS xxv 1.

    Turf-Wall turret 49*b*TW: CW² xxxv 234.

Vallum hereabouts: CW² xxxvii 171.

Turf-Wall milecastle 50TW: CW² xxxv 220.

Vallum at milecastle 50TW: CW² xxxvii 166.

    Turf-Wall turret 50*a*TW: CW² xxxv 234.

Patrol-track on Vallum: CW¹ xiv 185, CW² xxxvii 170.

    Turf-Wall turret 50*b*TW: CW² xxix 306; xxxv 232.

Milecastle 51: H 153, Gordon, *It. Sept.* 80, M 56, B³ 266 (210), CW² xxviii 384; xxxv 254.

Vallum at milecastle 51: CW² xxxvii 158; in original state, CW² xxii 398.

Coombe Crag quarry and forgery: CW² xxx 120, lxviii 22.

Lanerton Quarry: Hodgson, *Hist. North.* II iii 440.

    Turret 51*a*: CW² xxviii 382, lxxiii 67.

    Turret 51*b*: CW² xxviii 382, JRS xlix 104, AA⁴ xliii 170.

Milecastle 52: M 57, B³ 268 (211), CW² xxxiv 147, xxxv 247; inscriptions CW² xxxiii 238, xxxvi 1.

Signal-tower on Pike Hill: CW¹ i 214, CW² xxxii 145, xxxiii 271, RHW 140.

    Turret 52*a*: CW² xxviii 382, xxxiv 148.

Milecastle 53: M 58, B³ 269 (212), CW² xxxiii 267.

    Turret 53*a*: PSAN¹ i 237, CW² xxxiii 262.

    Turret 53*b*: CW² xxxiii 270.

Milecastle 54: M 60, B³ 275 (217), CW² xxxiv 144, xxxv 236.

Clay Wall here: CW² xxxv 244.

    Turret 54*a*: CW² xxxiv 138.

    Turret 54*b*: CW² xxxiv 131.

Milecastle 55: M 60, B³ 275 (217), CW² i 81.

    Turret 55*a*: CW² xxxiv 131.

Vallum hereabouts: CW² i 77.

Milecastle 56: M 60, B³ 275 (217), CW² i 82, CW² ii 390, iii 346.

    Turret 56*b*: CW² xxxiv 132.

CASTLESTEADS

General accounts: H 154, M 61, B³ 276 (218), CW¹ i 204, CW² xxii 198, RHW 203.

Excavation report: CW² xxxiv 159.

Altars: CW² lxxv 91.

Sculptures: LS 471-6.

Course of Vallum: CW¹ xv 354, CW² ii 385, iii 339.

The Stanegate, Boothby and Brampton

The Stanegate: CW² xxxvi 188.
Castle Hill fortlet: CW² xxxiv 154, JRS xli 55, RHW 140.
Stanegate cuttings at Quarry Beck and Pottscleugh: CW² xxxvi 188.
Old Church fort: B³ 284 (224), CW² xxxvi 172, RHW 138.
Tile and pottery kilns: CW² lxvi 1, lxxi 35.
Hawkhirst site: M 64, Hodgson *Hist. North.* II iii 233, CW¹ xv 359, CW² xxxvi 179, RHW 139.
Stanegate at Buckjumping: M 70, CW² xxxvi 184.
Watchcross camp: H 108, 154, M 72, B³ 288 (227), CW² xxxvi 170, RHW 138.
Stanegate at High Crosby: CW² xxxvi 183, RHW 137.

From Castlesteads to Stanwix

Milecastle 57: M 61, B³ 276 (218), 285 (225).
  Turret 57*a*: CW² xxxiv 132.
Milecastle 58: M 70, B³ 286 (226).
Wall hereabouts: *Archaeologia* xi 64.
Vallum hereabouts: CW² iii 340, M 90.
  Turret 58*b*: PSAN² vii 221, CW¹ xiii 465.
Milecastle 59: M 71, B³ 287 (226), PSAN² vii 221, CW¹ xiii 465.
Milecastle 60 and neighbourhood: M 71, CW¹ xiii 462, xiv 191, 393, 405, B³ 289 (228).
Bleatarn Quarry: CW¹ xiv 405.
Wetheral Cells Quarry: RIB 1004.
Gelt Quarry: CW² lxviii 22, RIB 1007.
White Moss: CW¹ xiii 460, xiv 392.
Milecastle 61: PSAN² vii 220.
Milecastle 62: M 72.
Milecastles 63, 64: M 73.

Stanwix

General accounts: H 155, 265, M 74, B³ 290 (231), CW¹ ix 174, CW² xxxi 69, xxxii 147, RHW 205.
Excavations, 1940: JRS xxxi 129-30, pl. xii.
Inscription of 167: RIB 2026.
Cemetery: CW² lii 154.
Sculptures: LS no. 482-5.
The Vallum: CW² xxxiii 275, xxxiv 155, xxxv 257; JRS *loc. cit.*

CARLISLE AND THE STANEGATE

General accounts: H 114, 409, M 76, B³ 293 (232), CW² xxiv 95, lii 155, RHW 136.
Roman name: JRS xxxviii 57.
Early history: CW² xvii 235.
Excavations: CW² lv 59, lxiv 14, *Brit.* v 410.
Platforms: CW¹ xii 344, lxiv 14.
Walls: CW² lxxiv 211, Bede, *Vita S. Cuthberti*, 27.
Small finds: CW¹ vii 114.
Carvetii Inscriptions: JRS lv 224, no. 11, RIB 933.
Coins: *Numis. Chron.*⁷ viii 63.
Sculptures: LS nos. 491-2, 494, 500-3.
Bridge: CW² lii 148.
Cemeteries: CW¹ iv 325, CW² lxxiv 8.
Scalesceugh: CW² lxxiii 79.

FROM STANWIX TO BURGH-BY-SANDS

Milecastle 66: RHW 208.
The Wall bridging the Eden: CW² lii 148-153.
Shawk Quarries: Hutchinson, *History of Cumberland*, ii 439.
The Wall passing Carlisle: CW¹ ix 167, CW² xxxii 149.
Milecastles 67-70: PSAN⁴ iv 186.
Grinsdale Roman camps: M 79, OS, AA³ v 262.
Doudle Beck: M 79.
Wall at Beaumont: JRS xviii 196.
Milecastle 71: CW² lxi 39.
Wall at the Manor-house: CW² liv 109.
Speergarth Holes, timber foundation of Wall: AA² xii 171, CW¹ ix 177.
Wall east of fort: CW² xxiii 8.

BURGH-BY-SANDS

General accounts: H 156, 266, M 81, B³ 299 (236), CW¹ i 151, RHW 208.
Excavations, 1922: CW² xxiii 3.
Turret 71*b*: CW² lxi 38.
Solway fords: CW² xxxix 152.

FROM BURGH-BY-SANDS TO DRUMBURGH

Milecastle 72: CW² lxi 35.
    Turret 72*a*: CW² lxi 34.
    Turret 72*b*: CW² lii 15.

Stone and Turf Walls, Watch Hill: CW² xxxv 213.
Milecastle 73: B³ 300 (237), CW² lii 15.
The Wall and Burgh Marsh: CW² lii 16.
Milecastle 76: CW² lxi 31.
Wall east of Drumburgh: CW¹ xvi 92, lxii 60.

DRUMBURGH

General accounts: H 157, M 85, B³ 301 (238), RHW 209.
Roman name: RHW 210.
Excavation reports: CW¹ i 209, xvi 81; CW² lii 9.
Harbour: CW² lii 14.
Road to Kirkbride: CW² lii 41.

FROM DRUMBURGH TO BOWNESS-ON-SOLWAY

Turret 76*a*: CW² lii 14.
Vallum from Glasson to Bowness: CW² xxxv 214, DUJ xxix 29.
Wall at Glasson: *Brit.* v 412.
Sunken forest of the Solway: AA¹ ii 117.
Milecastle 78: CW² xxxv 217.
Turret 78*a*: CW² lii 14.
Wall west of Port Carlisle: CW² xxxi 144.
Wall east of milecastle 79: CW² lii 22.
Milecastle 79: CW² lii 17.
Turret 79*b*: CW² xxxv 217.

BOWNESS-ON-SOLWAY

General accounts: H 157, 267, M 87, B³ 303 (240), CW¹ i 212,
CW² xxxi 140, lxxv 29, RHW 211.
Excavations: CW² xxxi 140, lxxv 29.
Vicus: CW² xxxix 327, lx 13.

KIRKBRIDE

General accounts: CW² lxiii 126, lxxv 58, *Brit.* iii 308.
Roads: CW² lii 41, xlix 75.

CUMBRIAN COAST GENERAL

H 134, CW¹ v 128, CW² xxix 138, xlvii 78, lxix 65, lxx 40, RHW
126.

FROM BOWNESS TO BECKFOOT

End of the Wall: H 158, M 87, CW² xi 352 (Bainbrigg 1601).
Running ditches: *Brit.* vii 236, *Arch. Journal* 132 20.
Towers 0*a*-1*b*: CW² lxix 65-79.

Milefortlet 1: CW² liv 36, pl. 1.1., lxii 67, lxx 35, *Brit.* vii 311.
Milefortlet 2: CW² lxix 70.
    Tower 2*b*: CW² xlvii 82, xlii 67.
Milefortlet 3: CW² xlvii 82, lxii 61.
    Towers 3*a, b*: CW¹ 128, CW² xxix 146, xlvii 82.
Milefortlet 4: CW² xlvii 82, liv 54, lxii 67.
    Towers 4*a, b*: CW² xlvii 82.
Milefortlet 5: CW² xlvii 85.
Moricambe in Roman times: CW² lxii 56.
Milefortlet 9: B³ 364 (289), CW² liv 36, pl. I.2, lxii 62.
Milefortlet 12: CW² lxvi 38, lxix 60.
    Tower 12*a*: CW² lxiv 38, lxix 55.
    Tower 12*b*: CW² lvii 22.
Milefortlet 13: CW² lxvi 41.
    Tower 13*a*: CW² liv 40.
    Tower 13*b*: CW¹ v 258, CW² lxvi 40.
Area 14-14*u*: CW⁰ xxi 270.

BECKFOOT

General accounts: CW¹ iv 318, v 136-48, CW² xxxvi 76, lviii 58,
    JRS xli pl. IV.2, RHW 214.
Inscription: RIB 880.
Vicus: Arch. Journal 132 29.
Cemetery: CW² xlix 32, lv 51, lviii 57, lxii 68.
Tombstone fragment: CW² lviii 182.

FROM BECKFOOT TO MARYPORT

Milefortlet 15: CW² lvii 21.
    Tower 15*a*: CW² liv 36, lvii 18.
Milefortlet 16: B³ 365 (289), CW² lxx 35, lxxiii 350.
    Tower 16*a*: CW² xxxviii 157, liv 32, lvi 62.
    Tower 16*b*: CW² liv 42, JRS xlv 149 no. 25.
Milefortlet 17: CW² lxii 63.
Milefortlet 20: CW² lxx 23.
    Tower 20*b*: CW² lxiii 142.
Milefortlet 21: CW² lxiii 143, lxx 36.
    Tower 21*a*: CW² lxiii 140.
    Tower 21*b*: CW² lxiii 142, lxvi 37
Milefortlet 22: CW² lxiii 143, lxx 36.

MARYPORT

General accounts: H 109, 279, B³ 365 (289), CW² xv 136, xxiii 142,
    xxxvi 85, lviii 63, lxx 42, *Archaeologia* ii 54, x 140, CW
    extra series xxii, RHW 216.

Excavations: JRS lvii 177, 204 no. 14.
Vicus: CW¹ v 237-57, CW² xxiii 151, xxxvi 85.
Altars: CW² xxxix 19, liv 268.
Parade ground: CW² xxiii 148.
Site by river: CW² xxvi 415.
Netherhall collection: CW² xv 136, xvi 284, xxvi 419.

SOUTH OF MARYPORT

Positions of milefortlets: CW² lxx 42.
Milefortlet 26: CW² lxx 43.
    Tower 26*a*: CW¹ v 124, CW² xxix 144.
Tottergill: CW² xlviii 217.

BURROW WALLS

General accounts: H 483, B³ 371 (294), CW² xxix 157, lxvi 42,
    lv 30, RHW 223.
Inscription: RIB 806.
Excavations: CW² lv 30-45.

MORESBY

General accounts: B¹ 366, B³ 371 (294), AA² v 138, CW² xlviii 42,
    xlix 218, RHW 224.
Garrisons: CW¹ ix 294, RIB 800-1.
External excavation and *Praetorium:* CW² li 176.
Tombstone: JRS liii 160 no. 5.

SOUTH OF MORESBY

Itunocelum: H 103, *Archaeologia* xciii 10, 36.
Haile altar: CW¹ vii 150, CW² xxviii 369, RIB 796.
Braystones finds: CW² xlviii 218.

RAVENGLASS

General accounts: CW¹ ix 296, CW² xxi 42, xxv 374, xxviii 353,
    lviii 14-30.
Name: *Brit.* i 70.
Casual finds: CW¹ iii 17, CW² iii 396, xxi 42, xxv 374, xxx 223,
    xlviii 219, PSAN² ii 322, JRS xxxiv 79.
Walls Castle: CW¹ iii 23, vi 216, ix 297, CW² xxviii 356.

OUTPOSTS IN GENERAL

Archaeologia xciii 1-50, NCH xv 63-129, *Brit.* iii 36, RHW 227.
Glasgow Arch. J. ns iii (1974) 34-42.

M

From Corbridge to Risingham

Stagshaw Camp: MW 21-2.
Portgate to Four Laws: MW 22-6.
Devil's causeway: MW 22, R 103, AA⁵ i 50.
Milestone at Waterfalls: MW 26, NCH xv 76.
Milestone at Risingham: LS 643, NCH xv 76 n.5.
Swine Hill camp: MW 26, NCH xv 118.
Four Laws: NCH xv 101, AA⁴ xlix 131.
Rob of Risingham: B³ 338 (268), NCH xv 87, AA⁴ xiv 108.

Risingham

General accounts: H 234, MW 27, B³ 331 (262), NCH xv 66 *et seq.*,
    AA¹ iii 150, AA⁴ xiii 170, RHW 235.
Excavations: AA⁴ xiii 184.
Inscriptions: RIB 1234-5.
Townfoot altar: AA⁴ xlv 103.

From Risingham to High Rochester

Dere Street: MW 28-34.
Dargues Camp: MW 29-30, NCH xv 118.
Blakehope: H 396, MW 30, NCH xv 70, JRS xlv 84, RHW 240.
Bagraw Camp: MW 32, NCH xv 120.

High Rochester

General accounts: H 241-4, MW 33, B³ 313 (248), NCH xv 66
    et seq., AA⁴ xiii 170, RHW 242.
Excavations: B² 300, 450, AA² i 69, AA⁴ xiii 171.
Tombs: B³ 330 (261), NCH xv 104, AA⁴ xii 200=RIB 1288.
Sculptures: LS no. 583-9.

From High Rochester to Cappuck

Dere Street: NCH xv 120, *Rox.* ii 463.
Camps by Rochester: MW 35-6, NCH xv 120.
Foulplay Head: MW 39, B³ 313 (248), NCH xv 124.
Chew Green: MW 41, B³ 313 (247), NCH xv 69 *et seq.*, AA⁴ xiv
    129.
Brownhart Law: *Rox.* ii 379 no. 798, PSAS lxxxiii 170.
Woden Law: *Rox.* i 169 no. 308.
Pennymuir camps: R pl. xxii, PSAN⁴ vii 107, *Rox.* ii 375, no. 794.

CAPPUCK

General account: *Rox.* ii 381 no. 803, PSAS xlvi 446, lxxxv 138.
Name: *Archaeologia* xciii 14.
Inscriptions at Jedburgh: RIB 2117-8.
Camps beside: JRS li 121.

FROM CAPPUCK TO NEWSTEAD

Dere Street: *Rox.* ii 466.
Eildon Hill North: *Rox.* ii 310 no. 597.
Rubers Law: *Rox.* i 103 no. 145, PSAS xxxix 225.

NEWSTEAD

General accounts: Curle: *A Roman Frontier Post* (1911), *Rox.* i 25,
ii 312 no. 604.
Excavations: Curle, PSAS lxxxiv 1.
Camps and annexes: JRS xlviii 87, li 121, lix 118.

ROAD NORTH FROM CARLISLE

H 409, R 104, CW² liii 28, SWS 1-6.

NETHERBY

General accounts: H 271, B³ 355 (281), CW² liii 6-39, RHW 229.
Chance finds: *Archaeologia* ix 222, x 139.
Baths: R 197, pl. xlvi.
Hadrianic Inscriptions: RIB 974.
Sculpture: LS no. 775-86.

BIRRENS

General accounts: H 114, 341, PSAS lxxiii 254, Macdonald &
Barbour, *Birrens and Its Antiquities* (1897), SWS 95,
RHW 227, A Robertson, *Birrens (Blatobulgium)* (1975).
Name: *Brit.* i 69, Robertson *loc. cit.* 3.
Excavations: 1895, PSAS xxx 81; 1936-7, PSAS lxxii 275; recent,
Robertson *loc. cit.*
Inscriptions: Hadrianic, CW² liii 21, *Trans Dumfries & Galloway
Soc.*³ xxxviii 142, RIB 974; Antonine, RIB 2110.
Altars: RIB 2096, 2107-8.
Annexe and cropmarks: R pl. xxiv, JRS xxxiii 50, xli 57, SWS
pl. I, *Trans. Dumfries & Galloway Soc.*³ xxxviii 132.
Burnswark: PSAS xxxiii 198, *Antiquity* xiii 286, SWS 97.
locus Maponi: NCH xv 97, *Archaeologia* xciii 15, *Trans. Dumfries
& Galloway Soc.*³ xxxi 35, 39.

THE MAIDEN WAY AND GILLALEES BEACON

Maiden Way: *Arch. Journal* xi 1-22, CW² xxii 178, xxiv 110.
Name: CW¹ xiv 196, 420.
Gillalees Beacon: B³ 264 (208) and plate, CW² i 82, xxxiii 241, xxxviii 198, RHW 233.

BEWCASTLE

General accounts: H 270, B² 321, CW² xxii 169, xxxi 137, RHW 231.
Excavations: CW² xxxviii 195.
Baths: CW² xlix 216, liv 265.
Hadrianic inscription: RIB 995.
Cocidius: *Archaeologia* xciii 34, NCH xv 86, AA⁴ xiv 103, RIB 986-7.

INDEX

347